Mission from the Perspective of the Other

Mission from the Perspective of the Other

Drawing Together on Holy Ground

TIM NOBLE

☙PICKWICK *Publications* • Eugene, Oregon

MISSION FROM THE PERSPECTIVE OF THE OTHER
Drawing Together on Holy Ground

Copyright © 2018 Tim Noble. All rights reserved. Except for brief quotations in critical publications or reviews, no part of this book may be reproduced in any manner without prior written permission from the publisher. Write: Permissions, Wipf and Stock Publishers, 199 W. 8th Ave., Suite 3, Eugene, OR 97401.

Pickwick Publications
An Imprint of Wipf and Stock Publishers
199 W. 8th Ave., Suite 3
Eugene, OR 97401

www.wipfandstock.com

PAPERBACK ISBN: 978-1-5326-5048-2
HARDCOVER ISBN: 978-1-5326-5049-9
EBOOK ISBN: 978-1-5326-5050-5

Cataloging-in-Publication data:

Names: Noble, Tim, 1962–, author.

Title: Mission from the perspective of the other : drawing together on holy ground / Tim Noble.

Description: Eugene, OR: Pickwick Publications, 2018. | Includes bibliographical references and index.

Identifiers: ISBN: 978-1-5326-5048-2 (paperback). | ISBN: 978-1-5326-5049-9 (hardcover). | ISBN: 978-1-5326-5050-5 (ebook).

Subjects: LCSH: Missions—Theory. | Ignatius, of Loyola, Saint, 1491–1556.| Carey, William, 1761–1834. | Innokentiĭ, Saint, Metropolitan of Moscow and Kolomna, 1797–1879.

Classification: BR127 N625 2018 (print). | BR127 (epub).

Manufactured in the U.S.A.   08/29/18

Scripture quotations are from New Revised Standard Version Bible, copyright © 1989 National Council of the Churches of Christ in the United States of America. Used by permission. All rights reserved worldwide.

This book is a result of the research funded by the Protestant Theological Faculty of the Charles University as part of the project "Progress Q01—Theology as a Way of Interpreting History, Traditions and Contemporary Society".

Contents

Preface | vii

Introduction | 1

Part 1: The Other
1. Encountering the Other in the Scriptures | 15
2. Mission Encountering the Other | 44
3. The Other as Given | 76

Part 2: The Missionary
4. Saint Ignatius of Loyola: Mission as Service of the Other in Love | 95
5. William Carey: A Particularly Baptist Missionary | 116
6. Bishop Innocent Veniaminov and Russian Orthodox Mission in Alaska | 145

Conclusion | 174

Bibliography | 183
Index | 205

Preface

As with many other things in life, the beginnings of this book owe as much to accident as design. My doctoral research had involved me in the study of Emmanuel Levinas and Jean-Luc Marion, and the insistence on the irreducibility of the other stayed with me in my reading and teaching of missiology. It was only when I was asked to produce a paper on the ethics of proselytism and was reading about the etymology of the word that I was struck by the idea that will be central to this book—the proselyte (*prosēlutos* in Greek) is, literally, "the drawing near one." What, I asked myself, would it look like if mission was conceived from the perspective of this other, this one who draws near?

My teaching had been, anyway, leading me in this direction, with a special interest in the "addressee" of mission. Who is mission for, and does that really make any difference? Looking at people like William Carey and Saint Innocent (Veniaminov) who have a prominent role in the second half of this book, and coming from a background where the third person whom I examine, Saint Ignatius of Loyola, was a key figure, I realized that, if there was anything in what I wanted to say, then great missionaries would, however unconsciously, have been aware of the need to take the other seriously.

The results of my research are what I present here, and this is not the place to rehearse the argument. However, it is the place to record my thanks and indebtedness to people and institutions. I start with the latter, since one of the claims that I want to make in the book is that the person is always part of a community. Three academic communities have a claim to this work. The first is (or was) the International Baptist Theological Seminary (IBTS) in Prague, where I taught missiology for nine years.[1] A number of the ideas contained in this work were first tried out with students and fellow staff there, and they were always a welcoming and challenging other for me. My

---

1. The institution has now moved to Amsterdam, where it has adopted the name of International Baptist Theological Study Centre.

inclusion of William Carey is one way of expressing my gratitude for being able to work for the European Baptist Federation, the owners of the seminary, for the years I did, and for all that I have learned through contact with Baptists and other Evangelicals from Europe, North America, Africa, and Asia.

The second institution is the one under which I am employed at the moment, the Protestant Theological Faculty of Charles University in Prague. However, in one way or another, my contact with the Faculty goes back much further, and it has always been a place where I have felt personally welcomed and accepted. Third, there is the Catholic Theological Faculty of Charles University, where I worked in the field of contextual theology. The fact that Christian mission, whilst always rooted in particular traditions, is or should be for the glory of God rather than simply the advancement of one denomination to the detriment of another, is a key assumption of my work and, I hope, my life.

There are many people to thank, too many to name all of them. Nevertheless, I want to thank two former rectors of IBTS in Prague, Keith Jones and Parush Parushev, for their support and encouragement. I want also to thank my students in contextual missiology, who have helped me sharpen and reflect on the ideas contained here. I am grateful to Zdenko Širka, the librarian for the last five years of IBTS's time in Prague, and to his predecessor, Katerina Penner, for their help. I would also like to acknowledge my gratitude to Katerina's husband, Peter Penner, an inspiring missiologist who has taught me a lot.

Part of the work for this book was done under the auspices of a grant project, "The Churches' Response of Welcome to the Migrant Other," (NF-CZ07-ICP-4-334-2016), supported by the Norway Grants, and carried out in cooperation with the School of Mission and Theology in Stavanger, Norway, part of the VID Specialized University. This project looked at the way in which churches do or should react to the migrant crisis in Europe and is one way of trying to put into practice the ideas discussed in this book. The book itself is a result of research funded by the Protestant Theological Faculty of the Charles University under the programme Progress Q01: Theology as a Way of Interpreting History, Traditions and Contemporary Society and supported by the Charles University Research Centre No. 204052, "Theological Anthropology in Ecumenical Perspective," under the leadership of Professor Ivana Noble of the Ecumenical Institute of the Protestant Theological Faculty of Charles University in Prague.

Because of circumstances, though the thinking and reflecting behind this book spread back over a number of years, it had to be written rather intensively. I could not have done this without the support, both academic and personal, of my wife, Ivana. As with my doctorate, I find that I have ended up writing about similar issues to ones that she had dealt with—when we were in the library on one research trip, we were both using the same books about Ignatius and Ignatian spirituality at the same time. But she has proved, as always, a sharp, constructive and challenging reader, and, for all its faults (and I am aware of at least some of them), this book is much better for her help.

The central claim of this book is that the encounter with the other in mission is mutually enriching for the missionary and the addressee of mission. So perhaps it is only right to finish these acknowledgements with recognition of all those, known and unknown, who throughout the centuries have drawn near to the proclaimers of the good news, however imperfect many of them (of us) have been, and have enriched the Christian faith with their stories, their gifts, their talents. Without them, our faith would be impoverished, our lives more dull, our journey harder.

Introduction

The aim of this book can be simply stated. It sets out to examine what Christian mission looks like when the perspective of the other—the one to whom mission is addressed—is given a key role. Christian mission always involves three interrelated subjects. The first is God, and the other two are the missionary and the other. I want to rescue this third, this other, seeing her or him not as a problem that mission has to overcome, but as a blessing and a gift, without whom mission is impossible.

This book, then, is an attempt to see how an encounter can happen that allows the other to have a voice in mission. Reflecting on my own experiences of attempts to evangelize me and in listening to and reading about other people's tales of their encounters with missionaries in various forms, I have been frequently struck by their monological form. Essentially, the missionary says: "I know everything about God, you know nothing, and my task is to transfer my knowledge to you so that you will become like me." This is what the Brazilian educationalist Paulo Freire called the banking model of education.[1] But worse still, it models a way of following Christ and of being church that is inherently destructive and reductive. What is brought by the other is largely without value, certainly if it cannot be colonized in a Christian form, and the best path to follow is to abandon whatever one has of one's own and vest oneself in the clothes of the missionary.[2]

But, in arguing for the need to engage with the perspective of the other in order to revitalize Christian mission, a few points of clarification are already called for. The most important is that this is not a book that seeks to cast doubt on the necessity or possibility of mission. Entirely to the contrary, my interest is to see how mission can be more effective, for

---

1. See Freire, *Pedagogy of the Oppressed*.
2. In some cases literally—see, for example, Ruether, "Heated Debates," on attitudes to clothing in one particular setting.

both the missionary[3] and the addressee of mission. I will seek to show that, through a mission that enables a significant role for the other, the faith of the missionary is also deepened, and new insights into who God is are granted to the church. And, through hearing and experiencing the word of God in action, the other is enabled to come to a deeper understanding of who they are and where they belong within creation. Ultimately, the Christian missionary wishes the other to experience the transforming power of Christ in their lives and to follow Christ. But that choice and decision can only ever be made freely, and perhaps only ever be truly known to God.

I also do not wish to claim that the culture of the other is beyond reproach and is to be accepted in its entirety without comment. Whether we use an Augustinian language of original sin or a more Irenaean language of human incompleteness and immaturity, it is clear that there are things in our lives and our world that are not perfect, because we have seen or can imagine better versions of them. Even at such a broadly pre-theological level, it is possible to engage in dialogue with people about elements of their own lives and their cultures that do not appear compatible with Christian life, even if, as we will see later in the book, precisely what such elements are is not always so obvious.[4] Even at the risk of making mistakes, it seems to me that a critique of culture is a key contribution that Christian mission can make, but it can only do it in conversation and allowing its own critiques to be criticized and challenged themselves. Often what we call Christian is, of course, simply our own equally questionable cultural assumptions, and it is only by allowing these to be purified that the missionary can truly speak out against the shortcomings of the other.

So, at one level, this book is—I hope—an eminently practical response to a real problem. However, for reasons I will explain shortly, it will not give instructions about how to do mission, if by that is understood a list of strategies and procedures, even though it arises from and responds to a need that is becoming increasingly recognized in missiological literature. To

---

3. I will use "missionary" to refer to the person engaged in mission, regardless of where they do this. So, I am not thinking only about people going away to another place, or even people who are employed in some form or other as missionaries. I am thinking of the vocation of all Christians to share their faith and to witness and pass on what they have received. Prescriptively then, if not actually, "missionary" is simply a synonym for Christian.

4. I am thinking of the different attitudes toward the caste system in India, as expressed by Roberto de Nobili and William Carey, which I discuss in chapter 5. Another long-standing issue has been the question of polygamy, and to what extent it is possible to be polygamous and Christian. At this juncture, I merely point to these examples to show that it is not as simple as we sometimes make out to say that there is one single Christian approach to life.

articulate the question that underlines this book, I turn to Michael Barram. one of the leading writers of the Gospel and Our Culture Network (GOCN)[5] in America.

At the 2008 meeting of the American Academy of Religion another member of the GOCN group, George Hunsberger, presented a paper, entitled "Proposals for a Missional Hermeneutic: Mapping the Conversation."[6] Hunsberger suggested four ways in which a missional hermeneutics[7] could be approached. He speaks of a missional direction to the story of the Bible, a missional purpose to the story, the missional locatedness of the readers, and finally, the missional engagement with culture. To sum up very briefly, a missional hermeneutic seeks to see the Bible as a story about mission and for mission, and it seeks to find the hearer of the story as placed and part of a culture. In making these points, Hunsberger was trying to be descriptive, categorizing the works of other prominent North American writers linked to the GOCN.

After Hunsberger's lecture, Barram offered a brief response.[8] Although Barram broadly welcomed the paper, he offered some critical questions. Here I cite what for me is the key paragraph of his response:

> I continue to be struck and frankly a bit uncomfortable with the interpreter-centric assumptions implied in the four "streams." It should be clear that not only do we as the interpreting community ask questions of the text, but also the text asks questions of us—indeed, we might say, biblical texts ask hard, challenging questions about our questions. Moreover, although some of the proposals take context quite seriously, I wonder if we have dealt adequately with the context of the other, that is, the context of the one who is engaged—in whatever form—by the missional community. How does the encounter with the other challenge the power and privilege so often presupposed in the community's understanding of its "sentness"—and indeed, of its appropriation of the gospel? I wonder if a missional hermeneutic

---

5. The Gospel and Our Culture Network (often abbreviated as GOCN) first started in the United Kingdom and arose principally out of the work of Lesslie Newbigin. On the American network, which is now by far the most vigorous, see http://gocn.org/network/about-us/what-and-why/.

6. Hunsberger, "Proposals." Hunsberger is author of a major work on Newbigin: Hunsberger, *Bearing the Witness*.

7. Very simply put, "missional hermeneutics" is an approach that emerges especially out of the GOCN movement, and seeks to read the Bible and Christian life missionally, that is to say, from the perspective of mission as the interpretive key. Mission is not, thus, an added extra, but the lifeblood of Christian existence.

8. Barram, "Response."

would be even more robust if we could come up with a "stream," or at least a focused question, that actually privileged the perspective of the other confronted by mission.[9]

Like Barram, I am uncomfortable with the "interpreter-centric" nature of much of the writing on and—as far as I can observe—practice of mission today.[10] Theology and spirituality and other forms of Christian life may finally be trying to move from focus almost entirely on the individual to focus on the community, but all that that move really changes in mission is a rephrasing from "it's all about me" to "it's all about us." However, just as theologians are starting to move from the twentieth-century concentration on ecclesiology to consider more broadly theological anthropology,[11] so perhaps it is time for mission to move beyond looking inward, and to start looking out to embrace the whole of creation. At the very least, the need is to move from what in grammatical terms would be the exclusive first person plural ("you and I but not him or her") to the inclusive ("you and I and him and/or her").

Simply to do this, to start with the other as human being, and therefore daughter or son of God, is already to recognize their otherness as potential blessing, and thus to renounce any claims to the superiority that Barram alludes to. My attempt in this book is to develop this fifth stream of a missional hermeneutic that attempts to take seriously the other, the one encountered in mission. This other is seen not as a problem to be overcome, or as a "pagan" to be converted, but as one who journeys with us on the path of faith, where we can learn together what it is to be disciples of Christ.

It should be clear that I will not be able to supplant the other, and speak for them. In that sense, the perspective of the other remains inescapably other. We can only ever learn what the other wants to give us by entering into contact with that other and engaging in a form of kenosis, not clinging to our own beliefs and certainties for our own salvation, but being ready to abandon all to be filled with the power of the risen Lord in all its transformative glory. This is why I do not seek to explain how mission should be done from the perspective of the other. In part this is because I am not sure that mission, anyway, is something that should be susceptible

---

9. Barram, "Response," para. 8.

10. Of course it would be wrong to overgeneralize, and there are, no doubt, many individual counterexamples. I think that what Barram refers to is, however, a widely observable trend. In part, this is because the "interpreter"—the missionary—is the most easily changeable element in the equation. We can change what we do, and not what the other does. But my point—and I think Barram's—is that we need to listen to this other first, and let the other change us too.

11. For example, see Ware, *Orthodox Theology*, 25.

to strategies and plans and points and programs. It is true that to do the work of God is to engage in something serious and wonderful, and the missionary should prepare for this seriously and in wonder (through deed and prayer, one might say). But the only real "strategy" is to let God talk and to encounter the other, and see what happens.[12]

But even if we cannot say what the other will command in the missionary encounter, I believe that we can point to ways of encounter that will allow the other to have a voice, and in that sense we can create a hermeneutical stream that is other-centered. To do this is already, at least in many countries of Europe, but elsewhere too, to make a counter-cultural statement. It denies that the other—however we denominate that other[13]—is a threat or problem and affirms them as a blessing and a gift. It is never otherness that is the problem, only sameness.[14] Thus my affirmation is not merely that mission can be done with the other, but that without the other there can be no mission. Mission needs the other human, just as it needs the Other, God.

The claim that mission depends on the other also means that, strictly speaking, it is not possible to give a specific definition of mission. Mission in this perspective will always include a process of learning about God in encounter with the other, and thus to do mission is a part of learning what mission might be. Needless to say, not every other will want to dialogue. In both the Matthean and Lucan accounts of the mission discourse of Jesus, the disciples are told to go to towns and only stay where people welcome them and are prepared to engage with them.[15] Dialogue cannot be enforced, and the other is free to reject or to welcome—and, as Luke's Gospel tells us, the kingdom of God is still near at hand. But those who do welcome the

---

12. Actually, I think that in the best cases this is what good missionaries have always done, regardless of what they think they are doing at a more rational level and regardless of the demands of mission boards and sponsors.

13. According to race, gender, religious belief, sexual orientation, socio-economic status, or whatever else we use to categorize otherness.

14. I will refer briefly to Emmanuel Lévinas, but this is one of his great contributions to contemporary thought, one that finds echo in Christian theology too.

15. Matthew 10:11–14 reads: "Whatever town or village you enter, find out who in it is worthy, and stay there until you leave. As you enter the house, greet it. If the house is worthy, let your peace come upon it; but if it is not worthy, let your peace return to you. If anyone will not welcome you or listen to your words, shake off the dust from your feet as you leave that house or town." The equivalent in Luke 10:8–11 says, "Whenever you enter a town and its people welcome you, eat what is set before you; cure the sick who are there, and say to them, 'The kingdom of God has come near to you.' But whenever you enter a town and they do not welcome you, go out into its streets and say, 'Even the dust of your town that clings to our feet, we wipe off in protest against you.'"

missionary are those with whom she or he will learn what it means to be engaged in the mission of God.

THE STRUCTURE OF THE BOOK

The book is divided into two parts. The first seeks to set out the ground for including the other in discussion about mission through a series of dialogues, with Scripture, with contemporary missiologists, and finally, in order to help establish the other as a partner for missional hermeneutics, with a contemporary philosopher, Jean-Luc Marion. The second part takes three historical missionaries and examines how in their writings and in their lives they sought, even if not always perfectly, to respond to the stranger, to the other whom they encountered.

I begin with a consideration of some of what the Bible has to say about the other. Chapter 1 examines some interpretations of the use of the word *gēr* ("stranger," "resident alien") and related terms in the Old Testament. It then goes on to discuss the translation of the word into Greek in the Septuagint. This necessitates first a consideration of the Septuagint as translation, followed by an investigation into the most common translation of *gēr* as *prosēlutos*, with its root meaning of the one who is coming near, or towards. Because by the time of the New Testament *prosēlutos* had gained a more specific technical sense,[16] the word itself is largely replaced in New Testament texts, when used, by a related term *paroikos*. The encounters of Jesus with the religious other, especially in Matthew, are finally taken as paradigmatic for the way in which the other can lead us to understand more deeply what mission is.

In the second chapter I look at how the engagement with the other has been dealt with by contemporary missiologists.[17] The aim of this chapter

---

16. By this stage, as we will see, it is perhaps closer to the idea of proselytism. On the development of the term, see Johnson, "Proselytism and Witness"; Ocaríz, "Evangelización"; Marty, "Introduction."

17. I refer to more literature on this theme in the second chapter especially. One important contribution that came out after I had written the main body of this book is the October 2015 issue of the *International Bulletin of Missionary Research*, entitled "Engaging Mission: Hospitality, Humility, Hope." The articles in this volume approach the issue of the other in mission. Especially important for my perspective is DeBorst, "At the Table," which uses the story of the disciples on the road to Emmaus as the basis for a reflection on the importance of allowing the other to act as host. Other works on similar themes include Jeong, *Mission from a Position of Weakness*, on the position of the "missionary" in regard to the other; Glaser et al., *Announcing the Kingdom*, with pages 120–21 on the alien in the OT, and pages 169–70 on proselytes in the NT; Muck, "History of Religion," 70, who says "method [in missiology] begins at the point of faith

is not to give an exhaustive account of everything that has been written on the subject, Instead, I turn principally to the work of David Bosch and of Stephen Bevans and Roger Schroeder, especially as they discuss the nature of dialogue in mission. As leading writers on mission, these authors serve as representative and offer us an overview of what missiologists are reflecting on in regard to the other. Especially the idea of prophetic dialogue will help see how mission involves a coming together of pilgrims. This is always risky, but in order for mission to be productive, and to be shared and multiplied, risks have to be taken, investment has to be made.[18]

However, in itself, dialogue may not be enough. For often it fails to enquire about the nature of the other with whom I engage in dialogue, and assumes that this other is some kind of version of myself—even the fact that we think we can dialogue with them can imply that. The third chapter, then, moves on to the search for an adequate hermeneutic for being engaged by the other. To talk about these *prosēlutoi* who draw near, I turn specifically to the language of phenomenology.[19] In particular, I draw on the French

---

in God—a faith that acknowledges God's initiating activity in creating and sustaining human life, including scholarly activity. God's initiating activity creates a sense of responsibility that precedes and sets bounds for all subsequent activity . . . Missiologists often describe this in terms of 'call'. Perhaps the closest non-theological equivalent is Immanuel [sic] Lévinas's description in philosophical terms of pre-reflective contact with the other, a contact that in itself contains a responsibility of action"; Dorr, *Mission*, 16–73, on dialogue, as much internal as external; Moreau et al., *Introducing World Missions*, on relating to people of other cultures (233–43) and of other religions (265–73); and perhaps closest to what I aim to do in my work, but in more limited form, Gittins, *Ministry*, especially 40–60 and 142–60. In this latter section, he speaks of missionaries "choos[ing] to become servants and learners" (151), though I would prefer to see it in terms of a divine necessity rather than a strategic choice; Werner, *Wiederentdeckung*, 64–84, who writes on the concept of *Konvivenz*, a concept normally associated with the German missiologist Theo Sündermeier, though Werner does not quote him directly; for a negative take on the turn to the other, see the noted conservative evangelical missiologist David Hesselgrave in *Paradigms in Conflict*, especially 81–115 on interreligious dialogue, which he basically opposes.

18. The implicit reference to the parable of the talents here is not meant to support an economic model, but it does remind us that risks have to be taken, and only thus can the Word of God be spread. Although it is hardly the most ecumenical of documents, the lines written by Saint Edmund Campion (1540–1581), and known as "Campion's Brag" (or more properly, his "Challenge to the Privy Council"), on his commitment to the reconversion of England, contain a powerful expression of the risks involved in mission: "The expense is reckoned, the enterprise is begun; it is of God, it cannot be withstood." The text is available in various places online; for example, http://www.catholictradition.org/Saints/campions-brag.htm. For more on Campion and his influence on English Catholicism, see, for example, Kilroy, *Campion*.

19. The use of phenomenology is not that common in missiology. There is, however, a fascinating article from 1979 that to some extent begins to explore what I am doing here, though as far as I can discover the work never made much further progress. See

phenomenologist Jean-Luc Marion, and his concept of "givenness." Marion will give us a way of thinking the other and indeed the self that does not need to restrict either to what we already know. His insights will give us the possibility not to encounter and categorize but to allow the other to come to us, to encounter us. Only then does the search for meaning begin.

The second part is primarily historical. This needs a few words of comment. It is of course a common feature of missiological writing,[20] and in that sense one that needs no defense. It would have been possible to have looked at the implications of what I say through consideration of contemporary issues in mission, such as interreligious dialogue, migrant churches, or the vexed and complex issue of mission in Europe,[21] to name but a few. These are important and serious questions and would have served my argument well. However, I have chosen to use historical examples for two reasons.

The first is that today it is almost impossible to ignore the other. Thus, one would expect that in dealing with contemporary issues there would be at least lip-service paid to the role of the other. It then becomes very hard, however, to separate out what is real attention to the other and what is there because it is expected, and indeed to decide when an attitude such as attention to the other becomes so deeply-ingrained as to be natural, something that I would, of course, see as a positive. In looking at the past, however, there were no such strong cultural expectations, and thus no external

---

Gilliland, "Phenomenology." Dean Gilliland (1928–2013) was a long-time worker in Nigeria, where he was head of a theological college and especially interested in Christian–Muslim encounters. See Gilliland, "My Pilgrimage."

20. Almost any work on missiology will include at least brief examples from history. Both Bosch, *Transforming Mission*, and Bevans and Schroeder, *Constants in Context*, contain significant engagement with the history of mission. See also, for example, Dahling-Sander, *Leitfaden*, 51–110; Eitel, *Mission*, 219–29, 245–82; Luzbetak, *Church*, 84–105; Moreau et al., *Introducing*, 93–195; Pachuau, *Ecumenical*, 3–50; Shenk, *Changing*, 141–76; Sunquist, *Understanding*, 23–175; van Engen, *Mission*, 115–24; Verstraelen, *Missiology*, 211–62. The names are listed here in alphabetical order. They come from different continents and denominations and understandings of mission, but all of them use history as part of their argument. Many other examples could be given, but this can serve as a very short indicative list. I can adopt here the summary in Shenk, *Changing*, 2, on his guiding principles for discerning what he calls the mission frontier for today: "The second guiding principle is to reflect carefully on the experiences of the missionary church in previous generations. There we find episodes of true creativity where the gospel has been communicated in its integrity and in the idiom of people."

21. Good starting points for these areas are the recent volumes in the Regnum Edinburgh 2010 series. On interreligious dialogue, see Behera, *Interfaith Relations*; on migrant churches, see Chandler and Yong, *Global Diasporas*. On mission in Europe, see, among others, Wrogeman, "Mission"; Paas, "Mission from Anywhere to Europe"; Paas, "Making"; Jackson, "'Mission-Shaped.'" On how those from outside viewed Europe, see especially Becker, *Europe*.

reasons for indications of attention to the other to be present. Thus, if it is, the case for today is made *a fortiori*.

It would also seem plausible that if in some form attention to the other is an important part of Christian mission (rather than simply an expression of a modern or post-modern fad), then it will have been practiced and experienced in the lives of missionaries through the centuries, whether it was something that they gave explicit information about or not. Of course, the other side of this that has to be acknowledged from the start is that I am reading the history of these missionaries through a particular lens. But this is not to be untrue to historical research or practice.[22] Rather it is to acknowledge that the other is present as a "character" in the drama of history, however we understand that discipline, and that people have had to react in some way to that presence—through hostility, ignorance, acceptance, or love, to name just some possibilities. My aim, then, is not to pass judgement on the three missionaries I examine from some position of assumed superiority, but to engage with them also as others who come to us and from whom we can learn. This learning is emphatically not to do with repetition or imitation in the strict sense, because we do not live in the same time and place. But it is to claim that "the saints" (the holy ones of God, that is, all who have followed in the footsteps of Christ) are people we can hope to learn something from about the nature of discipleship. Precisely what that "something" is is one of the points of the book.

The second part begins, then, with an examination of Saint Ignatius of Loyola's contribution to the understanding of Christian mission. I start by looking briefly at how mission is presented in Ignatius's *Spiritual Exercises*, as a response in love and in service of God and of the other. I then move on to see how this response was articulated in a more systematic way in the *Constitutions of the Society of Jesus*, in which Ignatius, aided by his early companions, set out where and how Jesuits should engage in the mission entrusted to them by the church. Finally the chapter examines some concrete examples of how Ignatius thought that mission should be practiced in welcoming love for the other who drew near.

In chapter 5, I look at William Carey, an English Baptist who was instrumental—with a little help from his friends—in setting up what quickly became the Baptist Missionary Society, and who did a lot to instill an interest in mission among British Baptists and other evangelicals. I first examine Carey's important text on the need for mission, and then consider Carey the missionary in his encounter with India. With Carey we will see the tension

---

22. On the reasons why people write history, see Burrow, *History of Histories*, and the discussion in Judt and Schneider, *Thinking*, especially 257–60 and 264–69.

that exists in mission as encounter, between the baggage (theological, cultural, psychological) that the missionary brings with them and the painful and growing awareness of its inadequacy. Is it better to hang on to what we have and know, even if it does not really correspond to the needs we perceive, or is it better to take the risk of letting go of the past in order to become more deeply rooted in a different present? This, we will see, was the challenge that Carey faced.

The subject of my sixth chapter is Saint Innocent (Veniaminov). Innocent was a Russian Orthodox priest, and later bishop, who worked for some thirty years in Alaska, then part of the Russian Empire. He was a generation younger than Carey, from a very different Christian tradition, working in a completely different part of the world, with its own culture and languages and challenges. Like Carey, he went as a missionary with his family, and had to face the difficulties of life in harsh and unfamiliar surroundings, learning languages and cultures. In other respects, their lives were very different. Innocent came to an already established and, broadly-speaking, officially recognized ecclesial setting. But Innocent too had to find out how to relate to the others among whom he lived, and to allow himself to be changed by the love he received from them, and the sixth chapter tells this story. The conclusion draws out some of the major points that are developed throughout this book.

Before beginning the journey, a few further observations are in order. The basic idea of this book is, I think, straightforward. Christian mission should be done with the other and in love, and in this way the missionary and the addressee of mission will be transformed. Clearly then I am focusing here on the how of mission, rather than on the content. There are two reasons for this. The first is that the argument itself demands that the content cannot be predetermined, at least not the precise content. This is because, to repeat, what it is to do mission will ultimately be learned only with and through the encounter with the other. It was Marshal McCluhan who many years ago now insisted that "the medium is the message."[23] The second reason is more pragmatic, since I presume that most people engaged in mission have some idea of what it is they want to proclaim, based on Scripture and church/tradition.

I am also aware that my examples and the authors I draw on are not unproblematic. Most of the authors and all three examples are men, and certainly in Part Two choosing a woman missionary would have been

23. The phrase occurs in several places in McCluhan's writings. It was introduced, as the title of the first chapter, in his work *Understanding Media*. See also McCluhan, *Counterblast*, 31. This is not the place to discuss his work, however. For a recent work by a former co-worker, see Logan, *McCluhan*.

informative.²⁴ As mission changes its focus, it will also be important to move from what is essentially a Western or at least European perspective to a more global one. It is, I would say, a prerequisite of my argument here that in order to understand what mission means in encounter with the other, that other will have to decide that they want to help, hence the provisionality of my claims about mission. This, though, is a methodological necessity rather than terminal indecision.

Finally, I repeat that this book seeks to be also a celebration of the need for and possibility of mission. In presenting the other as the key for understanding what mission is, I am not denying the value or importance of Christian mission, but arguing that it has so much more to give and to learn. It will involve humility, risk, humiliation,²⁵ but it will also enable the encounter in mission to be one of love and service; and love and service in mission are not optional extras—they are the Way.

---

24. As just one example, I can mention here the Scottish missionary in Nigeria, Mary Slessor (1848–1915), a fascinating figure and one who would fit very well into the themes of this book. On Mary, see Hardage, *Mary Slessor*.

25. See chapter 4 of this book on Saint Ignatius of Loyola for the background to this.

PART 1

The Other

1

Encountering the Other in the Scriptures

To begin the investigation of the place of the other in mission, I want to examine one way the irruption of the human other in the Bible is treated. In a number of important texts,[1] the Hebrew Scriptures draw Israel's attention to how it is to deal with the stranger, or resident alien, whom it most commonly refers to as the *gēr*. So, in this chapter, I start by examining the role and place of the *gēr* in the Old Testament. Who are these people, what do they demand, and why are they important? Then I proceed to look at the translation of this term into Greek in the Septuagint, before moving on to a brief investigation of the translations of the word in the New Testament. I conclude with a bridging reflection on some key encounters between Jesus and those who presented themselves to him as other. Although I shall primarily be looking at the use of three particular expressions (*gēr—prosēlutos—paroikos*),[2] I shall also briefly attend to other images used to talk of the encountered other in the Bible. Methodologically, I will draw on studies of the relevant words and concepts, in order to understand better the narratives in which these words and concepts appear. I do this to

---

1. Further references to these texts will be given throughout this chapter.

2. In what follows, I will use only transliterations or translations of Hebrew and Greek, and that for two reasons: first, to underline that this is not an exegetical work, and secondly because the use of other alphabets excludes those who do not know them and goes against the spirit which is intended for this book. Those who wish to consult the originals will be in a position to do so, and others can work with translations, since part of my argument is that translation is one of the key ways that the other is encountered and through which the other contributes to mission.

see one way in which the Bible narrates the encounter with the other, and to see how this can help in developing a non-ideological understanding of mission.

I am not, then, engaging here in an exercise in the field of Biblical Studies, or even directly of exegesis, at least not in terms of detailed textual, historical, and form studies of particular Biblical verses. This work has already been done by others more qualified than I, and there is no need to repeat what they have done. Rather, I am investigating whether in the way the *gēr* is viewed in the Bible, there is anything that sustains an understanding of mission as encounter, as two people[3] who come, each from their own—and, therefore, to the other, alien—place, to a meeting ground. Does the treatment of the *gēr*, the *prosēlutos*, give us a useful concept for talking about this encounter?

To ask this question is almost automatically to raise a subsidiary one. The Old Testament describes a fundamentally rural community, even if it is one that is becoming increasingly urbanized, with the consequent weakening of more ancient forms of social bonding.[4] This is true whether we date particular passages about the *gēr* to before or after the Exile. Thus societal structures and relationships are obviously very different than what we experience in most of Europe today. Indeed, in the last few years it has been claimed that for the first time the majority of the world's population lives in urban settings.[5] As we shall see, it is also true that the precise referent of the term *gēr* is open to some question.[6]

A simple substitution (the *gēr* in the Old Testament as either human subject or object of mission) will therefore not do. For one thing, it would reduce Christian mission to welcoming the outsider in a setting where

---

3. Because I understand human existence as ineluctably relational, the use of the singular here is not meant to restrict this encounter to any two given individuals. Any such encounter always includes a wider community and culture. However, it is also true that most encounters of any depth happen not at some abstract level of cultures and communities, but between individuals or, at most, small groups of people.

4. See van Houten, *Alien*, 73.

5. For some statistical grounding for this, see the report by the Population Division of the Department of Economic and Social Affairs of the United Nations Secretariat, *2010 Revision* and *2014 Revision*. According to this report, in 2014, 54 percent of the world's population was urban, and 46 percent rural. The report explains what these two terms mean.

6. Brazilian theologian Clodovis Boff distinguishes between what he terms "a correspondence of terms" approach and "a correspondence of relations." The first understands words as being identical in meaning then and now (Israel enslaved in Egypt, the poor enslaved now, for example). The second argues, rather, that it is how God responds in analogous ways to very different settings that is important. See Boff, *Theology and Praxis*, 142–46. See Noble, *Poor in Liberation Theology*, 112, where I discuss this further.

Christians are an overwhelming majority, which is not the case in most places in the world, with the possible exception of the Americas. Rather, I would contend, we need to see how God relates to the world—to his creation—and then seek to find a way of acting analogously in a very different setting.

THE *GĒR* IN THE OLD TESTAMENT: BIBLICAL NOTIONS OF OTHERNESS

The Old Testament has several words for talking about those who are not the children of Israel.[7] These include *nōkhrī*, *zār*, *tōschāb*, and *gēr*, the one that will most preoccupy us in this chapter.[8] One important thing to note already is, therefore, that it would be wrong to see Israel as having a simplistic view of those who are not an integral part of it by birth. Rather, as Joel Kaminsky argues, there are at least two very distinct groups of "other" for Israel.[9] Whilst seeing itself as "elect," Israel encountered the other as both what Kaminsky calls "anti-elect" and as "non-elect."

The "anti-elect" are those who in some sense deliberately exclude themselves from God, those "who are deemed to be enemies of God and whom Israel is commanded to annihilate."[10] For all that the texts dealing with them are problematic in terms of the often violent approach they suggest, Kaminsky considers that the anti-elect are a fairly small proportion of those surrounding Israel.[11] By far the larger category is that of the non-elect, those who are not Israelite, but who dwell peacefully either within Israel itself or alongside Israel.

Given that the first group of the anti-elect is almost by definition excluded from the possibility of peaceful and transformative encounter,[12] I

---

7. As Langer, "Jewish Understandings," 257, notes, the term "Jew" or "Jewish," though of Hebrew origin, is not a self-designation of the people in Old Testament times, but the word used by outsiders. In this, of course, as Acts 11:26 reminds us, they have something in common with Christians.

8. See Schnabel, "Israel," 37. Schnabel goes on to say that in "the prophetic literature the *nōkhrī* and *zār* are mentioned with reference to other nations that potentially or actually oppress Israel" ("Israel," 38).

9. Kaminsky, "Election." The implications of this distinction for the attitude to migrants in Europe and elsewhere is, I think, obvious.

10. Kaminsky, "Election," 399.

11. See Kaminsky, "Election," 400–408. Noting that these texts are indeed a problem, Kaminsky also shows how later Jewish tradition sought to work with them, in order to find ways of overcoming the violence inherent in them.

12. Either because of the attitude of the group concerned—so a form of

will not at the moment attend to it.[13] My interest, then, in what follows, lies in the non-elect, a group that, says Kaminsky, is comprised of those "individuals, groups, and nations who are neither members of the people of Israel, God's elect, nor are they to be counted among those who are utterly beyond the pale of divine and human mercy in the Israelite imagination, the anti-elect."[14] Kaminsky goes on to argue that the treatment of these people is complex, and cannot be reduced to simple categories of either exclusion or inclusion.

This claim, along with Eckard Schnabel's remark that "[n]either the Torah nor the prophets contain any hint that Israel has a historical mission to bring members of other nations to a saving knowledge of YHWH,"[15] should introduce a note of caution from the outset. The stranger in Israel is always in a kind of in-between position, and the fact that their well-being needs to be legislated for in itself suggests that the reality was far different. In this sense, the heading that Schnabel gives to his treatment of the various categories of "pagan other" is helpful: he speaks of "Israel's Relationship to her Pagan Neighbors as Tolerant Reserve." Both "tolerance" and "reserve" are, however, important qualities and so now we can turn to a more detailed examination of the particular use of the word *gēr* in the Old Testament.

The *gēr*: The Other Dwelling among Us

The Hebrew word *gēr* can be translated as "alien," an English word that already in its etymology implies otherness.[16] It starts therefore, as an exclusive

---

self-exclusion—or because of being excluded more or less a priori by the people of Israel. This latter is of course in many ways highly problematic and remains a difficulty when any form of stereotyping of the other takes place. Schnabel, "Israel," 38, notes that "prophets anticipate a time when Israel . . . dominates the foreign nations herself." As evidence, he directs the reader (see Footnote 15) to the following texts: Isa 25:2, 5; 60:10; 61:5; Jer 30:18; and Joel 4:17. The last is presumably Joel 3:17, and it, along with the other texts cited, do not seem to me to warrant the use of the word "dominate."

13. There are also passages in the New Testament that make it clear that not everyone will accept the proclamation of the kingdom. That message is an integral part of the various missionary instructions that Jesus gives his disciples. Those households or towns that do not welcome Jesus's followers decide against the kingdom that the disciples have come to proclaim, and Chorazin, Bethsaida, and Capernaum will suffer a worse fate than Sodom and Gomorrah (cf. Matt 10:14–15 and 11:20–24).

14. Kaminsky, "Election," 409.

15. Schnabel, "Israel," 38.

16. The root "al-" or "all" goes back, it would seem, to a Proto-Indo-European (PIE) word, meaning "beyond." "c. 1300, 'strange, foreign,' from Old French *alien* 'strange, foreign'; as a noun, 'an alien, stranger, foreigner,' from Latin *alienus* 'of or belonging to

definition, speaking of someone who is not "one of us," but comes from beyond our boundaries. To speak of exclusion is not necessarily to pass a negative judgement or to imply inferiority. It can be simply a statement of fact. This person was born elsewhere and has come from that other place to be with us. How we welcome or conversely reject her or him is a separate and subsequent question.

In her work on the treatment of the *gēr* in the law codes of Israel,[17] Christiana van Houten seeks to show how this treatment developed over time. She argues for a progressive change in the attitude to the *gēr* from the pre-Deuteronomic tradition, through the Deuteronomic law code, to an exilic or post-exilic Priestly code. Although van Houten recognizes that the law codes are predominantly normative rather than descriptive, she nevertheless wants to claim that the behavior they posit as the norm should be at least in principle possible.[18] This means that whether or not the *gēr* was actually treated in this way in Israel, there was a reasonable expectation, and a deeply felt wish on the part of the compilers of the law code, that he or she would be. In her conclusion, van Houten sums up her findings as follows:

> What began as legislation pertaining to a stranger needing hospitality and justice in the Covenant Code changed in Deuteronomy to legislation dealing with a class of vulnerable, landless people and created a system of support which gave them economic stability. It encouraged the Israelites to be just in their social dealings, but did not encourage them to allow the outsider to join the community. This was also the case for the first level of redaction of Priestly laws. However, in the second level, in addition to the laws that treated aliens as outsiders and inferiors, there was also legislation [that] allowed the outsider to join the community and be on equal terms with the Israelite.[19]

It is not necessary to accept all of van Houten's conclusions, especially on the weight to be given to different strata of the law and her attempts to assign different redactions to particular periods.[20] Nevertheless, she both draws attention to and gives a plausible narrative for understanding the

another, not one's own, foreign, strange,' also, as a noun, 'a stranger, foreigner,' adjective from *alius* (adv.) 'another, other, different,' from PIE root *al-* (1) 'beyond.'

Meaning 'residing in a country not of one's birth' is from mid-15c. Sense of 'wholly different in nature' is from 1670s." This information comes from the Online Etymology Dictionary at https://www.etymonline.com/word/alien.

17. Van Houten, *Alien*.
18. Van Houten, *Alien*, 159.
19. Van Houten, *Alien*, 164.
20. See, for example, the comments of Pressler, Review.

change in approach to the *gēr* in Israel's history. Because, for my purposes, the precise details of the history of the development of Old Testament legislation and attitudes to the alien are not so important, I will broadly accept her findings. I do this not because the matters in question are unimportant, but because any account of the attitude to the alien is going to have to construct some explanatory narrative, and what really interests me is the way in which proximity brings about change. Whether this change amounted to a full-scale acceptance of the other as one who was either on the verge of becoming or already in some sense a child of Israel is not, for what I am looking at here, so central.

I now turn to look at some key texts that link the treatment of the *gēr* in Israel with Israel's own history. The first of these is Exod 22:21 (22:20 in the Hebrew text and some other translations), which reads "You shall not wrong or oppress a resident alien, for you were aliens in the land of Egypt." There is some discussion among scholars as to whether the motivational clause is a Deuteronomist addition or not.[21] Apart from this there are also questions about the historicity of the tradition of slavery in Egypt, which are too well-known to need to be rehearsed here.[22] However, the identifying myth of Israel by the time even these earlier laws were being written includes the motif of slavery in Egypt, and it is this that is most interesting.

Christiana van Houten suggests that the command of Exod 22:21 and the framing one in Exod 23:9 ("You shall not oppress a resident alien; you know the heart of an alien, for you were aliens in the land of Egypt") are to be taken within the context of law courts.[23] The justice that was not available to Israel as alien in Egypt is now to be made accessible to those aliens who dwell in its midst. The implication of this is that, because justice is ultimately an attribute of God, all who come before God come with the same rights and responsibilities. In this sense, the motivational clause would be unnecessary, but it nevertheless serves as a reinforcement of the command. Remembering its own experience of being denied justice, Israel should be even more ready to ensure that all who dwell in its land should have equal protection against oppression.

We can already see here that the *gēr* is not simply a problem to be resolved, but has a significant function as witness and reminder of God's activity on behalf of his people. Simply through their presence, the *gērīm* serve to recall Israel to a rightful attitude and place before God, and this

---

21. For example, van Houten, *Alien*, 53–54, concludes that it is not, whilst Bultmann, *Der Fremde*, 166–74, seems to think it likely that it is.

22. The classic work remains Gottwald, *Tribes*.

23. Van Houten, *Alien*, 55.

necessarily includes justice for all, since God's self-revelation is as a God of justice.[24] The passage from Exod 23:1–9 constantly reminds us of this. But in order for the practice of justice to be observed, so in order for Israel to fulfil its covenant with the Lord, the other, represented by the alien, the widow, the orphan, the poor, stands in a position of something akin to power.[25] It is only because the other stands there that Israel can see its task of doing God's justice and can recall its own experiences of injustice and God's liberating act.

However, it is not only for the sake of justice that Israel is called to welcome the stranger, but also out of love. Thus, in Deut 10:19 we find the command "You shall also love the stranger, for you were strangers in the land of Egypt." This comes within a passage (10:12–22) that is portrayed as a discourse of Moses, recalling his own encounter with God, and his people's journey from slavery[26] to freedom. According to Christoph Bultmann, this passage can be seen as a kind of introduction to the Deuteronomist law.[27] He dates this passage to the second decade of the sixth century BCE, so around the time of the return from exile.[28] The commandment to love stems from the fact that the *gēr* has no place to belong, therefore nowhere to receive the practice of love. Bultmann writes: "For the interpretation of the word [*gēr*] as a social type 10:18b[29] offers a confirmation, insofar as the sentence shows that the *gēr* is an independent person, not belonging to any "house," living on the borders of a minimum necessary for existence and for whom a responsibility is laid on the community who are addressed in the cultic language."[30]

---

24. This is a very common theme in liberation theology, which has often now come to see the option for the poor as an option for those whom in Spanish or Portuguese are called the *injustiçados*, the "injusticed." On this, see Vigil, "Opção."

25. I will allude to this later on, but I am thinking here in terms of Lévinas's observation that I am a hostage to the one who I am called on to substitute. See Lévinas, *Otherwise*, 112–18.

26. In the Deuteronomic law code itself, the motivating clause refers rather to Israel as slaves and not as aliens: cf. Deut 5:15–16 (on keeping the Sabbath); 16:12 (as a motivation for keeping all the laws regarding the Feasts); 24:17–18, 21–22. See Bultmann, *Der Fremde*, 126.

27. Bultmann, *Der Fremde*, 121.

28. Bultmann, *Der Fremde*, 123–24.

29. The text of Deut 10:17–19 is as follows: "For the LORD your God is God of gods and Lord of lords, the great God, mighty and awesome, who is not partial and takes no bribe, who executes justice for the orphan and the widow, and who loves the strangers, providing them food and clothing. You shall also love the stranger, for you were strangers in the land of Egypt."

30. Bultmann, *Der Fremde*, 127.

Thus, as Israel itself was once in a position of having no "house"[31] to which to belong, since it was placed in slavery as part of Pharaoh's household, it must now recall this and act with love towards the alien. The love of the alien is not, of course, an abstract sense of pity, but rather summarizes what the other commandments enjoin—allowing the gleaning of the land, not keeping the cloak at night, and other very practical examples of bearing life to those whose lives are threatened. If Bultmann is correct in his dating of this passage to the post-exilic period, it takes on extra force. The Israelites were not, at least for the most part, slaves in Babylon, but they were exiles, aliens, unloved, and the memory would still be fresh. Now that they have returned, the lawgiver is eager to remind them not to forget their recent experiences, but to use them as an additional incentive to love even more those among them who are undergoing something similar. People who are all in a sense *gērīm* meet in a particular spot, and each must practice love towards the other.

One final passage that will repay examination is Lev 19:33–34: "When an alien resides with you in your land, you shall not oppress the alien. The alien who resides with you shall be to you as the one born among you; you shall love the alien as yourself, for you were aliens in the land of Egypt: I am the LORD your God."[32] One way of reading this text is to take it in conjunction with the requirement in Lev 19:18 to love one's neighbor as oneself.[33] Thus, the main emphasis is not on avoiding injustice in the court but rather on allowing for socio-economic justice.[34] The love of one's neighbor demands also the love of the alien, of the *gēr* who resides in the midst of Israel. It is part of van Houten's overall argument in her book that the *gērīm* became increasingly assimilated, or at least were increasingly given permission to assimilate if they so wished.[35] Thus, the *gēr* was to be loved as Israel loved itself, because the *gēr* was potentially, if not yet actually, part of Israel. Moreover, part of Israel's love for itself was to become reconciled with its history, to remember its Lord's intervention in its history and the liberation that the Lord had brought to his people.

---

31. This idea will also influence the translation "*paroikos*."

32. The NRSV translation is slightly altered because "citizen," which the NRSV uses, seems a rather anachronistic choice for *ezrah*.

33. See van Houten, *Alien*, 142. See also on this, Kaminsky, "Loving."

34. van Houten, *Alien*. See also Bultmann, *Der Fremde*, 177, who argues that the form of Lev 19:33–34 shows that it should be understood as forbidding oppression (*Bedrückungsverbot*). Bultmann offers here a detailed analysis of the *Formgeschichte* of the text.

35. Schnabel, "Israel," 38–39, also points out that foreigners could join the community of Israel.

The picture of the *gēr* that is emerging, then, is of one who is increasingly seen as central to Israel's own self-understanding. In her examination of Jewish conceptions of the religious other, Ruth Langer notes that "the Jewish understanding of the non-Jew builds from an understanding of self as a member of this holy community in contrast with an outside world that lives according to a different (or non-existent) relationship to God."[36] But this sharp division was muddied by the presence of the *gēr*, who inhabited a somewhat intermediary status between the two.[37]

The beginning of Israel's story as recounted in the Bible, the story of Abraham, portrays Israel as a blessing for the nations.[38] It would appear, though, that the story of Israel can also be understood as portraying the *gēr* as in some sense a blessing for Israel. This is because of all that the *gērīm* bring to Israel, in terms of recalling it to a correct appreciation of what God has done for it, by offering it a chance to practice the love for the lost and abandoned that God himself had shown to his people. One way of seeing this dawning realization is by looking at the way in which the term *gēr* was translated in the later Jewish diaspora, when the Scriptures were rendered in Greek, and it is to this that we now turn.

THE SEPTUAGINT: UNPACKING THE LAYERS OF ENCOUNTER

The preceding section has served as an introduction to one of the main metaphors that I am employing in this book, that of *prosēlutos*. This is by far the most common translation of *gēr* in the Septuagint. It was either a neologism created by the translators themselves[39] or, more recent evidence indicates, taken from colloquial Alexandrian speech.[40] Before concentrating on the particular word, I want, however, to look at the Septuagint itself as translation, because the very act of translation is also central to what I am addressing. The first contact with the other for many missionaries, and certainly for William Carey and Innocent Veniaminov whom I consider later,

---

36. Langer, "Jewish Understandings," 257–58.
37. See Langer, "Jewish Understandings," 264n26.
38. Gen 12:1–3. For a detailed analysis of this, see Wright, *Mission of God*, 199–220.
39. See van Houten, *Alien*, 182.
40. On this topic, see Moffitt and Butera, "New Evidence." They bring evidence from a manuscript from roughly the third century BCE to show how the word *prosēlutoi* was used in a legal case that was not related either to the Jewish community or to religion. Thus it is likely, they argue, that *prosēlutos* was a common word in Ptolemaic Alexandria, signifying approximately what *gēr* did in Hebrew.

is with a language teacher, and the act of translating Scriptures has always been important,[41] so how did the first Scripture translators go about their task?

The Septuagint is, among other things, a contextual translation. It would, moreover, become, even if this was not its original intention, a way of allowing the *gēr* who did not speak or understand a Semitic language to approach the God of the Bible. At the same time, the act of translation forced the translators to reflect on their own faith, on what they wanted to say about this God, how this God had revealed himself to them. In accepting the gift of another language, they were allowed to express something of who they were, as individual translators and as part of a people.

This people, at least in the context of the translation, had moved from being a majority who had to decide on how to deal with the minority who dwelt among them to being themselves *gērīm*, strangers dwelling in another's land, marked out by their religious practices and the alphabet and language it used, from those around them. Put like this, however, the matter is over-simplified, since it runs the risk of the kind of racist language that demands that those of a different skin pigmentation or religious belief should not be allowed to remain in a particular setting but should "return home." This demand is made even though the people in question may have been born and grown up in the new setting. For the community for whom the Septuagint was written, the Jews are essentially a migrant group, like any other migrant group, with children who are bi-cultural, or even generations for whom the tales of the "home" country are simply that. This brings about a re-negotiation of concepts of belonging and strangeness, and it is this re-negotiation that I want to address now.

Here the mythical "history" of the Septuagint is interesting. As the authors of an introduction to Septuagint studies note, "[s]trictly speaking, there is really no such thing as *the* Septuagint."[42] In other words, at least in that respect, the legendary story of the 72 translators remains that, a nice story but with little historical foundation. But the earliest source that speaks of the translation, the *Letter of Aristeas*,[43] may still contain some genuine memories of what seems to have been an initial translation of the Pentateuch, always the most central part of the Hebrew Bible.

There are two factors in the *Letter of Aristeas* that I wish to pick up on, the part allegedly played by Ptolemy II Philadelphus and his librarian, and

---

41. See the well-known article by Andrew Walls, "Translation Principle," in Walls, *Missionary Movement*, 26–42; on the Septuagint in particular, see pp. 30–36.

42. Jobes and Silva, *Invitation*, 30. Italics in original.

43. See Jobes and Silva, *Invitation*, 33–37. For the text of the *Letter*, see Hadas, *Aristeas*.

the bargaining position that Aristeas, the purported writer of the document, adopts in relation to the Ptolemy. The evidence is overwhelming that the document could not have been written by a contemporary, and thus this is clearly a subsequent account.[44] However, as I have already made clear, the stories that people tell about themselves are an important element of who they take themselves to be, and this is regardless of whether these stories are factually correct in every sense. Even given the probability that Aristeas's[45] letter is intended to be a form of propaganda to defend his opinion in a possible conflict with other groups in the community,[46] it is still clearly an attempt to narrate a justification of this translation and to create a new story for the community to adhere around. So, the elements of purported contemporary history that Aristeas puts in are important in showing how the Alexandrian Jews were to view their own history and present.

The first thing, then, to take from the letter is that the translation came about as a request from the king. According to Aristeas, the librarian Demetrius of Phalerum[47] told the king

> "I am informed that the laws of the Jews also are worthy of transcription and of being included in your library." "What is to prevent you from doing so?" the king replied; "all the necessary means are at your disposal." But Demetrius said "Translation is required; in the country of the Jews they use a peculiar script, just as the Egyptians employ their arrangements of letters and they have their own language . . ." When the king learned these particulars he gave word that a letter should be addressed to the High Priest of the Jews, in order that the design above mentioned might be carried to completion.[48]

The initial impulse for the translation in this narration comes, therefore, from the other, and moreover not just from any other, but a privileged other, the king of the territory in which the diaspora community resides. Emissaries are sent[49] to the high priest in Jerusalem, as a result of which

44. After a lengthy discussion, Hadas, *Aristeas*, 54, argues for a date around 130 BCE, something like 125 years after the events are meant to have taken place.

45. Whatever the actual author was called, I will use Aristeas to describe them.

46. Cf. Jobes and Silva, *Invitation*, 34, and 35.

47. This is historically inaccurate, and one of the many reasons why scholars reject this as a contemporary account. Demetrius was an official under Ptolemy I Soter, but was opposed to the succession of Ptolemy II Philadelphus, and moreover, was never librarian. See Hadas, *Aristeas*, 96–97 (note to paragraph 9 of the *Letter*).

48. Hadas, *Aristeas*, 97 and 99. On this topic, see also Müller, *First Bible*, 46–58, here especially 47–48.

49. Named as Aristeas (himself) and Andreas; Hadas, *Aristeas*, 115.

translators return to Egypt. At least in the terms of the letter itself, Aristeas seems to imply that neither he nor his fellow emissary is Jewish, so they are in Jerusalem as *gērīm*, or *tōschābīm*, travelers from outside, who yet come to ask for help. The translators then return, with their language skills, to give the king what he seeks. So, according to Aristeas, the genesis of the translation of the Pentateuch lies in a joint mission of encounter.

The second important point for the contextualization of the translation can be found in the decision of Aristeas to link the mission to Jerusalem with a request to the king for the liberation of Jewish slaves in Alexandria. These had come or been forcibly removed to Alexandria following military campaigns by Ptolemy I and those who were not deemed fit for the military had been enslaved, according to Aristeas, on the demand of the Ptolemy's soldiers who had wanted recompense for their service.[50] The number of these slaves is given as around one hundred thousand.[51] It should be said that there is no link made here by Aristeas directly to the Exodus story and the liberation of the Jewish people from enslavement under the Egyptian Pharaoh, so we must be careful about reading too much into the parallel. In fact, Aristeas's motivating clause is that the law that Philadelphus is so keen on having translated is valid for all Jews, so it would be strange to send this request to the high priest, whilst holding the people in slavery, with the implication being perhaps that they would not be able to uphold this law anyway.

But, even if Aristeas himself does not draw out the parallel to the story of Moses, the text is suggestive enough for our purposes to allow this as a possible reading. In this, I am in agreement with Noah Hacham, who argues that the *Letter* is intended as a new Exodus story.[52] Hacham suggests that the underlying ideology of the book can be summed up as follows:

> a combination of total loyalty to Judaism and deep and active involvement with the Hellenistic world and culture. This combination is revealed in the writer's affection for and identification with the Hellenistic world on the one hand, and in the logic and justice attributed to the laws of the Torah, the central place of God, and the importance of the Land of Israel, Jerusalem, and the Temple on the other.[53]

One way of understanding the Septuagint, then, is as an expression of this encounter between the two worlds, of a way of remaining loyal to

---

50. See Hadas, *Aristeas*, 101.
51. See the note in Hadas, *Aristeas*, 104; the reference to the number is at 103.
52. Hacham, "Letter."
53. Hacham, "Letter," 2.

Judaism's foundational text and at the same time to the culture and world that is also now Aristeas's own, and in which the translation is embedded. But, Hacham claims, "the request for the liberation of the Jews and their actual liberation is one of the central issues in *Aristeas*."[54] In other words, this motif of liberation from slavery is not simply some kind of plot device for getting Aristeas to Jerusalem, but is at the heart of the argument being made in the *Letter*.

In detailing the similarities and differences between the Exodus story and the story of liberation in *Aristeas*,[55] Hacham notes that the differences all have one thing in common, namely that the writer of the *Letter* is happily settled in Ptolemaic Egypt, which is now his country. Perhaps even more interesting for me is the way in which Aristeas puts into the mouth of Eleazar, the high priest in Jerusalem, words from the discourse in Deuteronomy 10 that contains the passage discussed in the previous section. In fact, the scriptural quotation given in the text "Thou shalt remember what great and marvelous things the Lord thy God did in thee"[56] comes from two verses of Deuteronomy, 7:18 and 10:21, in their Septuagint version.[57] But in Eleazar's use of the words, they have nothing whatsoever to do with Egypt, or Israel's experiences there. Now they are related to an explanation of the food laws and other laws, which had, it would seem, become less intelligible to the Jewish diaspora community.[58]

If Israel is now *gēr* in Egypt, it is in a very different manner to before. God's love for his people in Egypt is now made manifest in a new way, since it is now, according to Hacham, the Ptolemy who assumes the role of Moses and gives the law to the people.[59] The story is thus not only, as previously noted, to do with establishing the act of translation as legitimate, but "[i]t seems that the purpose of reformulating a foundation story such as the Exodus, the building of the Tabernacle, and the giving of the Torah is updating and adaptation, thereby formulating a new foundation story."[60] Hacham claims that it does this in two ways, by legitimizing the residence of Israel in

---

54. Hacham, "Letter," 5.

55. Hacham, "Letter," 5–9.

56. Hadas, *Aristeas*, 161 (*Letter of Aristeas*, para. 155 and note).

57. The quotation from Deut 7:18 very consciously leaves out the reference to Pharaoh and the Egyptians—the full verse reads: "Do not be afraid of them [the surrounding nations]. Just remember what the LORD your God did to Pharaoh and to all Egypt."

58. Cf. Hadas, *Aristeas*, 66.

59. Hacham, "Letter," 12.

60. Hacham, "Letter," 14.

Egypt, a land with which it traditionally had problems,[61] and by showing the divine rationale and favor for Jewish residence in the land.[62]

The final point that needs to be made is that the *Letter* sees the translation as bringing about a deeper union between the Jews and the "Greeks," or Hellenized Egyptians. In cultures where table fellowship was so important, the refusal of Jews to eat with outsiders was often taken as an insult and led to hatred of Jews in various quarters.[63] So, part of what the letter is trying to do is offer an *apologia pro vita sua* of the Jewish community—why is it that we act in this way? Thus neither the *Letter of Aristeas* nor most especially the translation of the Law itself is simply for Jews, but an explanation to those among whom they live of what they do and why they do it. So, as Hacham concludes, everything that serves to

> provide a new account of the foundation stories of the Israelites, namely the Exodus from Egypt, the giving of the Torah, the construction of the Tabernacle, and perhaps the settlement in the Land of Israel—as taking place in Egypt, or as a result of the activities of the gracious Ptolemaic-Egyptian king—in order to provide a religious justification for residence in Egypt and to create friendly relations between Jews and foreigners in Egypt, is in line with this ideology. Moreover, if the *Letter of Aristeas* should be viewed in this manner, it should not be viewed as just another book emanating from this ideology, but rather, as a book that attempts to create a foundation story for this ideology—the foundation story of the Hellenistic Jewry.[64]

In writing this work, Aristeas has moved beyond seeing enmity as a natural state between the two cultures in which he lives, and has recognized that in the act of translating the Scriptures bridges are being built that will enable each to bring the best of what it has to the other. The Septuagint is thus the first act in a history of biblical translation that goes on till today.

At the heart of this translation, is the recognition of what it means to be *gērīm*, those who have come from one place to another, and found there a dwelling place, safety, welcome, acceptance. In finding this, the recipients also want to give the best of what they have, the revelation of their God, which they believe is for all. This is at heart a missionary enterprise, not because they want people to become Jews,[65] but because it is a way of com-

---

61. Though there were exceptions to this, as Kaminsky, "Election," 410, points out.
62. Hacham, "*Letter*," 14–16.
63. See Hacham, "*Letter*," 18.
64. Hacham, "*Letter*," 19.
65. Something that was very difficult, though it may well have been a result of this

municating their faith to the other in a way that is intelligible to that other, without betraying what they believe. It also reinforces the obvious point that to be alien is a relational and mutual concept. If you are alien to me, I am also alien to you, and thus paradoxically it is our awareness of otherness that is precisely what we share and what unites us.

The ways in which the communication between the groups happened were, no doubt, varied. I want here briefly to focus on just one reading of the Septuagint translation, suggested by John Beck, namely to see the translators as storytellers.[66] I do this because at the heart of any missionary encounter there is a sharing of stories, both the personal stories of the missionary and the other, and the story of the life, death, and resurrection of Jesus Christ, the Son of God.[67] The importance of narrative in theology in general and in missiology[68] in particular has increased greatly in recent decades, and although it is an approach that brings its own problems,[69] in this case it is a useful starting point.

The question is not so much, for my purposes, to do with particular narrative techniques, but with the way in which the storyteller responds to the "audience." In many ways this is a subdivision of the idea of dynamic equivalence in translation. The concept of dynamic equivalence, developed by Eugene Nida,[70] looked to bring about a similar response in the recipient of the message as that evinced in the recipient of the message in its original language. Thus when the storyteller narrates the story in a new setting (linguistic, cultural, religious), she or he seeks ways to enable the hearer to respond in the same way in which the original hearer responded.[71]

translation that more and more people became interested in Judaism, and the Jewish community had to develop policies of how to accept people into their midst in a more formal way. On this, see Langer, "Jewish Understandings," 260–62. In passing, it is perhaps interesting to note that the Hebrew for conversion is *gerut*, from the same root as *gēr*—see 260n15 of Langer's article. See also Goodman, *Mission and Conversion*, who argues persuasively that there was no widespread Jewish missionary enterprise in the first century, prior to the development of Christian mission, and that the main point of the Septuagint was to make the Scripture available to Jews themselves, most of whom no longer understood much, if any, Hebrew. On this too, see Walls, *Missionary Movement*, 30.

66. Beck, *Translators*.

67. To paraphrase somewhat the beginning of the Gospel of Mark.

68. See, for example, Adeney, "Why Biography?" and van Engen et al., *Footprints of God*.

69. See Mauz, "Theology and Narration."

70. Most developed in Nida and Taber, *Theory and Practice*. Nida would later come to prefer the term "functional equivalence." Among many discussions of Nida's work, see Constantinescu, "Nida's Theory."

71. For further reflections on this aspect of translation, and the problems associated

Translating Otherness in a Foreign Land

What does all this mean for the decision made by the Septuagint translators when it came to translating *gēr*? As Karen Jobes and Moisés Silva point out, when it comes to translating a word, "the semantic range of a given word is usually not identical to the range of its corresponding word in another language."[72] Clearly Greek had other words for stranger, and the Septuagint uses them, even to translate *gēr*. It can use *xenos*, as it does in Job 31:32, or *g(e)iōras* as in Is 14:1. But by far the most frequent words[73] are *paroikos*[74] and *prosēlutos*.[75] In keeping with the preceding paragraphs, we can ask what different stories are being told by the use of these words. Partly it may be a question of personal preference, but, given that both words are used in the same text, it clearly cannot be reduced to the idiolect of the translator.

In fact, it would seem that there is a fairly clear distinction, expressed already in the chosen Greek words, that explains the choice. When forms of *paroikos* are used, they generally refer to Israel itself, in its condition of "exile," from its land or its God or those who are in exile from the community. Thus texts that refer to Israel in Egypt, most commonly in reminding it of its previous status, almost always use *paroikos*, with its associated sense of being outside the home.[76] The perspective is, perhaps naturally, an Israelite one—where are we in relation to the other?

On the other hand, *prosēlutos* is almost always used to refer to the other who is present in Israel. Again, the word is self-explanatory: the reference is indeed to those who have come to Israel, those who have joined their lot to that of the people of the covenant. It is neither necessary nor greatly informative to concentrate in detail on all these passages, so I will merely make a few general remarks.

---

with it, see Charlesworth, "Translating Religious Texts."

72. Jobes and Silva, *Invitation*, 87.

73. According to Schnabel, "Israel," 37, 37n9, *gēr* is translated 77 times as *prosēlutos* in the LXX, and 11 times as *paroikos*.

74. For example, Gen 15:13; 17:6; 18:3; 19:9; 23:4; Exod 2:22; Lev 25:3; Deut 23:8; 1 Chr 29:15; Ps 39 (38):13; 119 (118):19; Ezek 20:38 (numbers in parentheses refer to the corresponding chapter in the LXX).

75. For example: Exod 12:48; 20:10; 22:20; 23:9, 12; Lev 16:29, 17:3 (not in Hebrew), 8, 10, 12, 15; 18:26; 19:10, 33; 20:2; 22:18; 23:22; 24:16, 22; 25:23, 35, 47; Num 9:14; 15:14, 26, 29; 19:10; 35:15; Deut 1:16; 5:14; 10:18; 12:18; 14:29; 16:11, 14; 24:14, 17, 19; 26:11; 27:19; 28:43; 29:10; 31:12; Josh 9:2; 20:9; 1 Chr 22:2; 2 Chr 2:16; 15:9; 30:25; Ps 94(93):6; 145(146):9; Isa 54:15; Ezek 14:7; 22:7, 29; 47:22; Zech 7:10; Jer 7:6; 22:3; Mal 3:5.

76. This is the image that is picked up, as we shall shortly see, in the New Testament, where it is *paroikos* that is used in Eph 2:19 and in 1 Pet 2:11.

One is that, as we have seen, the *gēr* is particularly apparent in the law codes. Now, in itself, this does not change in the translation of course, except that precisely the idea of *Torah* and its frequent Greek equivalent *nomos* are not identical (in Nida's terms, they are not entirely dynamically or functionally equivalent).[77] However, and in a sense regardless of the precise understandings of the two terms, the normative dimension of dealing with the stranger continues to be important. The other is not so alien as to remain outside the legislation of God, but is rather now included within the divine economy. This affording of a divine status to the other has to be held on to, since the amount of attention given to it does suggest that it is honored more in the breach.

But the granting of a privileged status to the *prosēlutos* cannot be pushed too far. This is perhaps most obvious in an interesting addition to the Greek text in Lev 17:3-4. The NRSV translation of the Hebrew text reads: "If anyone of the house of Israel slaughters an ox or a lamb or a goat in the camp, or slaughters it outside the camp, and does not bring it to the entrance of the tent of meeting, to present it as an offering to the LORD before the tabernacle of the LORD, he shall be held guilty of bloodshed; he has shed blood, and he shall be cut off from the people." The Greek text adds to the words "anyone of the house of Israel" the phrase "and of the proselyte." In itself, this is perhaps minor, and yet it does point to the fact that the *prosēlutos* is not simply given advantages but that it is taken for granted that she or he is also bound by the same restrictions as the people of Israel.

We will return to this facet when we discuss the New Testament, but before we go on to do that, another point needs to be recalled. Whatever the precise provenance (or provenances) of the Septuagint translators and translations, all of them come from a situation of what we might term migration. The Jews themselves are both *paroikoi*, as the people of Israel are in the translations, and at the same time, from the perspective of the peoples among whom they live, *prosēlutoi*. Whether this was a deliberate choice or not, it can be seen as a way of boosting the minority community, by giving it a doubly blessed status, reminding them of the Lord's care for both *paroikoi* and *prosēlutoi*.

One possible support for this is found in the Septuagint translation of Lev 16:29. The Hebrew is translated as "This shall be a statute to you forever: In the seventh month, on the tenth day of the month, you shall deny yourselves, and shall do no work, neither the citizen nor the alien who resides among you." "The alien who resides among you" is rendered in the LXX

---

77. See Jobes and Silva, *Invitation*, 88, including the corrective in footnote 3.

as "*ho prosēlutos ho proskeimenos*,"⁷⁸ the alien who is settled among you. Although again this is not a huge difference, it does make two things clear. The present passive participle suggests some agent, who may be God or may be some foreign power, but it implies that it is not the choice of the people to be where they are. At the same time, and in something of a counterpoint, it also implies a certain degree of permanence.

The relation between the translation of *gēr* and the situation of Jewish community life in the diaspora at the time of translation is taken up in an Appendix by Christiana van Houten. She sees the Septuagint as "the fundamental document of Hellenistic Judaism."⁷⁹ van Houten follows W. C. Allen in arguing that "*prosēlutos*" is used to refer to the "proselyte," and that occasions when Israel is described as proselyte⁸⁰ can be explained because they are always in cases when Israel is reminded of its status in Egypt, and thus its subsequent responsibility towards the other in its midst. She argues briefly, then, that the use of the term "*prosēlutos*" is a coinage by the translators of the Septuagint to deal with the phenomenon of interest in Judaism among non-Jews in Alexandria and elsewhere. She concludes by noting that "what began perhaps as reforming legislation in the restoration period to allow the indigenous population to join the cultic community of the returnees has become a practice in Alexandria which allows converts to join the Jewish community several centuries later."⁸¹

However, and rightly in my opinion, Allen's methodology is found wanting by Matthew Thiessen, who argues that it is simply wrong to translate *prosēlutos* as "proselyte" and to draw too hasty conclusions about conversions to Judaism from its presence in the Septuagint.⁸² Thiessen argues that Allen set out from the principle that the Septuagint could be regarded as something like a single translation unit, something that ignored the very different settings of the various translations, and indeed the nature of the texts they were translating from. By separating out the uses of *gēr* and *paroikos* and *prosēlutos* in the various OT books, Thiessen makes a convincing argument that the translators did not have converts in mind, but, as the phrase is frequently rendered in the New Revised Standard Version, "resident aliens." Nevertheless, I am not so convinced that *paroikos* and *prosēlutos*

---

78. On this, see Wevers, *Notes*, 257. Wevers points out that this is not a one-off, but that the same use is found in other verses of Leviticus: 17:8, 10, 12–13, and 25:6.

79. Van Houten, *Alien*, 179.

80. The reference is to an 1894 article, Allen, "Meaning." The discussion in van Houten focuses on the Pentateuch, and she points to Exod 22:20, 23:9, Lev 19:34, and Deut 10:34, where Israel is reminded of its status in Egypt. See van Houten, *Alien*, 181.

81. Van Houten, *Alien*, 183.

82. Thiessen, "Revisiting."

are complete synonyms in Deuteronomy, Ezekiel, and 1–2 Chronicles, as he suggests.[83] As I argued previously, whilst they may refer to the same group of people, they do so from different perspectives.

None of this, of course, brings us any closer to knowing precisely why the translators of the Septuagint, or at least one of them, decided to use *prosēlutos* to translate *gēr*. That question is, to all intents and purposes, unanswerable, and even if, *per impossibile*, we could talk to the translators themselves, anyone who has ever engaged in any kind of translation work will be aware that they would probably not be able to give a very satisfactory answer. And yet in doing so, they have provided us with a word-image that is helpful. It refuses to leave the stranger in our midst as some kind of monolith, a problem to be dealt with, but adds a dynamism to the presence of the one who has drawn near, who has come to be with us. Furthermore, the one who comes closer is in some sense transient, since one movement can be easily followed by another, in which the *prosēlutos* moves away. We can now turn to a briefer consideration of how the *gēr* was seen in the New Testament.

THE OTHER IN THE NEW TESTAMENT

Not surprisingly the New Testament writers take over a number of the words used by the different Septuagint translators, so we find, for example, *prosēlutos, paroikos, xenos*, and *allotrios*. There are however some differences. So, in the New Testament, *prosēlutos* is used exclusively to describe converts, or potential converts, to Judaism. There are only four such references, one in Matthew (23:5) and three in the Acts of the Apostles (2:11; 6:5; 13:43).

Of these, the Matthean reference is from the discourse against the Pharisees: "Woe to you, scribes and Pharisees, hypocrites! For you cross sea and land to make a single convert, and you make the new convert twice as much a child of hell as yourselves." Two brief points can be made here. By this stage, whatever the original use of the word in the Septuagint—and even more so in the Hebrew Scriptures—it is clear that *prosēlutos* has come to have a technical religious sense,[84] of one who draws near to Judaism with the intention of becoming eventually incorporated into the people of Israel.

---

83. Thiessen, "Revisiting," 349.

84. See Goodman, *Mission and Conversion*, 72. Goodman writes: "the word was *becoming* a technical term among Jews for a converted gentile, and had been doing so since the time of the Septuagint translation of the third and second centuries BCE, but . . . its meaning was not yet confined to this sense alone" (italics in original).

Traditionally this has been taken to indicate that Rabbinic Judaism was a missionary religion. However, as Martin Goodman has argued, there is little convincing evidence for this prior to the development of Christianity, and in this verse most probably the "proselyte" is the one who accepts the Pharisaic form of Judaism.[85] But second, it reminds us of the relationship between coming to Israel—in whatever form—and being beholden to the law. The general interpretation of this verse is that Jesus condemns the Pharisees, not for their missionary activity, whether *ad intra* or *ad extra*, but for making those who followed their form of Judaism subject to the full rigors of the law.[86]

It is also perhaps significant in this respect that the three uses of *prosēlutos* in Acts all refer to proselytes who have or at least are on the cusp of taking a further step, from Judaism to becoming followers of Jesus. Thus in Acts 2:10-11 the proselytes are among those who respond with amazement to Peter's speech, with the implication that they are among the three thousand (cf. 2:41) who were baptized that day. Acts 6:5 speaks of those who were chosen as deacons, and names one of them as Nicolaus, a proselyte of Antioch, and Acts 13:43 tells of Paul and Barnabas preaching in the synagogue of Antioch in Pisidia, the first of the three great set speeches by Paul in Acts. After the discourse, we are told, many Jews and devout proselytes came to learn more from Paul and Barnabas. Perhaps here there is a hint of what Augustine would famously say several centuries later, that the restless traveler after God will only finally come home through the encounter with the Risen Lord. At least it serves to encourage the possibility of moving towards fullness of life in God.

The two most striking uses of the *gēr* vocabulary of the Old Testament in the New Testament are found in Eph 2:19 and in the opening chapters of 1 Peter. Ephesians 2:19 reads: "So then you are no longer strangers and aliens, but you are citizens with the saints and also members of the household of God." "Strangers and aliens" is a translation of the Greek *xenoi kai paroikoi*. This combination does not appear in the Septuagint, nor precisely does the combination in Eph 2:12[87] that begins the argument ("remember

---

85. See Goodman, *Mission and Conversion*, 70–74. A somewhat different—though as far as I can see, largely unargued—position is adopted by Matthews, *First Converts*.

86. The whole chapter of the curses against the Pharisees has also been critiqued, but that is not my main interest here. However, see the brief but suggestive paper by Lattke, "Call to Discipleship."

87. However, see Exod 2:22, where Moses names Gershom thus, because *paroikos eimi en gē allotria* ("I have been an alien residing in a foreign land"). However, Eph 2:12 uses *apēllotriōmenoi* (translated here as "alienated") rather than *paroikos* and employs *xenos* for stranger. This at least suggests that such terms are, if the later parallel is to have any sense, more or less synonymous.

that you were at that time without Christ, alienated from the commonwealth of Israel, and strangers to the covenants of promise, having no hope and without God in the world" [NRSV translation slightly modified]). Here it is perhaps interesting to note that the language of *prosēlutos*, which may have been used in an Old Testament parallel, is no longer available, and that moreover the imagery has changed. The transitory dwellers have found a permanent home in God, and have a new city, that of the saints, with whom they are *sumpolitai*. Here then *paroikos* and *xenos* are seen as negative characteristics, perhaps reflecting the social world of the early Christians, where the threat of homelessness and non-belonging in social terms was ever-present.[88]

The other place where *paroikos* is an important term is in 1 Peter. The precise nature of the letter need not detain us here,[89] but it is worth considering the nature of the foreigner, a term applied by Peter to his addressees on three occasions (1:1, 1:17, and 2:11). Two words are used, *paroikoi* and *parepidēmoi*, which could be understood as "resident aliens" and "visiting aliens."[90] Thus the letter begins with words of greeting to the *parepidēmoi* of the Diaspora in Asia Minor. The *parepidēmoi* were those who were not settled, but were on the road, for a number of reasons. As Fika Janse van Rensburg points out, these words are not simply metaphorical, "[r]ather, the addressees were, already before their conversion to the Christian faith, 'visiting and resident foreigners' in the literal socio-political sense of the words."[91] Although there were also some more positive understandings of the word and, van Rensburg argues, it may indicate that they had been previously *prosēlutoi*, or at least God-fearers,[92] the word no doubt also indicated their daily experience as migrants, and people who were discriminated against.[93] The restrictions they faced on a daily basis were real enough, and,

88. See, for example, Edgar, *Social Setting*.

89. See for a brief discussion, van Rensburg, "Constructing," esp. 2–3. He accepts the Petrine authorship of the letter, thus dating it prior to 70 CE, but for my purposes it does not matter whether this is indeed by Peter or by someone else, and for the sake of convenience, I will use "Peter" to designate the writer of the letter.

90. Or, to put it in slightly more friendly, if wholly anachronistic language, the *paroikoi* had work permits, the *parepidēmoi* tourist visas.

91. Van Rensburg, "Constructing," 6.

92. On this, see also Seland, "πάροικος καὶ παρεπίδημος." He argues that the words do refer, at least in part, to the semantic domain of proselytes, but that their meaning is transformed here to refer to the situation of Christians in the region that Peter addresses.

93. van Rensburg, "Constructing," 7, and see especially footnote 27. This is not entirely germane to my argument, but the situation of the foreigner is also interesting in terms of the relationship to the law. As "aliens," they were not able to engage with the

as with other discriminated groups, they perhaps wore their designation, however pejoratively it was intended, as a badge of pride.

It is against this background that the small Christian communities addressed by Peter are to be understood. As the British biblical scholar David Horrell has argued, in this respect the choice of descriptors in 2:9, *genos*, *ethnos*, and *laos* is highly significant.[94] Here the writer of the letter is setting about the construction[95] of an alternative setting for those who are viewed—and in many ways indubitably are—*paroikoi* or *parepidēmoi*. This is a necessary basis for any language of stranger, since the alien is only ever relatively so, and always inhabits two worlds, the one where she or he is labelled "alien," and the one where she or he has a "positive"[96] belonging. Thus, the language of race, nation, and people serves to strengthen the *oikos* to which or from which the addressees are *paroikoi*.[97] It should be noted that this is at least an attempt at a positive identity formation, rather than what we also get in the New Testament, where the identity is much more over against the negativity of the "world."

Thus, when Peter speaks to the people as *paroikoi kai parepidēmoi* in 2:11, he is doing so within a particular context. These words in the singular, *paroikos kai parepidēmos*,[98] are used by Abraham in Gen 23:4, when he seeks permission from the Hittites for a burial place for Sarah. They also appear, again in the singular, in Ps 39:12 (LXX 38:13), where the psalmist calls on God for help, describing himself as *paroikos kai parepidēmos*.[99] van Rensburg sees the letter as addressing how the Christians should live, as

---

legal system, and as people who had left Judaism, they were also seen as outside the law of Israel. In that respect, Paul's call to move beyond the law can be seen as a typically Pauline move of emphasizing, rather than ignoring, the apparent weakness of a position. To be beyond the law is not a problem but a blessing.

94. See Horrell, "'Race,' 'Nation,' 'People.'"

95. See Horrell, "'Race,' 'Nation,' 'People,'" 136–37, on the social construction of ethnicity.

96. There are, of course, all sorts of problems here, which two thousand years of Christian history have displayed all too clearly. Any form of nationalism or, in Horrell's terms, ethnoracial identity, can be abused.

97. The best-known work on this topic remains Elliott, *Home for the Homeless*, here 24–49, though reference to other works cited here will make it clear that Elliott's reading is not uncontested.

98. In both cases, *paroikos* translates *gēr*, whilst *parapidēmos* is used to translate *tôshāb*.

99. See more on this in Seland, "πάροικος καὶ παρεπίδημος," 249–52. In reading this, however, Thiessen's deconstruction of Allen's arguments, which Seland follows to some extent, should be borne in mind.

Encountering the Other in the Scriptures

strangers and sojourners, in both real and metaphorical terms.[100] But they do this against a particular backdrop, and part of what they are encouraged to do is, as it were, to find a way of burying their dead, of leaving behind them their old lives, and reconfiguring them, not so that they alienate themselves even further from the world in which they find themselves, but so that they can relativize the impact of that world in comparison with the true home, people, race, and nation to which they belong, that of Christ.

It is also true, as Torrey Seland argues, that, just as it was for Abraham and for the psalmist, the state in which they find themselves is a temporary one (*ton tēs paroikias umōn chronon,* as 1:17 puts it, "the time of your exile"), that began with their conversion.[101] Thus, they find themselves on a journey,[102] and the exhortations in the letter are something like rules for travelers. But they are real travelers, and the designation in the Septuagint for the alien who resides among you, "*ho prosēlutos ho proskeimenos,*" is echoed in John 1:14, (*ho logos sarx egeneto kai eskēnōsen en hēmin*). To be a resident alien, to dwell among others who do not receive you, was the lot of Christ, and is the lot of the Christian.

A Brief Word on the Vulgate

The importance of the Vulgate translation of *gēr* or *prosēlutos* does not lie so much in the actual nature of the translation, but in the possibilities that it will open up for my argument later on, so here I only want to note briefly the most common ways in which the words were translated into Latin. The most frequent translation is a literal translation of *prosēlutos*, namely *advena*. On occasions the translation *peregrinus* is employed, and on three occasions in 1–2 Chronicles, the transliteration *proselytus* is chosen, though in 2 Chr 15:9, where it would have made as much sense as elsewhere to use that translation, in fact *advena* is preferred.

Thus, it would seem that the Vulgate follows rather closely the Septuagint in its translation here, including using *peregrinus* especially to translate *paroikos*. This taking over of the Greek word in its Latin form has, I would argue, some unexpected advantages, since it emphasizes again the dynamic nature of the other, as the one who draws near, who comes towards. It also

---

100. Van Rensburg, "Constructing," 2

101. Seland, "πάροικος καὶ παρεπίδημος," 257. Seland's further argument is based on his conviction that 1 Peter can and should be read in the light of Philo, as expressing a more general Jewish background and thought. See also Seland, "Common Priesthood."

102. The Vulgate translates *parepidēmoi* in 2:11 as *peregrinos*, whereas in 1:1 it uses *advenis*, the term more associated with its translation of *prosēlutos*.

allows us to see an eschatological dimension, which will enable the *chronos paroikias* to change into a *kairos prosēluton*. I will return to these dimensions later.

JESUS AND THE ENCOUNTER WITH THE OTHER IN THE GOSPELS

In this section, I want to begin to move the discussion on by reflecting on some of the encounters with the other—with the *prosēlutos*—that Jesus had in the Gospels. As a Jew, well-versed in the Jewish Scriptures, Jesus would obviously have known very well the tradition regarding the treatment of the resident alien. What is interesting in his encounters with non-Jews is the note of tension that is often present, between an exclusivity and an inclusivity.[103] It appears to be the role of the other to help clarify and resolve this tension. To whom is Jesus sent? This is the question that has to be answered in the course of Jesus's ministry, and it is a key one for the early church, too.

The first point to make is the well-known one that there is ample evidence to suggest that the encounter with the other who came to him had a profound effect on Jesus, especially as the story is recounted in the Gospel of Matthew.[104] Immediately after the Sermon on the Mount we find a series of healings and other miracles that serve to concretize the teaching gathered in the preceding chapters. The first two both feature people who "came to him" (*prosēlthen autō*)[105]—first the leper, who worships him, and second, the centurion, who does not consider himself worthy of having Jesus enter his house. The leper says to him, "If you choose, you can make me clean." This other does not command Jesus to heal him but to make a choice, but it is still in a sense a command, asking Jesus to decide about the nature of his ministry. Does he welcome or continue to exclude the other? By choosing to make the man clean (*thelo*—"I want [to]"), he sets a pattern for his ministry from the beginning. It is one that responds positively to those seeking restitution

---

103. On this see, with special attention to Matthew's Gospel (on which I will primarily focus in this section), Senior, "Between Two Worlds." The article focuses on the encounter between Judaism and the gentile world as reflected in Matthew.

104. On this topic, see an excellent reflection by Matthey, "Pilgrims," esp. 122.

105. Matt 8:2 (*proselthōn prosekunei autō*) and Matt 8:5 (*prosēlthen autō*).

to the community, especially those who are marginalized through illness, gender,[106] religious belief, or race.[107]

Thus, when the Roman centurion—whatever his ethnic origin, he was a representative of an oppressive colonial power and, perhaps even more to the point, ritually unclean[108]—comes to him, as one who understands, perhaps even abuses, the language of command and response, he asks Jesus to heal not himself but someone else,[109] a servant (*pais*, which can of course also mean child).[110] The response of Jesus is clear. He is amazed (*ethaumasen*, filled with wonder) "in no one in Israel have I found such faith."[111] The faith of the other, coming from a different background, socially, ethnically, religiously, transforms the way in which Jesus views the other, for now he comes to realize that faith (response to the givenness[112] of God) is possible not just in Israel but outside.

To concentrate on Matthew is not just because the Gospel contains some of the clearest narrative examples of how Jesus is moved by the other

---

106. The story of the woman who had been bleeding for 12 years is found in this section of Matthew, in 9:20–22, within the story of the young girl who has died. See the comment of Burchard, "Matthäus," 287: "It is in this connection important to note that the three individuals to whom Jesus does good are disadvantaged—an outcast, a pagan, a woman."

107. The centurion is not a Jew, so ethnically and religiously he differs from those around him. Admittedly, in Matthew, he is not specifically identified as non-Jewish, but the overwhelming implication is that he is. On this, see, for example, Burchard, "Matthäus," 278–80.

108. See Smillie, "Even the Dogs," 78–84, who details the considerable gentile presence in Palestine at the time of Jesus. Thus, these encounters are not so rare as is sometimes proposed, which makes them both more likely, and more threatening. On the colonial experience, see also p. 91 of "Even the Dogs": "As a commanding officer of the hated Roman army of occupation, this outlander represents the far end of the spectrum of those to whom the Jewish Messiah ministers."

109. On the "economics" of this request, see Anderson, "Healthy Economics," 2 (of 16). She sees this encounter as a series of "transactions" between, in this case, Jesus and the centurion, who acts as a "Supplicant on behalf of Another," in Anderson's phrase.

110. There are conflicting opinions on which translation is best here, though the majority, perhaps influenced by Luke 7:1–10, are inclined to assume it is a servant (however, the Johannine parallel in 4:46–53 can also be taken as favoring "son" or "child"). See Burchard, "Matthäus 8,5–13," 281n15, and, in an otherwise rather strange article, the discussion in Shaffer, "Harmonization," 40–41. The very fact that Shaffer is so concerned with a perceived need to harmonize two texts from different Gospels gives a good indication of the kind of article this is. However, it has some useful information in as well.

111. See Matthey, "Pilgrims," 124. The "such great faith" that Jesus finds here contrasts with the little faith he finds in his disciples in 8:26.

112. I will refer much more to the concept of givenness in chapter 3, in relation to the work of Jean-Luc Marion.

whom he encounters in his mission. The Gospel is also, arguably, the most explicitly missionary.[113] The second great discourse, in chapter 10, is the missionary discourse,[114] the sending out of the disciples, which, of course, does not actually happen until the end of Matthew.[115] The mission here, though, is still to the "lost sheep of the house of Israel" (Matt 10:6), not to the gentiles or Samaritans (10:5). The encounter that most allows the change of the final commission to the disciples (Matt 28:19), to make disciples of the whole world, is that with the Canaanite woman (Matt 15:22–28). Initially Jesus refuses to acknowledge her or her command to "have mercy"[116] on her and her daughter.[117] He will not even agree to send her away, since that would constitute engagement with her,[118] and "I was sent only to the

---

113. Matthey, "Pilgrims," 122: "Matthew's gospel has often been considered a 'bestseller' for missionaries." Matthey's intention, however, is to get beyond the appeal of the so-called "Great Commission" to show that Matthew is a great deal subtler and richer.

114. On this, apart from works mentioned in the next footnote, see Cuvillier, "La construction narrative," esp. 165–70. The "displacement" that Cuvillier refers to in his title is precisely from the exclusive to the inclusive (or particular to universal) mission.

115. For more detail, see Weaver, *Matthew's Missionary Discourse*. See also Brown, "Direct Engagement," for a broader account of the nature of the Matthean discourses. She comments on the missionary discourse's incomplete nature on pp. 24–25.

116. Matthey, "Pilgrims," 125, notes how these words have become part of the liturgy (though they are also present, for example, in Matt 17:15, another example of what Anderson, "Healthy Economics," sees as a microeconomic exchange between Jesus and a supplicant on behalf of another—here a man with a sick son). The words of the centurion in Matt 8:8, "Lord, I am not worthy to have you come under my roof; but only speak the word," are—as Matthey also says—contained in some Christian liturgies.

117. On this topic, see Smillie, "Even the Dogs," 93, who notes that Jesus's first words seem "cold and harsh," and his "subsequent refusal sounds insulting."

118. There are various possible interpretations for this. Guardiola-Saenz, "Borderless Women," gives a highly ideological interpretation, seeing the woman as a victim of oppression. In some ways, of course, she is right, but as Gundry-Volf, "Spirit," esp. 516, argues, the woman would probably have been upper-class, and in coming from Tyre would have been seen by the Jews as a representative of an oppressive people. The two positions are not necessarily mutually exclusive, of course, and Guardiola-Saenz is, I think, right in her condemnation of the initial exclusive attitude displayed by Jesus and the disciples (or at least by the Gospel writer in his account of the meeting). See also Presler, "Mission is Ministry," 201: "Matthew characterizes her identity as different not only ethnically and nationally but also by the term 'Canaanite,' which in Israelite history evoked religious abhorrence and national enmity."

lost sheep of the house of Israel."[119] But the woman comes to him (here *elthousa*), kneels,[120] and says "Lord, help me."

Even this command is not enough to convince Jesus. His reply sounds rather pat,[121] like the kind of put-down line a politician might use when they realize they cannot win an argument: "It is not fair (*kalon*, good) to take the children's food and throw it to the dogs." By introducing the concept of what is "good" or just into the conversation, Jesus seems to be trying to regain the moral high ground. The mother's reply is devastating in its simplicity—even the dogs get to eat of the crumbs that fall from the table, and, implicitly, that too is good and fair.[122] The effect of this on Jesus is immediate.[123] This time he is not even astounded, because the sheer physical presence of the other does not permit even astonishment or wonder, which would be a form of possession and destruction. All he can do is exclaim, for the only time in the Gospel, that in this woman he has met someone of great faith (*megalē sou hē pistis*).[124] And this is enough to bring about the cure of her daughter. From this point on there is no restriction of the missionary activity of Jesus himself or his disciples.

At the same time, in keeping with the fact that, as we will see time and again, the missionary is also *prosēlutos*, the one who comes, it is worth noting that in John's Gospel Jesus is portrayed in the prologue as the one who comes and is not accepted (John 1:11). Later in the first chapter of the Gospel it is in his coming to John (*erchomenon pros auton*, John 1:29) that Jesus is first proclaimed—"Behold the Lamb of God." Verbs of movement are not without significance in John's Gospel. Jesus is the one sent by the Father who

---

119. However, as Cuvillier, "La construction narrative," 171–72, notes, in the story of the Canaanite woman, it is only the part about the lost sheep that is repeated. He interprets this as a broadening of understanding of who the lost sheep are—now not just the people of Israel as traditionally understood, but "all those who await a word of healing from Jesus."

120. Matthey, "Pilgrims," 125–26, points out that kneeling is a gesture of discipleship.

121. It has been suggested that this is a kind of proverbial saying: see, for example, Cadwallader, "Out of Wordlock," 265. Cadwallader focuses on the Markan version, which contains the additional phrase "Let the children be fed first," but the general point is valid. See also Gundry-Volf, "Spirit," 517.

122. See Smillie, "Even the Dogs," 93–94; Guardiola-Saenz, "Borderless Women," 78; Gundry-Volf, "Spirit," 518–19.

123. See Presler, "Mission is Ministry," 201: "The woman expanded Jesus' understanding of his calling to include a sending to the Gentiles."

124. Gundry-Volf, "Spirit," 519–20, expresses it like this: "Jesus rises up to her faith in him as Lord of Gentile as well as Jew, of oppressor as well as victim. When he marvels at her faith . . . he does so not as one who has simply tested her faith and approved it, but as one who is himself inspired by her faith." It is, though, worth mentioning that in Mark there is no word about the woman's faith.

in turn sends out his disciples (John 17:18), and the Father sends the Spirit (John 14:26). Jesus is the one who makes the Father seen.[125]

SUMMARY

As I have made clear, this chapter has no pretensions to be a work of detailed exegesis for its own sake. Nevertheless, it has been both important—as it always is for any theology—and informative to return to the biblical stories, and look at how the other is treated there. A first important point to be drawn from this treatment is the unusually positive regard for the resident alien that is displayed in the books of the Old Testament. Presuming that ancient peoples were as averse to the presence of the stranger as their modern counterparts, it is hard not to be struck by the way in which the rights of the stranger are repeatedly and powerfully re-affirmed by appeal to Israel's own founding myth as a people who had lived as resident aliens in an oppressive world. In this sense, the stranger is a reminder of the blessing that Israel has received from its God. More than a threat, or an oddity, the stranger becomes a necessity.

The two major translation choices for *gēr* in the Septuagint are *prosēlutos*, the drawing near/approaching one, and *paroikos*, the one who is close to (but therefore not in) the house.[126] These translations, the first of which especially is echoed in the Vulgate translation (*advena*), carry various implications. The first emphasizes the point already noted, namely, the relational nature of any description of someone as "alien" or "stranger." They are so both in relation to another person, who does not consider themselves in those terms, and in relation to a particular time and place. But precisely by crossing the boundary, coming nearer, the stranger at the same time destroys the imagined boundary.[127] Simply by being able to identify someone

---

125. As Jean-Luc Marion puts it "[t]he depth of the visible face of the Son delivers to the gaze the invisibility of the Father as such" (Marion, *Idol and Distance*, 8).

126. The word has some relation to the etymology of the English word "foreign," the one at the doors. See http://www.etymonline.com/index.php?term=foreign: "Foreign (adj.): c. 1300, *ferren, foreyne* . . . from Old French *forain* 'strange, foreign; outer, external, outdoor; remote, out-of-the-way' (12c.), from Medieval Latin *foranus* 'on the outside, exterior,' from Latin *foris* (adv.) 'outside,' literally 'out of doors,' related to *foris* 'a door,' from PIE *dhwor-ans-*, suffixed form of root *dhwer-* 'door, doorway'. English spelling altered 17c., perhaps by influence of *reign, sovereign*. Sense of 'alien to one's nature, not connected with, extraneous' attested late 14c. . . . Replaced native *fremd*."

127. This is the argument of Guardiola-Saenz, "Borderless Women," in her interpretation of the Canaanite woman.

as a stranger, they in fact cease to be so, since I already have some interaction with them.

The second translation, *paroikos*, is more important in the New Testament, by which time *prosēlutos* had, for the most part, a more technical meaning. But the *paroikos*, especially in 1 Peter, offers a further insight into what it is to be a disciple of Christ, which is well summed up in the Vulgate translation of *peregrinus*. Their home is now in Christ, and yet they are still not there, so they live also among others, who however will regard them as strangers and aliens.

In the following chapters I will develop these points more fully in terms of a theology and practice of mission that will require focusing on both the "missionary" and the "missioned." Both are *prosēlutoi*, and their journey is towards a meeting point. On that journey they bring with them their own gifts and their own weaknesses and areas of ignorance. They are also both called to be *paroikoi*, to step outside of the door of their house to encounter the other, with all the risks and benefits that involves. I will especially concentrate on how this meeting must be a meeting in love, for as God loved Israel when it was in the position of stranger, so Israel (and by extension the follower of Christ) is to welcome and love the stranger.

So it is that in the next chapter I will turn to current missiology. How have writers in the field of mission studies tried to deal with the challenge posed by the other? I will start with some reflections on the development of mission over the past hundred years to show how missiologists and missionaries have become gradually more aware of the wealth to be found in attending to the other. Then I look at some well-known attempts to encapsulate this approach into some kind of method, before turning to reflections on the role of dialogue in mission, as the first step in allowing oneself to be confronted by the other. This investigation, which will be necessarily expository, since I want to allow the voice of contemporary writers on mission to be heard, will demonstrate both how far the reflection on the role of the other in mission has come, and what still needs to be done.

2

Mission Encountering the Other

In the previous chapter I looked at how the encounter with the resident alien was reflected on in the Old and New Testaments. From this first investigation, it is already clear that the other who comes to us is both blessing and challenge to our prejudices and our certainties. The other is a blessing as a reminder of the good that God has done and—at least implicitly therefore—continues to do. Our God is a liberating God, who hears and responds to the cry of his people, and the other who comes to us, especially the other in need, is a permanent reminder of this liberating intervention. But at the same time, the other brings challenges, as we saw with the encounters of Jesus with the centurion and Canaanite woman in Matthew's Gospel. The exclusive certainties that were assumed are opened up to question.

So, in this chapter, I turn to contemporary missiologists, to see what they have had to say on the subject of mission's addressee, the "other" who is encountered in and who draws near in any form of Christian mission. I will begin with a very short excursus on the "other" as presented in the work of Emmanuel Lévinas, the Lithuanian-born French philosopher. This will help clarify the way in which I understand the term, though it cannot and will not serve as a definition, something that in Lévinas's understanding would be precisely impossible.

Having set the scene in this way, I will seek to trace in broad terms the development in understandings of mission over the past century, using as framing points the Edinburgh World Mission Conference of 1910 and the smaller conference held to mark its centennial in 2010. This will show us what has been done to give a more central role to the voice of the other who comes, whilst also indicating some of the remaining *lacunae*. The attempts to give more space to the other form the basis of several readings of the methodology of contextual theology, so I will consider them briefly as suggesting how the other can be given more solid space in reflection on mission. Finally, in this chapter, I will focus in on dialogue as one way of being confronted by the other.

A BRIEF REFLECTION ON EMMANUEL LÉVINAS

My reading of this other is heavily influenced by Emmanuel Lévinas (1906–1995),[1] and so it is only right that I very briefly consider his work now.[2] Lévinas's key concern was to find a way out of the reduction of all to sameness, what he called "totality."[3] His proposal was that, first, there must be a move from the primacy of metaphysics to the primacy of ethics, and secondly, then, that ethics is concerned with the relation between the I and the other. So, in his book *Autrement que Savoir*, Lévinas comments, "The term ethics for me always means the fact of encounter, of the relation of an I with an other."[4] As someone deeply rooted in the tradition of Judaism, he also always saw this other in primarily Old Testament terms:

> To hear [the] destitution [of the Other] which cries out for justice is not to posit an image for oneself, but is to posit oneself as responsible both as more and as less than the being that presents itself in the face. Less, for the face summons me to my obligations and judges me . . . More, for my position as *I* consists in being able to respond to this essential destitution of the Other, finding resources for myself. The Other who dominates me in his transcendence is thus the stranger, the widow, the orphan to whom I am obligated.[5]

---

1. For a biography of Lévinas, who was born in Kaunas, Lithuania (then part of the Russian Empire) in 1906 and died in Paris in 1995, see Malka, *Emmanuel Lévinas*. Lévinas studied under Husserl and Heidegger, was imprisoned in the war—during which most of his family in Lithuania were murdered by the Nazis—and then worked for many years as head of the École Normale Israélite Orientale, the leading Francophone institute of higher education in Judaism. Later he held positions in Poitiers, Nanterre, and the Sorbonne.

2. I have considered Lévinas's contribution in more detail in Noble, *Poor in Liberation Theology*, especially 74–83. I draw on that treatment in what follows. In terms of what I talk about in this chapter, see also Hall, "Conversing with Others," with brief reference to Lévinas on p. 7.

3. The title of his first major philosophical work is *Totality and Infinity*.

4. Lévinas, *Autrement que Savoir*, 28, in Júnior, *Sabedoria da Paz*, 271. I translate here from the Portuguese.

5. Lévinas, *Totality and Infinity*, 215; cf. 78 and 251.

Thus, a Lévinasian reading also reminds us that this encounter with the other, here specifically including the *gēr*, is always an "ethical" encounter, not in the rather loose sense of implying a particular form of behavior according to one or other ethical system, but in terms of fundamental relationship.

Moreover, Lévinas also insists that there is an almost absolute responsibility to respond to the command of the other.[6] For Lévinas, as soon as Jesus looks at the face of the Canaanite woman, he is in some sense obliged to do what she asks. As he famously writes in his second major philosophical work, *Otherwise than Being*, "A subject is a hostage."[7] Thus, specifically in relation to my theme, the missionary is always in some sense the hostage of two others[8]—namely of Christ and of the other encountered in mission. But these others cannot be defined, for, as the final word of the title of Lévinas's *Totality and Infinity* (*infini* in French) reminds us, the other is unbounded, the one who cannot be reduced to sameness, to the I. Thus, again in Lévinas we see that the other is a blessing, as my only guarantee of freedom, and a challenge, as the one whose command I must obey. In this chapter, I want to look in more detail at how missiologists have viewed this commanding other.

FROM EDINBURGH TO EDINBURGH: ONE HUNDRED YEARS OF ENCOUNTER[9]

The discussion[10] over the role of the other raises the question as to how the mission of the church and the churches can lead to the building up of the body of Christ in such a way as to include this other in a radically constructive way. My response to this question begins with a significant moment in early twentieth-century mission history, the World Mission Conference

---

6. I deliberately say "almost absolute," since Lévinas also introduces the concept of the Third to maintain justice—my responsibility to the other is absolute unless it involves harm to a Third. He writes: "My resistance begins when the evil which [the Other] does to me is done to a third who is also my neighbor" (Lévinas, *De Dieu*, 134, in Júnior, *Sabedoria da Paz*, 91).

7. Lévinas, *Otherwise than Being*, 112. In other words, the other who commands or gives the power to command (as he writes in *Totality and Infinity*, 178) is ultimately the one who has power over me and holds me hostage, since without that other I cannot exist.

8. On this in relation to questions of multiculturalism, see Elolia, "Let us Break Bread."

9. This section draws heavily on Noble, "Addressing the Other," which I have, however, adapted for the purposes of this book.

10. See more on this in Bosch, *Transforming Mission*, 368–89.

Part 1: The Other

and Greek Churchmen were to be considered as coming within the province of the Conference, as Foreign Missions."[17] To the credit of the organizing committee, they were able to accept that "Roman and Greek Churchmen" were Christians.[18] At stake here, though, is where the borders of "otherness" lie, and what degree of otherness is acceptable.[19] This question will reoccur in terms of relation to culture. Underlying the decision to exclude particular territories from consideration as missionary regions was, however, something more problematic. Who has the power to locate the other in a particular place? Who can decide what counts as a church, or whether someone has or has not heard the gospel? This is the danger of trying to "define" the "infinite" and is not merely a historical question.

In 1910, the world was still being carved up, predominantly amongst the European superpowers, and the British Empire was approaching its peak. The implication was that the world could be divided into categories[20] according to the whim of the leading nations,[21] not so much salvation his-

---

17. The question was put by Bishop Montgomery, the Secretary of the Society for the Propagation of the Gospel, cited in Stanley, *World Missionary Conference*, 52

18. There were several problems faced in dividing the world up into Christian and non-Christian. On some of the problems involved in formulating the statistics for the Conference, see Stanley, *World Missionary Conference*, 60–64. See also Kim, "Edinburgh 1910 and Edinburgh 2010" (esp. 5), a lecture given at the Henry Martyn Centre in Cambridge in January 2010. Nearly all of Europe and Latin America were excluded from the Conference's remit, a fact described by Andrew Walls as "a major lacuna" in the conference. See Walls, "Commission One," 29–30. There were still some missions being carried out to indigenous groups in Latin America, but these were not as such represented in Edinburgh. On nineteenth-century Protestant views of Latin America, see Orozco, "'Not to Be Called Christian.'"

19. The decision to ignore these territories as mission territories led ultimately to what one commentator has called "the fatal flaw of Edinburgh 1910." See Dowsett, "Cooperation," in *Edinburgh 2010*, 250–62. It is debatable whether it was fatal, though it was certainly debilitating. Another Evangelical writer, the veteran missiologist David Hesselgrave, has placed the fatal flaw of Edinburgh 1910 and all subsequent ecumenical endeavors in the decision not to require any prior doctrinal consensus. See Hesselgrave, "Will We Correct."

20. The "heathen parts" were Africa and Asia, whilst the rest was considered part of Christendom.

21. On this, see Butlin, *Geographies of Empire*. Butlin's work begins with a wonderfully apt, if intentionally disturbing, quotation from a book published in 1893 by J. Scott Keltie, Assistant Secretary to the Royal Geographical Society. The book, *The Partition of Africa*, is described by Butlin, as "a helpful and generally even-handed chronicle of the history and geography of the 'scramble' for Africa" (*Geographies of Empire*, 1). The quotation from Keltie's book reads, "We have been witnesses to one of the most remarkable episodes in the history of the world. During the past eight years we have seen the bulk of the once barbarous continent [Africa] parceled out among the most civilized Powers of Europe" (Keltie, *Partition*, 1, quoted in Butlin, *Geographies of Empire*, 1).

held in Edinburgh in June 1910. This will offer a first approxim[ation of?]
what I mean by the encounter with the other, and why it is import[ant to?]
missionary enterprise.

Edinburgh 1910 and the Nature of the Other

The World Missionary Conference[11] was originally to have been [called?]
"The Third Ecumenical Missionary Conference."[12] One of the first t[hings the?]
planning committee had to deal with, before getting on to the non[-Chris-?]
tian other, was the question of the Christian "other." Who would be [wel-?]
come? It was clear from the start that there would be no Roman Catl[holic or?]
Orthodox participation,[13] because neither of these churches would d[ream of?]
attend. Nevertheless, from very early on, the main planners of the c[onfer-?]
ence, J. H. Oldham[14] in Scotland and John Mott[15] in the United State[s, were?]
keen to ensure the widest possible representation from mission bodie[s and?]
other denominations. They were particularly eager to make sure the [Angli-?]
can Church was represented, which meant coming up with a formul[a that?]
was acceptable to the Anglo-Catholic part of the Anglican Communic[n.?][16]

Of special concern was the way in which mission territories were [to be?]
defined, specifically "whether missions of Protestant Bodies among Ro[man?]

---

11. The major history of the conference is Stanley, *World Missionary Confer*[ence.?]
See also Ellis, *Century*.

12. This was because it followed two previous conferences held in London in 1[888?]
and New York in 1900. See Stanley, *World Missionary Conference*, 18-19 (and p. 3[6 on?]
the decision to change the title).

13. Greetings were read out to the conference from the Roman Catholic Bis[hop?]
Bonomelli of Cremona, acting on his own behalf and at the invitation of an Ameri[can?]
Episcopalian, Silas McBee. See Stanley, *World Missionary Conference*, 11-12 and 3[6.?]
The text of the greeting is to be found in Gairdner, *Edinburgh 1910*, 210-13. On Bish[op?]
Bonomelli, see Delaney, "From Cremona," which also contains the text of the messa[ge?]
(424-25). Bonomelli was a good friend and mentor of Angelo Roncalli, later Pope Joh[n?]
XXIII.

14. J. H. (Joe) Oldham (1874-1969) was a lay member of the United Free Presby[-?]
terian Church, and later an Anglican. On Oldham, see Clements, *Faith on the Frontie*[r?]
(on Oldham's role in the preparation and conduct of the Edinburgh 1910 conference[,?]
see 73-99).

15. John Mott (1865-1955) was a Methodist. For a biography, see Hopkins, *Mott*.

16. For this reason, it is perhaps too simplistic to say that the conference represented the Protestant churches, since the Anglo-Catholics would not have accepted this
description as reflecting who they were. On this topic, see Stanley, *World Missionary
Conference*, 9-10. Elsewhere Stanley, "Defining," 171, says that the Conference's delegates "spanned the theological spectrum of the non-Roman Catholic Western missionary enterprise," which is perhaps the best way to put it.

tory as salvation geography, where western civilization as much as Jesus Christ was the savior.[22] Apart from the ethical difficulties with such an approach, there were—indeed are—two other major problems, one practical, the other theological. Practically, it reinforced the often unreflected relationship between church and state, which saw Christianity as a part of the imperial enterprise.[23] The gospel belonged to the package of "civilization" that the West brought to, or wanted to impose on, the East (a more significant division in many ways at that time than North–South).[24] This is what Lamin Sanneh calls "global Christianity," and that he sees as being replaced by "world Christianity."[25]

---

22. The idea of salvation geography has been discussed in relation especially to the Holy Land. See for example, Jeschke, *Rethinking Holy Land*, and Šlajerová, *Palestinian Church Today*, especially 201–37. However, more relevant to what I mean by the term here is the essay by Ustorf, "Global Topographies," a stimulating account of the three different attitudes to encounter held by late nineteenth-century missionaries. See page 594 for a list and explanation for each of these three attitudes: emancipative-integrationist (*ex occidente lux*), racist-imperialistic (*extra occidentem nulla salus*), and egalitarian-inversionist (*ex oriente lux pro nobis*).

23. One of the commissions (Commission 7) in Edinburgh 1910 was devoted to the relationship with the governments in mission territories. Although missionaries were often critical of colonial government, it was more because of restrictions they felt were placed on their work, rather than because of any deep-seated rejection of the empire itself. On this topic, see Maluleke, "Christian Mission." See also Kim, "Edinburgh 1910 and Edinburgh 2010," 7–8. Butlin points out, *Geographies of Empire*, 356–57, that the story is more complex than at first sight might seem to be the case, and that missionaries were certainly not uncritical supporters of colonial and imperial policies, especially (and here there are echoes of what happened in Alaska, as we will see in chapter 6) when it came to maltreatment of native populations.

24. On the idea of the "*mission civilizatrice*," see Butlin, *Geographies of Empire*, 350–95, which includes his most specific treatment of foreign missions. See also Usdorf, "Global Topographies," 595–97; and Stanley, *World Missionary Conference*, 254–60.

25. Sanneh, *Whose Religion*, 22. The difficulty of any talk about mission in a post-colonial setting needs to be frankly acknowledged. But it is in part the purpose of this book to turn the attention from an egocentric (either "oppressor" or "oppressed") perspective to what might be termed an alliocentric perspective, in which the main focus is not on what I have done or what has happened to me, but on the other. For more on mission from a post-colonial perspective, see Ingleby, *Beyond Empire* and Abraham, "What Does Mumbai."

Master-Servant or Friend? Relating to the Other

One of the most frequently cited speeches[26] from the conference was that delivered by one of only eighteen Asian delegates out of a total of over 1200,[27] the Indian Anglican, V. S. (Vedanayagam Samuel) Azariah (1874–1945).[28] In his address[29] he considered the relationship between foreign missionaries and their indigenous fellow-workers.[30] Azariah noted how indigenous Christians were essentially treated as staff, as servants of the white paymaster. In his history of the conference Brian Stanley quotes a steward from the meeting, who recalled Azariah saying "Too often you promise us thrones in heaven, but will not offer us chairs in your drawing rooms."[31]

His plea, therefore, was for a radical re-ordering of the relationship from master-servant[32] to that of friendship. He argued that it was only when all worked together that the fullness of Christ would be known, and that "[t]his will be possible only from spiritual friendship between the two races. We ought to be willing to learn from one another and to help one another." He concluded by thanking the missionaries for all that they had done, and suggesting what further was needed: "You have given your goods to feed the

---

26. See, for example, Robert, *Christian Mission*, 54–56 and Ellis, *Century*, 11. See also Cracknell, *Justice*, 204 and n. 132 on p. 382.

27. One of these was a former Muslim from Turkey, eight were Indian, four Japanese, three Chinese, with one Korean and one Burmese. There was also one African delegate. For the figures, see Stanley, *World Missionary Conference*, 12–13. Part of the reason for this was the decision to limit participation to mission bodies with a certain annual expenditure on mission—see on this the introduction to Kerr and Ross, *Edinburgh 2010*, 5–6 (the starting figure was an expenditure of at least £2000 a year—comparisons are difficult, but that would be minimally ten times more today). This meant that the non-Western delegates were there mostly as part of American or British missionary bodies, though three were directly invited by the organizing committees.

28. See Stanley, *World Missionary Conference*, 121–30. See also Gairdner, *Edinburgh 1910*, 109–11, for an eyewitness report on the speech and its effect on its audience. Azariah was to be the first Indian Anglican bishop.

29. The address was part of the program of evening events. The main conference debates happened during the day, and in the evening there were talks open to the general public as well.

30. We can safely presume that the attitude of the missionaries to those who had not yet become Christian was certainly no better, and probably worse, than to their co-workers.

31. Stanley, *World Missionary Conference*, 124. Stanley notes that this remark did not make it into the official proceedings of the conference. Cracknell, *Justice*, 382 (endnote 132), identifies the steward as a recent Oxford graduate, H. L. Houlder.

32. Or perhaps, not altogether inappropriately, one might use the Hegelian terminology of Master-Bondsman, since the missionaries were also dependent in all sorts of ways on the indigenous Christians.

poor. You have given your bodies to be burned. We also ask for *love*. Give us FRIENDS!"[33] This impassioned request for a deep rethinking of the way in which the missionary task was carried out had something of a mixed reception at the Conference itself, which is one indication that it had struck a powerful chord.[34]

Already in 1910 it was clear to some at least that a purely centrifugal vision of mission, or missions, needed to be challenged.[35] Was there really a Christian center that was charged with taking the gospel out to the "heathen periphery"? This raises in a particular way the question of boundaries,[36] the place where aliens, as it were, change roles. There are various forms in which this question can be phrased, but here I want to use the categories of contact, conflict, or cooperation.[37] The most fundamental of these, of course, must be contact, and that at least took place, but the latter two—conflict or cooperation—define the nature of the contact.

Azariah's comment on not being offered a chair to sit on may serve as a starting point. The image that comes to mind is of the colonial missionary sat behind his (and it was predominantly though not exclusively his) large desk, covered with bibles, commentaries, papers, gazing to the doorway

33. Citations from Stanley, *World Missionary Conference*, 125.

34. See Gairdner, *Edinburgh 1910*, 110. It may also have had an effect on Gairdner himself. William Henry Temple Gairdner (1873–1928) was an important and interesting figure in his own right, an early proponent of Muslim-Christian dialogue, and in many ways the man who enabled the reception of the Edinburgh Conference. In the first issue of the missionary journal, edited by J. H. Oldham, that arose out of the Conference (at that point it was the *International Review of Missions*, but the final "s" has been dropped only with effect from the second volume of 1969 [58:2]), Gairdner wrote an important article, "Vital Forces," in which he speaks of the necessity of encountering the Muslim other as friend (see p. 55). See for much more on this and on Gairdner, Cracknell, *Justice*, 261–70, with this article and phrase quoted on 269.

35. That this was the predominant view, however, is not in question. On this topic, see Kim, "Edinburgh 1910 and Edinburgh 2010," 8–9. However, the ambiguity in the Conference's language is also noted in Okure, "Church in the Mission Field." There is a fascinating tension in Edinburgh 1910 between two very different understandings of mission. The dominant one certainly has the view that mission is about going out from Europe to the "world," but partly through the inclusion of reports and feedback from missionaries on the ground, this is tempered by a view of the missionary potential of the local churches themselves as agents in mission. See also Butlin, *Geographies of Empire*, 383–84.

36. Stanley, *World Missionary Conference*, 50. On the mapping of the empire, especially Africa, see Butlin, *Geographies of Empire*, 323–49. See also the article by Guardiola-Saenz, "Borderless Women," quoted in the previous chapter.

37. I take these from the subtitle of the following fascinating book: Apostolov, *Christian-Muslim Frontier*, which examines those places, especially in Europe, where Christians and Muslims have lived alongside each other and how they have related to one another.

where the indigenous Christian stands, waiting for instructions. The crucial space is that between the two.[38] Does the missionary rise and come round the desk to welcome the other who comes to him into the space, or does the space remain, an unspoken and unbridgeable gap? This is what has to be negotiated.

The basic point can be stated baldly and simply as follows: do "we" have a message to give "them," which it is incumbent on "them" to listen and respond to, or do all have a journey to undertake to discover together what the message is that together we must hear and respond to? Or to put it another way, is the word of God ours or God's? The assumption underlying much of the missionary work represented at Edinburgh 1910 was that God had, so to speak, lent or given "us" his word,[39] and it was "our" task to bring it to those considered as "poor benighted heathen."[40] It would be both too simplistic and unjust to say that the chief aim of late nineteenth and early twentieth-century missionaries was to produce good Europeans. Indeed, there is much in the responses and reports from Edinburgh that indicates the unease many missionaries felt.[41] Nevertheless, in most cases they represented a society and system that was fully implicated in the exercise of imperial power and that was confident of its own superiority in almost every aspect of life.[42]

What is lacking, and it is this that Azariah drew attention to, is the absence of any sense of mutuality, necessary for any form of discourse, and certainly for theological discourse. The non-Christian other was there simply as a potential Christian, perhaps in a similar way that the African or Asian was there at best as a potential European. An encounter that seeks to reduce all to sameness is violent and ultimately murderous, because it

---

38. In an engaging sermon reflecting on the story of the Roman centurion in Matthew that we looked at in the previous chapter, Alan Kreider speaks of the importance of liminality in mission—precisely moving across that space. See Kreider, "Testimony," especially here 83–88, on entering liminal spaces and what happens in them.

39. I think this is something of the criticism of Flett, *Witness of God*, on how the idea of *missio Dei* has been (mis)used.

40. The phrase seems to have been fairly common in nineteenth-century England, but is probably even older. Joseph Conrad's riveting reflection on the nature of empire, *The Heart of Darkness*, had been published only eight years previously, in 1902. Conrad's powerful portrayal of the intensely problematic and destructive relationships between colonizer and colonized can be helpfully read in conjunction with Azariah's speech to give a sense of the problem.

41. See Stanley, *World Missionary Conference*, 260–64. Stanley notes that the Commission Report tended to downplay the critical voices, especially from India, which questioned to some extent the exercise of colonial power, or at least the ways in which that power was exercised.

42. See Butlin, *Geographies of Empire*, 367–80.

refuses to be confronted by the face of the other in her or his otherness.[43] Azariah's challenge can be rephrased as demanding of the Europeans that they look him in the face and say "You are my brother," not as a potential if always inferior version of the I but precisely because you are other.

The motivating impulse of Edinburgh 1910 in terms of welcoming Christian others was predominantly pragmatic. Missionaries in the field saw that the work of Christian mission was being hindered by the obvious disunity among Christians, and it was felt that it would be more effective if the churches were seen to live out more visibly the unity they preached.[44]

Edinburgh 2010 and the Nature of the Other

The occasion of the centenary of Edinburgh 1910 was a useful moment for reflecting on the nature of Christian mission over the past one hundred years, seeking for similarities, and perhaps more importantly for differences. Of course, as David Bosch has argued, the paradigm shifts in theology (and by extension in mission) never see the complete annihilation of previous paradigms,[45] so we cannot and should not expect total transformation. Nevertheless, we can ask if the other has become more important in mission today, as a human person and child of God in their own right. It would certainly not be difficult to construct a narrative that points to an almost complete difference between the world of Edinburgh 1910 and that of today.[46] As several commentators have noted, perhaps the one constant is the fraction of the world's population that is Christian, roughly a third.[47]

However, apart from the static percentage of Christians, nearly everything else about mission and its context has changed.[48] The recovery of the

---

43. The implicit reference is here to Emmanuel Lévinas. One of the best commentaries I have come across on Lévinas (which I have cited previously) is by a Brazilian Jesuit, Nilo Ribeiro Júnior, and is entitled *Sabedoria da Paz*, or "*The Wisdom of Peace*," which is an excellent metaphor for describing what I understand of the nature of this encounter with the other, leading to the restoration of God's shalom.

44. On this topic, see the summary of Commission 8 of Edinburgh 1910 in Kerr and Ross, *Edinburgh 2010*, 233–35, and the following essay in the same volume: Kobia, "Cooperation," 241. See also Stanley, *World Missionary Conference*, 279.

45. Bosch, *Transforming Mission*, 186.

46. See, however, for example, Kim, "Edinburgh 1910 and Edinburgh 2010," 3–6, looking at some of the similarities of the world we inhabit.

47. For example, see "Theme Eight: Mission and Unity—Ecclesiology and Mission," in Balia and Kim, *Witnessing to Christ*, 208.

48. Bosch, *Transforming Mission*, 189, says this: "quite literally, we live in a world fundamentally different from that of the nineteenth century, let alone earlier times."

concept of (if not the actual phrase) *missio Dei* began in earnest at the International Missionary Council meeting in Willingen in Germany in 1952.[49] Since then it has become the defining concept in mission studies and has had a fundamental impact on the nature of the missionary enterprise itself. Previously missions were what the church did, either at home or mostly abroad. It was a God-given task, but in some sense external to God, or even really to theology.[50]

The introduction (or perhaps better re-claiming) of the idea of *missio Dei* has led to the restoration of the link between mission and the self-revelation of the Triune God. Mission is no longer one of the things the church has to do, but something that is integral to our existence as human beings created in the image and likeness of the God who sends. Mission, as the widespread use of the adjective "missional"[51] indicates, is perceived as a fundamental dimension of all aspects of Christian life.[52] To sum this up, mission is much more theological than it was in 1910, when missiology was still a very young discipline.[53]

Mission has also changed, even if we consider it in terms of the 1910 concept of missions. There is no longer "Christendom" and "heathendom," two broad blocks of opposing values. Mission is "from everywhere to everyone."[54] There is no Christian center exporting itself to the

---

49. The theological inspiration came primarily from Karl Barth. For a good brief introduction to this, see Bosch, *Transforming Mission*, 389–93. See also Balia and Kim, *Witnessing to Christ*, 201–2. For an excellent critical overview of the problems associated with too loose a use of the term *missio Dei*, see Flett, *Witness of God*.

50. Schleiermacher, for example, placed mission in practical theology.

51. Apart from the contributions mentioned in the introduction, see also from the Gospel and Our Culture Network, for example, Guder, *Missional Church*, and Hastings, *Practical Theology*.

52. As Bishop Stephen Neill famously remarked, "If everything is mission, nothing is mission" (Neill, *Creative Tension*, 81).

53. Gustav Warneck, generally regarded as the founding father of missiology, was unable to attend the Conference because of ill-health (he died in December 1910, at the age of 76). However, he did contribute to the preparation of the meeting. Warneck was named as professor of mission studies in Halle in 1896, the first such chair to be established in continental Europe. The first person to have taught mission at all at a university seems to have been John Breckenridge (1797–1841) at Princeton Theological Seminary in 1836. The first professor of what might now be called missiology was Alexander Duff (1806–1878), who was appointed to the new chair in evangelistic theology in Edinburgh in 1867. On these men and on the development of Protestant missiology, see Spindler, "Protestant Mission Study," 44–45. The first Catholic professor of missiology was Josef Schmidlin (1876–1944) at Münster in 1910. On Schmidlin, see Collet, "Comments."

54. Escobar, *New Global Mission*.

non-Christian periphery.[55] Apart from this, the nature of Christianity itself has changed massively with the spread of the Pentecostal movement in its various forms.[56] This has redrawn the boundaries of Christianity and added complexity to the negotiations over the nature of the Christian other,[57] let alone the non-Christian other.

In 1910 this latter non-Christian other was mostly seen in terms of exoticism,[58] and the general attitude was at best rather patronizing. Today there is, on the whole, more willingness to recognize the other as the one with and from whom I can learn. The problem for Christian mission is how to proclaim the good news of Jesus Christ without ultimately seeking to reduce the other to sameness, circumscribing the unknowability of the other within the limits of what I understand to be Christian life and faith.

This is not to suggest, as sometimes threatened to be the case in the 1960s and 1970s, that we should now abandon Christian missionary activity because it is inevitably destructive. It may, however, be useful to remember that the major imperative of what, for many, is the default missionary text, Matt 28:18–20, the Great Commission, is to make disciples.[59] The disciple is the one who follows the teacher, and the path to be followed is decided on by the teacher. In other words, Christian mission is about a liberation that allows people to follow wherever they are led. There is no one unique place where Jesus is to be found, not even the church. The Son of Man has nowhere to lay his head, has no address, but is always on the move, always indefinable.[60]

It is, as the reading of the scriptural evidence in the first chapter suggested, only through the challenge of the other, Christian or not, that we can have any hope of truly learning who we are and what it really means to be a

---

55. This is part of the thrust of Philip Jenkins's work. For example, see Jenkins, *New Faces* and *Next Christendom*. See also Janciles, "Migration and Mission."

56. On this point, see Synan, *Century*, and Robeck, *Azusa Street Mission*. For a good summary of contemporary Pentecostal theology, see Warrington, *Pentecostal Theology*.

57. Nowhere has this been clearer, perhaps, than in Latin America, where Pentecostalism has made great progress. The first Pentecostal missionaries—two Swedes who arrived via America—came to Brazil just months after the end of Edinburgh 1910. On relationships between liberation theology and Pentecostalism, see Noble, *Keeping the Window Open*, 58–71, as well as its bibliography.

58. See Stanley, *World Missionary Conference*, 95–97; and for confirmation from a participant, see Gairdner, *Edinburgh 1910*, 56–58. See also more generally Mikaelsson, "'Self' and 'Other,'" especially on representations of the other (mainly as "heathen" and "idolater") on pp. 94–98

59. Bosch, *Transforming Mission*, 73–74. In fact, Bosch entitles his entire section on the Matthean vision of mission "Making Disciples."

60. Luke 9:57–62.

follower of Christ in our world. Of course, we never undergo this encounter with some kind of *tabula rasa*, as if we suddenly forget all we know and have lived of our faith hitherto. But each encounter requires us to understand anew the faith that we proclaim and seek to live, to ask what it really means in the specific context of each time that we are confronted with and by the other. It is in the diversity of the encounters that we are enabled to find the wholeness and unity of our faith, a faith that demands that we live with others, welcoming and attending to their difference and diversity.[61]

MODELS OF CONTEXTUAL ENCOUNTER

It would be surprising if this diversity had not become apparent to missiologists, many of whom have a background in mission and thus personal experience of being encountered by the other. And indeed there has been increasing reflection on the contribution of the other to our understanding of faith. As a starting point in my examination of this reflection, I turn to Stephen Bevans, and his influential work on models of contextual theology,[62] as a key work on modes of encounter. In the revised edition of the book, Bevans looks at six models.[63] However, in the introductory chapters to the book, he is quite clear that "no one model can be used exclusively and an exclusive use will distort the theological enterprise."[64] Having said that, there is also no doubt that in certain contexts, different models may be more prominent. For my purposes, then, the two most important are the anthropological and the praxis models.

The anthropological model, according to Bevans, has, as its "primary concern . . . the establishment or preservation of cultural identity by a person of Christian faith."[65] As Bevans notes, the Gospel antecedents of this model can be seen in the encounter with the Canaanite woman that we looked at in the previous chapter. In terms of church tradition, we can think of Justin Martyr's concept of "the seeds of the word," which saw God already present and at work in all that is good in human life and thought.[66] The anthropo-

---

61. Compare Matt 25:36–45.

62. Bevans, *Models*.

63. Because I will not look at them all in what follows, and for the sake of completeness, the six are: the Translation Model, the Anthropological Model, the Praxis Model, the Synthetic Model, the Transcendental Model, and the Counter-cultural Model. This last was added to the second edition.

64. Bevans, *Models*, 32.

65. Bevans, *Models*, 54. For a brief summary, see Pears, *Doing Contextual Theology*, 25–26.

66. See Bevans, *Models*, 54. I return briefly to Justin Martyr later on.

logical model is such in two senses, in that it has at its center the human being, so that by "attending and listening to [a particular] situation . . . God's hidden presence can be manifested in the ordinary structures of the situation, often in surprising ways."[67] Secondly, though, it also draws on the insights of anthropology as a discipline, focusing on particular cultures as *loci theologici*.[68] Bevans insists that it is within different human cultures that God reveals himself, not as some extraneous element, but as an integral part of all that is good and of value in that culture.[69] It is within the culture itself that elements must be found that can serve as expressions of the gospel, as already manifesting the presence and activity of God.

To spell this out in terms of my argument, then, Bevans suggests that this way of doing theology seeks not to introduce God to an assumed "Godless" world, but to unveil or name in Christian terms the ways in which God is speaking through the culture and thus the way in which the culture itself is "missionary." Because there is much in this model that would correspond with what I am doing in this book, it is worth being particularly attentive to the critique of the model that Bevans himself offers. He points out that it can easily lead to a cultural romanticism, where genuine expressions of a particular culture are seen as necessarily good.[70] He also points out that in practice the model in its pure form is perhaps impossible, since the God who is manifested and whose presence is sensed is always spoken of in a particular way, which owes more to the insights of the first model Bevans considers, the translation model.[71]

From my perspective, then, the anthropological model is certainly a useful starting point. Indeed part of what I am doing here works from some of its presuppositions, most especially that, in the words of M. A. C. Warren, quoted by Bevans, "Our first task in approaching another people,

---

67. Bevans, *Models*, 55.

68. See Bevans, *Models*, 55. Bevans himself does not use Melchior Cano's phrase *locus theologicus*, which anyway is clearly adapted in this setting. For more on the idea of *loci theologici*, especially in liberation theology, see Araya, *God of the Poor*, 20: "Liberation theology is . . . a theology set in motion from *a point of departure* in the poor, the poor as interlocutor, as historical subject." The idea is critiqued by the Argentinian theologian Scannone in "Situación," 263–64.

69. See Bevans, *Models*, 56–57. For an example of what this means in practice, though with a more developed critical edge, see Noble, *Theological Interpretation*. The book examines how literature, film, and music can all serve as manifestations of a recognition of the presence of God in different cultures, even where Christian language to express that presence has been, to a large extent, lost.

70. See Bevans, *Models*, 60.

71. Bevans, *Models*, 61. This latter model starts from the one truth of the gospel, which it then seeks to "translate" into different cultural settings.

another culture, another religion is to take off our shoes, for the place we are approaching is holy. Else . . . we may forget that God was here before our arrival."[72] Nevertheless, apart from the problems noted by Bevans earlier, I would also say that the problem of determining what is a culture—and moreover seeing a culture as definitive of who people are—is one that should make us wary. In general, people are not simply specimens of a particular culture, at least not if we are to accept their genuine otherness. This is not to deny the importance of culture, but it is to warn against cultural reductionism, which can so easily lead to the worst kinds of nationalism, racism, and general exclusion. But whoever that other is, she or he comes to the encounter with the missionary as a bearer of God, as one created in the *imago Dei*.

The second of Bevans's models that I want to look at is the praxis model. The importance of this model, which, as Bevans puts it, "focuses on the identity of Christians within a context particularly as that context is understood in terms of social change,"[73] is in the primacy it gives to praxis. In scriptural terms, we could appeal here to Matthew 7:24 ("Everyone then who hears these words of mine and acts on them will be like a wise man who built his house on rock"; the hearing of the word necessitates its doing) or similarly James 1:22 ("be doers of the word, and not merely hearers"). Praxis, as Bevans himself notes, is a somewhat abused word, but he understands it in something akin to the use of the Frankfurt School.[74] Praxis is reflected action or acted-on reflection.[75] It is closely associated with a liberation theology approach.[76]

The first point to make is that praxis itself is always both context- and person-related, if not dependent. This is one of the reasons Bevans chooses to call the model "praxis" rather than liberation.[77] To put it simply, what one does is related to—even depends on—where one does it. But there is also a personal dimension. Praxis demands a practitioner, and each practitioner comes with particular experiences, needs, desires, ways of understanding, that also influence their interaction with the world around them.[78]

---

72. Warren, "General Preface," in Bevans, *Models*, 56.

73. Bevans, *Models*, 70.

74. See Bevans, *Models*, 71.

75. Cf. Bevans's citation of Berryman, *Liberation Theology*, 86 ("Praxis is 'action with reflection'") in Bevans, *Models*, 72.

76. See Noble, *Poor in Liberation Theology*.

77. See Bevans, *Models*, 73.

78. In some ways this is closer to what Bevans calls the transcendental model, which relies on the personal (not individual) engagement of the human being. But my focus here is on what happens in practice, what people do in relation to others, and thus

In terms of my argument, then, mission is a praxis that sees two practitioners (broadly the missionary and the addressee of mission) encounter in some new praxis. It is new, because if it is a genuine encounter, it will be both action and reflection, but it is no longer the previous action with reflection of either of those involved. Even if one or both of the parties thought that it was, in fact it has changed—the Christian missionary is confronted by the reality of the other, and the other is confronted by the reality of the Christian missionary. Both may remain steadfast in their previous convictions, but they do so now in the light of this new encounter, which has changed them.[79]

A reiteration and confirmation of Bevans's attempts to record these ways of doing theology can be found in the work of the great African missiologist, Lamin Sanneh, originally from Gambia, but for many years a professor in America.[80] Sanneh has produced a large number of influential and important works,[81] but here I examine briefly only one short book, written in the early 2000s, *Whose Religion is Christianity?*[82] In this work, Sanneh speaks of "the *indigenous discovery of Christianity* rather than the *Christian discovery of indigenous societies.*"[83] This approach re-centers the history of Christianity and its expansion in terms of the *prosēlutos*, the one who draws near, who comes to this faith, seeks to find what it has to say to them. Sanneh's book is also interesting because of the style in which it is written, a kind of question and answer format. He sees this stylistic device as an essential part of the approach to discussing religion, since it allows questions to be asked and responses to be given in a spirit of enquiry and openness that is mutually enhancing.[84] In the next few paragraphs I want to focus on some sections of Sanneh's book that are especially relevant for my argument.

First of all, following on from our previous comments on Bevans's praxis model, he makes the important point, in a discussion on the effects of Bible translation, that the "undisputed unintended consequences of actions

---

I stick to the praxis model here.

79. For a collection of texts examining how some of these encounters have been portrayed in literature through the centuries, see Hawley, *Historicizing*.

80. Sanneh has written an intellectual autobiography, *Summoned from the Margin*. In terms of my own understanding, Sanneh's work entitled *Translating the Message* remains very influential.

81. For a bibliography, see http://www.yale.edu/worldchristianity/TheWorksofLaminSanneh.shtml.

82. Sanneh, *Whose Religion*.

83. Sanneh, *Whose Religion*, 10; italics in original.

84. See Sanneh, *Whose Religion*, 5–6.

are beyond the control of the actors themselves."[85] The Holy Spirit should not be ignored in this context, of course, and at least a willingness to allow the Spirit to blow as it pleases should be one of the intended consequences of any action undertaken by a Christian missionary.[86]

Sanneh's argument is that Christianity becomes indigenized in different cultures because of what they bring to their encounter with it.[87] So, for example, he argues that the expansion of Christianity in Africa is due to "the end of colonial rule; the effects of mother tongue development, and Bible translation; indigenous cultural renewal and local agency; and the theological stimulation of the adoption of African names of God."[88] Christianity is growing in Africa because it is becoming a religion for Africans, rather than a European religion that was imposed from outside, along with so much else. This should not be over-romanticized or overstated. The encounters between Africa and Europe cannot be reduced to a single story, however tempting that is. Nor, indeed, can the fact be ignored that there have been mutual influences, and that African Christianity is also both source of inspiration for and inspired by other forms of Christianity. This is certainly the case in terms of theology itself, but even in terms of church life. Even when it is a case of reacting against something, what is reacted to clearly has an influence.

Nevertheless, Sanneh makes clear that for Christian mission to succeed[89] it is not simply a question of what the missionary brings, but how what the missionary brings is able to meet with and find a home with what the addressee of the mission brings. The strangers draw close and discover together something new. As Sanneh writes, the expansion of Christianity owes much to "a growing historical consciousness that God is alive in history through the specificity of language, culture, and custom."[90] Justin Martyr's contribution in the second century[91] may lead us to question just

---

85. Sanneh, *Whose Religion*, 25.

86. On this point, see Wells, "Christian Mission," 36–37.

87. On this topic, see the essays in Kaplan, *Indigenous Responses*, in which different authors consider how indigenous communities in parts of Africa, Asia, and Latin America utilized and assimilated the Christian story in ways that enabled them to maintain in some form their own culture.

88. Sanneh, *Whose Religion*, 41–42.

89. Without getting too bogged down in what "success" in mission actually entails, at least for the moment.

90. Sanneh, *Whose Religion*, 72.

91. On this and Justin's concept of *logoi spermatikoi*, see Dolejšová, *Accounts of Hope*, 80–83; and Noble, *Theological Interpretation*, 175–76. See also Trakatellis, *Pre-Existence*, 133–34.

how much this is really "a growing historical consciousness," and how much it is a rediscovery of a much older tradition. Justin was convinced that "the seed of reason" (*spermatikos logos*) was present in human history, wherever people acted according to what was good and right and just.[92] And this is precisely what Sanneh wants to argue for here.

Unanswered Questions

Both Sanneh's contribution and the models suggested by Bevans are helpful and I draw on them with gratitude. However, certain questions are left in the air. The first, already alluded to by Bevans himself in his critique of the anthropological model, relates to how culture is viewed. There is in some of what Sanneh writes the danger of the over-valuing of particular cultures that Bevans saw as a potential drawback to the anthropological model. I think Sanneh is aware of the danger,[93] but I am not convinced that he does enough to deal with the question. How does one prevent a culture from becoming, in the helpful language of Jean-Luc Marion, a conceptual idol?[94] The answer should perhaps be by making sure it is always confronted by the power of the gospel, but the more one insists on the culture as starting point for hearing the gospel, the harder it is to allow that to happen.

This is a reminder that, however much one desires to let the missionary encounter be shaped by the other, and indeed however much it actually is shaped by that encounter, there must always be an element of suspicion. This is the more so if it is accepted that there is no neutral point from which to judge cultures, and that even an assumed Christian standpoint will be at least entangled with cultural values that may or may not be entirely at one with Christian belief and practice. But on the other hand, there is no need to therefore abandon any hope of missionary encounter. It simply indicates the constant need for discernment related to the means, the methods, and the end of what is being done, and the humility to realize that, however sincerely that discernment is carried out, at times we might get it wrong. The encouraging corollary of the call to be perfect as our heavenly Father is perfect (Matt 5:48) is that it suggests that we are not yet at that point.

---

92. See, for example, Justin, "2 Apol. 13.3," in *Justin Martyr*, 83, 78. See also Trakatellis, *Pre-Existence*, 133–34; and Minns and Parvis, *Justin*. In this latter volume, the bilingual text of the thirteenth chapter of the Second Apology is on 320–21; see also the editors' comments in their introduction, 65–66.

93. See, for example, Sanneh, *Whose Religion*, 40–43.

94. See Marion, *Idol and Distance*; and Noble, *Poor in Liberation Theology*, 88–99.

The second problem with the material outlined previously is almost exactly the opposite of that just discussed. In the previous paragraph, I suggested that there can be no neutral place from which to view cultures. But these positions seem to assume in some sense that there is, at least in as far as something can be named a culture. Even Sanneh is at times prone to talk of "African Christianity" as if it was a monolith.[95] In this respect, the other is already assigned to a "culture," predefined as acting in a certain way, with assigned needs and desires and ways of acting. But to do this is to make the possibility of genuine encounter much harder.

Any encounter will always have to be based on a certain provisionality. Of course, as Hans-Georg Gadamer has helped us to see, in any encounter we carry with us our *Vorurteil*, our prejudice.[96] In this case it is our assumptions (to use the Heideggerian term)[97] about the nature of human beings and the way in which they live together that is at stake. We may be right in our prejudices, but they prevent us from the full encounter with the otherness of the other.[98] This is why I will not produce any strategy for encountering the other, since the other is not a problem to be resolved, but the very possibility of anything that I do, including mission. It is precisely the limitless possibility of the other that, it seems to me, is most powerful in teaching us something about the God whom we proclaim.

MISSION AS DIALOGUE

This other is one who is encountered, if at all, in exchange, and that means in dialogue. Dialogue is a complex term, but one that has begun to feature increasingly in writing on Christian mission. The question of the relationship between interreligious dialogue and mission is an area of ongoing debate,[99] but the reality of the encounter with other religions has clearly had an impact on contemporary Christian mission and has made clear the need to engage with the other. The nature of dialogue means that one needs to listen, and so this section will be somewhat more expository than others, as we listen to the voices of some leading missiologists. I start with the

---

95. Though he does also acknowledge that there are differences in it—see Sanneh, *Whose Religion*, 39–40.

96. See Gadamer, *Wahrheit*, 255–75.

97. Here "Vormeinung." See Heidegger, *Sein und Zeit*, §32, 200.

98. In Lévinasian terms, we are always in the world of the said, but must strive to get beyond it to the world of the saying. See Lévinas, *Otherwise than Being*, 5–8 and 45–48.

99. See Skreslet, *Comprehending Mission*, 150–51, who discusses this, and points out that even if interreligious dialogue is not directly missional in terms of an attempt to convert the other, it is nevertheless part of the church's missionary impulse.

Mission Encountering the Other

South African missiologist David Bosch, and his comments on dialogue and mission.[100]

Dialogue and Mission: Some Initial Reflections

For Bosch, the three major approaches to dialogue with people of other religions have adopted attitudes of respectively "exclusivism, fulfilment, and relativism."[101] But he finds these approaches "wanting. They are all too neat. They all work out too well. In the end everything—and everyone!—is accounted for."[102] Ultimately, there is no room for the otherness of the other. Rather, Bosch says, theology "needs dialogue also for its own sake."[103]

The reasons Bosch gives for engaging in dialogue are not all equally relevant for my purposes.[104] However, a brief summary of some of them will help explain something of the role of dialogue in encountering the other. In the treatment of the *gēr* in chapter 1 we saw that the stranger is first and foremost a blessing, and Bosch too notes that other religions should not simply be tolerated but embraced.[105] At the same time, the encounter with the other who draws near in their otherness demands of us a "witnessing to our deepest convictions, whilst listening to those of our neighbors."[106] This is because in dialogue and encounter "we go expecting to meet the God who has preceded us and has been preparing people within the context of their own cultures and convictions."[107] An encounter with the other is never an encounter with someone untouched by God, but always with a child of God created in God's image and likeness. Because of this, Bosch points out,

---

100. These are found in the section on "Mission to People of Other Living Faiths" in Bosch, *Transforming Mission*, 467–89. The subsection on "Dialogue and Mission" is from 483–89.

101. Bosch, *Transforming Mission*, 478–83, with the words in quotation marks from 478. What Bosch calls "fulfilment" would be more commonly referred to as "inclusivism," and what he calls "relativism" would normally be termed "pluralism." On this, see Pratt, "Christian Discipleship," in a section headed, intriguingly, "The 'Other' to whom Mission is Addressed," (329–31).

102. Bosch, *Transforming Mission*, 483. For a brief reflection on Bosch's treatment of Christian relations to other religions, see Anderson, "Theology of Religions."

103. Bosch, *Transforming Mission*, 483.

104. For an overview of the development of Bosch's theology that led him to this conviction, see Livingston, *Missiology of the Road*.

105. Bosch, *Transforming Mission*, 483–84.

106. Bosch, *Transforming Mission*, 484. On the importance of convictions in Christian life and theology, see McClendon and Smith, *Convictions*.

107. Bosch, *Transforming Mission*, 484.

all our dialogue should take place with an attitude of humility.[108] Humility is not opposed to witnessing to our convictions, but is an expression of our recognition of our own utter dependence on God.[109]

Bosch draws attention to the fact that otherness is intrinsic to religion, in that each religion is a world of its own, asking its own particular questions, and that therefore each should be treated differently.[110] Although I think Bosch's critique of Rahner's idea of the anonymous Christian is misplaced,[111] the important point being made is that the other should be allowed to be other in her or his otherness, rather than being transformed into some idealized (or idolatrous) version of what we think the other should be.

Ultimately, Bosch argues that dialogue is always necessary, because salvation is not simply post-mortem, but something experienced already.[112] Thus, to be a Christian is also always to be engaged with the world around us, including with people of other religions. Bosch manages, in a few pages, to get to the crux of the issue, and point both to the problems and to the

---

108. Bosch, *Transforming Mission*, 484–85.

109. The two different meanings of the word "apologetic" may help here. We do not need to apologise for our faith, but we do need to find an *apologia* that is not triumphalist. See Dolejšová, *Accounts of Hope*, for an attempt to outline a non-foundationalist *apologia*.

110. Bosch, *Transforming Mission*, 485–86.

111. Bosch's criticism is this: to call someone an anonymous Christian is to force the other, in the words of Küng, *On Being a Christian*, 78, into the Roman Catholic Church through the back door (cited by Bosch, *Transforming Mission*, 486). However, this is not really what Rahner is saying. Rahner is interested in how Christian theology can deal with the question of the other non-Christian in a way that does not exclude them from access to the salvific plan of God made manifest in Christ. In other words, this is an intra-Christian problem, or as Rahner says, it is "first and foremost a controversy internal to Catholic theology." See Rahner, "Observations," 280. This essay contains references to previous treatments of this issue by Rahner. In another essay, "The One Christ," Rahner reports a conversation with

> Nishitani, the well known Japanese philosopher . . . [who] asked me: What would you say to my treating you as an anonymous Buddhist? I replied: certainly, you may and should do so from your point of view; I feel myself honored by such an interpretation, even if I am obliged to regard you as being in error or if I assume that, correctly understood, to be a genuine Zen Buddhist is identical with being a genuine Christian, in the sense directly and properly intended by such statements. ("One Christ," 219)

On this, see also the work of Fletcher, who is more critical (and in a sense more in agreement with Bosch), in "Rahner and Religious Diversity," cited from Marmion and Hines, *Cambridge Companion to Karl Rahner*, here especially 241–46. In the same volume, see Duffy, "Experience of Grace," 52–55, who is more positive.

112. Bosch, *Transforming Mission*, 487. For a fascinating exposition of this question, see Castillo, *Pobres y la Teología*, especially 257–77.

possibilities. The attitude of "bold humility"[113] that so characterized Bosch's approach is seen here in full. Most importantly for my purposes is the fact that he both takes the "otherness" of the other seriously, whilst refusing as a consequence to abandon the imperative of mission. The other does not forbid, but commands mission, however complex and messy that might be in actual practice.

Mission as Prophetic Dialogue

I turn now to Stephen Bevans and Roger Schroeder.[114] In their book *Constants in Context* Bevans and Schroeder sought to do two things. They wanted to look at what they term the constants of Christian mission, those themes that have been of permanent concern to those engaged in missionary activity—christology, ecclesiology, eschatology, salvation, anthropology, and culture—but as played out in different contexts and in three broad patterns of engagement, which they label as Type A, B, and C theologies of mission, connected respectively to (A) mission as saving souls and extending the church; (B) mission as discovery of the truth; and (C) mission as commitment to liberation and transformation.[115] They then look at how these constants have been applied to mission activity through the history of the church. The part on prophetic dialogue comes at the end as a concluding chapter that attempts to set out criteria for mission today.

They argue that mission has two major tasks at the beginning of the twenty-first century. It must be dialogical and it must be prophetic. With regard to the first, they say, "the church . . . must be a community that not only gives of itself in service to the world and to the people of the world's cultures but learns from its involvement and expands its imagination of the depths of God's unfathomable riches."[116] The second task is seen in terms of the engagement of the church with the poor, with culture, and with other religions.[117] Thus the idea of prophetic dialogue is suggested as the overarching concept for considering Christian mission today.

---

113. Bosch, *Transforming* Mission, 489. See the title of Saayman and Kritziger, *Mission in Bold Humility*.

114. I concentrate here on Bevans and Schroeder, *Constants in Context*, and Bevans and Schroeder, *Prophetic Dialogue*.

115. The overview of these is given in Bevans and Schroeder, *Constants in Context*, 32–72.

116. Bevans and Schroeder, *Constants in Context*, 348.

117. Bevans and Schroeder, *Constants in Context*, 349. They draw here on the Asian Bishops' Conference here. For more on this see Chia, "Mission as Dialogue."

They look at this idea in relation to six areas: "(1) witness and proclamation, (2) liturgy, prayer, and contemplation, (3) commitment to justice, peace, and the integrity of creation, (4) the practice of interreligious dialogue, (5) efforts of inculturation, and (6) the ministry of reconciliation."[118] They then proceed to look at how these six elements of contemporary mission both coincide with their three theological types and with the practice of mission as prophetic dialogue. Bevans and Schroeder welcome the creative tension between the dialogical and prophetic as a necessary part of missionary engagement with the other. The aim of this tension, though, is not to produce some synthesis, but to maintain what might be termed a non-synthetic dialectics.[119] That is to say, both poles of the dialectic are seen as vitally important, and the place of Christian living is between, or rather within, both of them.

Some years later, Bevans and Schroeder brought together a new collection of essays that developed the idea of prophetic dialogue. In part it grew, they say, out of the realization that "prophetic dialogue functions much more as a *spirituality* than as a *strategy*."[120] The book works with a number of metaphors or *motifs*, one of which is that of dance. The obvious reference is to the common word play on the idea of *perichorēsis*, which, though in fact from the Greek *perichoreo* ("encompass" or "permeate") is often linked to *perichoreuo*, ("dance").[121] They want to remind us that mission precedes church and that the church—one might also add the Scriptures[122]—exists in order to provide a vehicle for the mission of God to happen in the world.

Positively, this relocates the center of all missionary activity to God,[123] and opens up space for welcoming the other as *angelos* and *euangelos*, as messenger and as bearer in their own right of good news for us. It also reminds us that the relatively absolute Other,[124] God, always remains beyond

---

118. Bevans and Schroeder, *Constants in Context*, 351. The six areas were developed by Bevans in conjunction with his colleague Eleanor Doidge: see Bevans and Doidge, "Theological Reflection."

119. See Noble and Noble, "Non-Synthetic Dialectics."

120. Bevans and Schroeder, *Prophetic Dialogue*, 2.

121. See Bevans and Schroeder, *Prophetic Dialogue*, 10, and endnote 7 on 158. On *perichorēsis*, see Hunt, *Trinity*, 16n25; and Fiddes, *Participating in God*, 71–81, and also Noble and Noble, "Non-Synthetic Dialectics," 277–78.

122. This may be one way of reading Wright, *Mission of God*.

123. Thus avoiding the very real dangers that John Flett points to in *Witness of God*, that the idea of *missio Dei* can actually end up doing away with the need for God.

124. To call God "Absolute Other" is to ignore the incarnation and the kenotic reality of Jesus Christ. The famous patristic aphorism, what is not assumed cannot be saved, makes the absolute otherness of God relative. God is indeed absolutely other than God's creation, and yet God has also chosen to welcome creation into participation in God

us. However many strategies and plans there may be, God is transcendent and calls us to transcendence too. This may counterbalance the dangers inherent in the apparent reliance on the social model of the Trinity, with its obvious tendency to some form of tritheism.[125]

The other point that can be made here is that to see the church in terms of mission (rather than to see mission as one of the tasks of the church, which is what has often happened) is to encourage an attitude of what the Russian hesychasts called non-possession. This idea was developed in fifteenth- and early sixteenth-century Russia,[126] especially in the life and writings of Saint Nil Sorsky, for whom the overarching concept of non-possession was central to all of his life and practice.[127] In terms of mission, the idea of non-possession seems to me to be a very helpful one. First, in conjunction with Bevans and Schroeder, it reminds us that mission is not something that the church owns, but that rather the church is, so to speak, possessed by the mission of God. And because mission is God's gift of himself to his church, every encounter is an encounter in and through gift, or givenness.[128] The other is not one we possess, but one to whom we are in thrall, and thus one who can command and teach us.

That is why, as Bevans and Schroeder go on to discuss using another motif, mission has moved from a focus on expansion to a focus on encounter.[129] As Donal Dorr puts it, "There is a two-way exchange of gifts, between missionaries and the people among whom they work."[130] Bevans and Schroeder understand dialogue as "an attitude of respect and friendship, which permeates or should permeate all those activities constituting the evangelizing mission of the church."[131] Here Bevans and Schroeder emphasize the

---

(what Orthodox theology calls *theosis* or deification).

125. See, for example, Holmes, "Three Versus One," 77–78, and Marambio, "Teorías recientes," 197–200, for a more analytical philosophical treatment of the issue.

126. For historical background, see Noble et al., *Ways of Orthodoxy*, 47–50 and 75–76.

127. I have dealt with Nil and the idea of non-possession in much more detail in Noble et al., *Wrestling with the Mind*, 81–97. A far more ample bibliography can also be found there.

128. This will be the thrust of the argument that I develop in the next chapter with reference to Jean-Luc Marion.

129. See Bevans and Schroeder, *Prophetic Dialogue*, 20, where they refer to Baziou, "Mission."

130. Dorr, *Mission in Today's World*, 16, cited in Bevans and Schroeder, *Prophetic Dialogue*, 20.

131. They draw here on the words of a document issued by the Pontifical Council for Inter-Religious Dialogue and the Congregation for the Evangelization of the Peoples, *Dialogue and Proclamation*, para. 9, which is cited in Bevans and Schroeder,

importance of "attitude," of dialogue not simply as some kind of strategy, but as a way of life, or, more fundamentally still, a spirituality, a new way of seeing the world.[132] Thus they give as characteristics of dialogue what might also be thought of as broadly "spiritual" characteristics—repentance, orthopraxis, confidence, and discernment.[133]

Mission as Repentance, Orthopraxis, Confidence, and Discernment

These four features of dialogue are worth further reflection. For the two authors themselves, repentance is connected more with the often very problematic history of mission. Certainly Christian mission has often been abused,[134] and sometimes it is simply necessary to accept that fact and to seek forgiveness and to act contritely. But I am not sure that the idea of repentance has to be so limited. At the heart of dialogue there is also a constant need for *metanoia*, for turning from self to the other, both to the other present to me, and through and with that other to God. The mission of Jesus began with the call to repentance (see Mark 1:14), and so mission must begin with a call to repentance, which is never simply for the other but for the missionary too. The failure to realize this is central to many of the problems of mission.

Attention to orthopraxis is a reminder that God is act and thus primarily God does.[135] Liberation theologians, starting with Gustavo Gutiérrez,[136] have reflected on the importance of orthopraxis, and argued that in the relationship between theory and praxis, praxis should be the dominant pole.[137] This retrieval of orthopraxis, for all that it is complex, should not be ignored. However, in terms of spirituality, what is perhaps most important

---

Prophetic Dialogue, 21.

132. Bevans and Schroeder, *Prophetic Dialogue*, 22.

133. Bevans and Schroeder, *Prophetic Dialogue*, 30–31.

134. The realization of this led to the debates between "ecumenicals" or "conciliarists" (broadly associated with the World Council of Churches) and "evangelicals," especially in the 1960s. On this, see McGavran, *Conciliar-Evangelical Debate*; and Bevans and Schroeder, *Constants in Context*, 260–64.

135. See Bevans and Schroeder, *Prophetic Dialogue*, 9–10, and the earlier comments on Bevans's praxis model on pp. 59–60.

136. Gutiérrez's definition of theology is well-known: "a critical reflection on Christian praxis in the light of the Word" (*Theology of Liberation*, 11). There are many other texts that could be quoted. For a discussion of the problematic relationship between orthodoxy and orthopraxis, see also Gutiérrez, *Truth*, 100–105.

137. See, for example, Boff, *Theology and Praxis*, 355–60.

is the reminder that, as the Letter of James makes abundantly clear, a faith or a relationship to Christ that is not lived out in active engagement with the other is hollow.[138] The importance of orthopraxis[139] as response to the other is imperative.

By confidence, Bevans and Schroeder mean the ability to trust the other.[140] This is both one of the most fundamental and often one of the most difficult elements of dialogue, because it entails vulnerability, the willingness to open oneself up to the other, whom one does not and can never fully know. Here the idea of non-possession may again prove helpful.[141] The missionary in encounter with the other cannot cling on to who she or he is, but must freely give themselves to Christ. Christians in many countries and situations are aware only too well of what this abandonment of self can bring, and whatever language is used to describe the opposition that proclamation and living of the gospel will inevitably bring, it is clearly a reality to be expected. And yet, we are called to trust, to confidence in the Spirit who will give us the words to speak (Matt 10:19–20).

Finally, all of this demands discernment. To engage in mission, to engage in dialogue with the other, to open oneself up to the other, is not to seek martyrdom or hate or rejection. A constant temptation to missionaries is to assume that rejection of the message they preach is a sign of the sinfulness of the other, rather than a sign of their own failure to submit themselves to the needs of that other. Sometimes they may be right, but honest and deep discernment is needed, both to reflect on the proclamation and invitation that is given, and to reflect on where God is already present and active in the person and culture with whom we dialogue. Although Bevans and Schroeder themselves do not specifically use this language, perhaps ultimately it could be said that at the heart of any praxis of dialogue there must first of all be a practice of prayer. Prayer is humble dialogue with God, a turning to God with confidence, with repentance, recognizing the close link between prayer and action.[142] In and through the Spirit, the will of God is discerned

---

138. On the Letter to James, see Kruger, *Pobres y Ricos*.

139. In the Lucan account of the sending of the 70 (or 72), the injunction is to cure and expel demons prior to proclamation.

140. They refer specifically to Pope Paul VI's encyclical *Ecclesiam Suam*.

141. See also chapter 4, and the fundamental attitude suggested by Saint Ignatius of Loyola in his *Spiritual Exercises*, where following Christ involves accepting poverty, leading to humiliation and humility.

142. As Jerome Nadal, one of the early companions of Saint Ignatius of Loyola, put it, the life of Ignatius was one of "contemplation even in action" (*sive* or *simul in actione contemplativus*). See Conwell, *Walking*.

and acted upon, and the testing of the discernment is in the relationship to the other who draws near.

The dialogue with God in prayer is arguably the most essential part of the qualifying adjective that Bevans and Schroeder apply, "prophetic." At first sight, it may appear that the prophetic element runs counter to the attention to the other. The prophet is the one who speaks and, even more fundamentally, does the Word of God, and the Old Testament prophets, and Jesus himself, speak and do this word regardless of the consequences that this proclamation and action will have for them. But attention to the other demands also a prophetic stance, and a speaking forth and a speaking for.

Mission as Teaching, Storytelling, and Trail-Guiding

First of all, as Bevans and Schroeder point out, a prophet must be one who listens and looks attentively.[143] It could be said that the prophet responds to the command of the other to understand and speak the truth of God. This need to speak God—in action or word—is a key impulse to mission, as Saint Paul makes clear (cf. 1 Cor 9:16). The compulsion to proclaim the gospel is not an exterior one, but interior. Bevans and Schroeder also speak of the prophet as teacher, storyteller, and trail guide,[144] and these three images of the missionary prophet can help us go further into the question of how it is possible to be a prophet and to be attentive to the other.

To teach is to dialogue. At its best, teaching is a mutual transfer of what, for want of a better word, we can call "knowledge," or, to use the phrase popular in ecumenical literature, "an exchange of gifts."[145] The teacher has something to give to the learner, but the learner also has something to give to the teacher, or, perhaps better, in any such situation, we are always both teachers and learners.[146] In mission it is the other who teaches me how to be a prophet to her or him, how to speak forth in word and deed the fullness of the gospel.

This is really about reading the signs of the times, a task that, as David Bosch noted, is both difficult, requiring as it does discernment, and necessary.[147] Theology will find its dialogue partner here also in other academic

---

143. Bevans and Schroeder, *Prophetic Dialogue*, 42.
144. Bevans and Schroeder, *Prophetic Dialogue*, 48–52.
145. See, for example, O'Gara, *Ecumenical Gift Exchange*.
146. This is also one of the claims of Freire, *Pedagogy of the Oppressed*—see especially pp. 75–118, which deal with the nature of dialogical education.
147. Bosch, *Transforming Mission*, 428–31.

disciplines,[148] because to read the signs of the times theologically requires recognizing that theology has something to learn about the world from others.

Much the same can be said about the act of storytelling and of being a trail guide. The importance of storytelling in mission and indeed in faith formation in general is well-attested.[149] Later on, when I come to consider Bishop Innocent in Alaska, we will see that storytelling is important not only to communicate the gospel, but to understand both the culture and the gospel. A storyteller tells stories always to a particular audience and the stories change according to the audience, perhaps not in the details, but certainly in the telling, as the storyteller reacts to the demands of the listeners. Here it will suffice to say that the missionary prophet as storyteller can only tell the story if previously they have listened to the story of the other, and learnt the narrative art of the other.

The trail guide is in some senses more directional. The point in having a trail guide is that someone at least will know the way and can show the others how to get to where they want to go. Nevertheless, as a starting point, at the very least this demands finding out where they do in fact want to go, so there must be some dialogue involved. But the trail guide can also be seen in terms of non-possession. The trail guide is acquainted with the trail, with some of its wonders and pitfalls, but she or he does not possess it, and through the new eyes of fellow-travelers, new wonders will be experienced and new pitfalls become apparent. Like the spiritual guide or accompanier or companion,[150] the trail guide's job is to point people on the way to making the path their own, so that they too may help people along it.

Mission in the Garden

The final metaphor I want to look at is that of the garden.[151] This continues the tension between the prophetic and the dialogical already seen, this time

---

148. This despite the criticisms of Milbank, *Theology and Social Theory*. For a critique of Milbank, see Noble, *Poor in Liberation Theology*, 120–22, and especially the work cited therein: De Schrijver, "Use of Meditations." Clodovis Boff's distinction between the autonomy and dependence of academic disciplines (in themselves autonomous, but relatedly dependent) remains apposite here. See Boff, *Theology and Praxis*, 57–61.

149. See, for example, Evans, "Matters of the Heart," and Wallace, "Storytelling."

150. See Barry and Connolly, *Spiritual Direction*, 10–11. As the title of their book makes clear, despite some misgivings, they feel that "spiritual direction" is still a term that has some usefulness.

151. Bevans and Schroeder, *Prophetic Dialogue*, 72–87. Unlike the other chapters

with reference to the presence of what is life-enhancing in each "garden" (Justin's *logoi spermatikoi*) and the "weeds," the presence in any and every culture of elements that choke the life out of the rest of what is there.[152] Schroeder says that one "approaches the 'other' with an initial attitude of discerning how God is already present (dialogue) and then eventually, together *with* the people, after developing respectful and mutual relationships, confronts the 'weeds' with the 'good news' (prophecy)."[153]

This confrontation occurs as a response to an important question that he raises: why is the missionary there in the first place?[154] Because the default answer to this question will be either, with Paul, to name the inner compulsion to proclaim the gospel, or to do with service to God, it is a question that is probably insufficiently reflected upon, at least in the first instance.[155] The idea of "mission-in-reverse" as understood by Schroeder's colleague Claude Marie Barbour and the other members of her Shalom community "means that by attempting to be totally present and open to the other, I encourage that person and myself to become more fully liberated."[156] I think that for Schroeder the answer to the question "why" is one to be discovered in the process, rather than known with certainty beforehand. There must indeed be some kind of initial response (and the default answers are by no means bad), but the depths of understanding the "why" will only become apparent through interaction with the liberating power of the Spirit at work in and through the other.

---

of the book, which are written in the first person plural, this one is written in the first person singular, since it reflects specifically on Roger Schroeder's own personal experiences.

152. Bevans and Schroeder, *Prophetic Dialogue*, 74. On the more positive image of the garden, see also Čapek, *Gardener's Year*, and comments on this work in Noble, *Theological Interpretation*, 21–24.

153. Bevans and Schroeder, *Prophetic Dialogue*, 75. In this book, Schroeder works with ideas developed by Claude Marie Barbour in Shalom Ministries in Chicago. On this topic, see Cairns, "Establishing Base Communities," and Barbour et al., "Shalom Ministries." The four principles of the community are "Mission-in-Reverse," "Developing Base Christian Community," "Contextualization," and "Bridge-Building" (Cairns gives them in a slightly different order).

154. A very interesting article, which has some relation to this question, is that by Bünker, entitled "Function of the Other." Bünker critically addresses the way "the other is perceived in calls to mission and what function this perception then fulfils" (343). But his perspective is formed by an interest, similar to mine, in the other to whom mission is addressed.

155. Of course, many missionaries do come to ask this question later—perhaps the classic example is Donovan, *Christianity Rediscovered*.

156. Cairns, "Establishing Base Communities," 36. It should not, therefore, be directly connected to ideas of "reverse mission."

Key to what Schroeder wants to say is the need for discernment and for understanding of what constitutes "good plants" and "weeds" in different cultures, and for the need to speak against the "weeds" when one encounters them. This is not a form of relativism. There are forms of behavior and interaction that may be relative,[157] but there are other things that are not. It may indeed be difficult to draw up a complete list that all Christians would subscribe to, but, for example, most Christians would agree that the inflicting of violence on another is, in most cases, wrong.[158] In other words, having entered the other's garden, got to learn their "plants," what they consider as beneficial and harmful, it is still possible for the missionary to act prophetically, pointing to what seems to be the presence and the flourishing and blooming of the seed of the Word, and to what is contrary to it.

SUMMARY

Through a few examples, taken however from among the most important contemporary missiologists, this chapter has focused on how those writing and reflecting on missiology have started to address the presence of the other in mission. Already more than twenty years ago, David Bosch, without using the particular language of otherness, was aware of the issue, and of the need for mission to come out of what he called dialogue. This challenge has been taken up and further developed in a series of writings by two leading American missiologists, Stephen Bevans and Roger Schroeder, especially in their recognition of the creative tension at the heart of the idea of prophetic dialogue.

It will be noted that, apart from a few references to the "*paroikoi*,"[159] there is little attention given in these writings to the New Testament

---

157. From my own experience of living in the Czech Republic, I could suggest several. In the Czech Republic, my wife tells me, men should enter a restaurant first (apparently in case there are barroom brawls going on), whereas in my native Britain, I was brought up to hold the door for women to enter first. Or, when we are out, there are differences about which side the man and woman should walk when together. The logic of both is perfectly sound, and in the end it really does not make a great deal of difference, but it is culture-relative. Of course, the fact that many of these rules are now considered problematic because of the relations of presumed power that they are taken to reflect simply adds to the complexity.

158. I am thinking here more of the kind of example that Schroeder gives, of domestic violence, rather than specifically of more military forms of state-approved violence, or even state-legislated killing in the form of executions. I think that both the latter are highly problematic, but these are areas—especially the first—on which it may be legitimate for Christians to disagree.

159. This is an image that has been taken up especially by Stanley Hauerwas. See

material, and as far as I can tell practically none to the *prosēlutoi* or *gērīm* in the Old Testament. And yet, one might argue that the material seems to cry out for an engagement with this dimension of the Scriptures, at least as a fruitful image for what is being talked about. Perhaps the best place to start is by abandoning any too sharp distinction between "us" and "them," and to admit that, just as Israel had the experience of being "*gēr*" as a foundational part of its identity, and thus should know how to react to other "*gērīm*," so mission is predicated on the missionary being always a stranger encountering strangers.

Otherness ceases to be a threat or a challenge, and becomes the greatest gift we have, because it is at the most basic level what unites us and what we have, paradoxically, in common. The one thing that I share with everyone else, regardless of who they are, is that I am not them, and they are not me. So, in order to understand each other, we are left with no choice but to draw near, to become *prosēlutoi* to each other, travelling together in search of what life has to offer, bringing what we have been given as *viaticum*, food for the journey.

Certainly there are risks involved, because those engaged in Christian mission follow Jesus of Nazareth, whose own journey led to life through death on the cross. As someone like Dietrich Bonhoeffer, in his work[160] and even more in his life, showed, there is no such thing as cheap grace, no following of Christ that does not entail facing the consequences that Christ faced. But the need to set our faces resolutely towards Jerusalem (Luke 9:52) is still there. The other, as with God, is *tremendum et fascinans*, and only through encounter can the fear be overcome and attraction satisfied.

It would be good to be able to answer the most obvious question in all this, which is what we might hope to learn from the other. But that question cannot be answered straightforwardly, because to answer it would be to discard the other as necessary and as gift. On occasions it may be that the other really has nothing to offer, that the exchange of gifts is one-sided, and that what we learn is that we cannot force the other to be other than she or he is. More often, we will learn about ourselves, about our God,[161] about what the mission of God entrusted to us is. At times the learning will be joyful, at times deeply painful, both life-affirming and life-threatening. But

---

Hauerwas and Willimon, *Resident Aliens*. However, Hauerwas, like John Howard Yoder, despite protestations to the contrary, seems to me too "Christian-centric," and thus ignores the reality of the other as a potential contributor to the life and mission of the church.

160. Most obviously Bonhoeffer, *Cost of Discipleship*.

161. This is what lies behind the idea of comparative theology. See Clooney, *Comparative Theology*.

the trail guide who Bevans and Schroeder spoke of always finds the trail new, because it is a new day with new people, and so what we learn from the other will always be new.

I have focused in this chapter on the notion of dialogue. But is it enough? The danger in dialogue is that both sides know what they want to say beforehand, and, even if they want to, find it hard really to listen. To do so requires recognizing the givenness of the other. This is clearly not without problems, and to help resolve these problems, I move in the next chapter to a consideration of the nature of gift, or more precisely of givenness, as the in-breaking of an experience of the love of God. To do this, I will step away briefly from direct reflection on mission to look at the work of the French phenomenologist Jean-Luc Marion.

3

The Other as Given

In the first chapter, I examined the other who comes, the *prosēlutos*, as this other appears in the Old and New Testaments. In these texts, we saw that the other has two functions, as reminder—blessing and challenge—and as self-identification. In the previous chapter, I looked at how writers on mission have increasingly tried to take into account the other, in all their otherness and complexity, as the one who helps make God manifest. The other, then, is not an accident or obstacle, but a fundamental given of human experience and life. In order to deepen the understanding of the other as given, I want now to turn away from the world of missiology to a contemporary French thinker, Jean-Luc Marion.

Marion's approach, drawing on his understanding of phenomenology, has the advantage of preventing the idolization of the stranger,[1] of the one who comes, and understanding, or better, receiving[2] this stranger as given. I draw on his insights because I think that he offers a language to speak about the other that welcomes the other without seeking to define her or him. In this sense he makes a contribution in two ways. First, he provides a hermeneutical approach that will aid and strengthen the development of a specifically missional hermeneutics. Second, he allows a restructuring of the relationship between the self—the "I"—and the other.[3] Despite the

---

1. I have written much more extensively on idols and icons in Marion, so I will not discuss it again here in any detail. See Noble, *Poor in Liberation Theology*, 88–99, and Noble, "Jean-Luc Marion."

2. Welten says the following: "Typically, a gift is *received*, not *understood*" ("Paradox of God's Appearance," 197; italics in original).

3. For a brief but excellent overview of this aspect, see Horner, "Gifted Self."

complex argument, the underlying point that he wishes to make is relatively clear. However, for the sake of the reader not versed in Marion's work or, more broadly, in phenomenology, I will intersperse my discussion with paragraphs explaining its more direct relevance to my undertaking. Marion will also offer a way of talking about God as *agape*,[4] understanding God not as Supreme Being but as love, as love given, love as a phenomenon that appears, given to us also through the presence of the stranger.[5] I begin with a short comment on Marion himself and his place in the current phenomenological discussion, before moving on to consider in more detail his book *Being Given*.

JEAN-LUC MARION: A BRIEF BIOGRAPHICAL SKETCH

Jean-Luc Marion was born in the outskirts of Paris in 1946, and studied first at Nanterre and the Sorbonne, before moving on to graduate study of philosophy at the highly competitive École Normale Supérieure.[6] Studying under such luminaries as Louis Althusser, Gilles Deleuze, and Jacques Derrida, he prepared his doctoral work in philosophy, and at the same time began a serious study of theology. He has long been a contributor to the French edition of the journal *Communio*, often thought of as a conservative Catholic response to the more open *Concilium*, and linked with theologians such as Hans Urs von Balthasar.

Marion's first work was on Descartes,[7] on whom he has continued to work throughout his career. But beginning in the late 1970s, and especially from around 1990, he began to work out his own particular take on phenomenology. This is not the place to go into this debate, and only where it is necessary for understanding the context of Marion's work will I provide more details. However, one of the underlying tensions that Marion works with is that between the demands of philosophy and the demands of faith. For a number of reasons, some pragmatic, Marion is at pains to mark some of his works (such as *Being Given*, which I consider here) as purely philosophical, even though, as Robyn Horner, a perceptive commentator on Marion, notes, "it is this book more than any other which reinforces the

---

4. For an examination of the biblical meaning of *agape*, see Spicq, *Agape in the New Testament*, and more specifically in the Johannine writings, see Segovia, *Love Relationships*, and more generally the classic work of Nygren, *Agape and Eros*.

5. On this, see Marion, *God Without Being*, especially 46–48 and 134–38.

6. For a brief biographical introduction, see Horner, *Jean-Luc Marion*, 1–12.

7. The founder of phenomenology, Edmund Husserl, also wrote extensively on Descartes, and the first book bearing Emmanuel Lévinas's name was his French translation of Husserl's *Cartesian Mediations* in 1930. See Malka, *Emmanuel Lévinas*, 39.

ambiguity of Marion's attempts to limit himself to philosophy,"[8] something that will become apparent in our discussion of this topic.

In this respect, Marion has been part of what another French phenomenologist, Dominique Janicaud, has termed (critically) the "turn to God" in French philosophy.[9] This interaction between philosophy and theology—with all its problems and ambiguities—thus also provides a first testing ground for the possibility of dialogue and encounter between two others. Because of the complexity in Germany after the war of dealing with Heidegger,[10] it is in France that phenomenology has most deeply taken root. Thus Marion is also firmly embedded in a long tradition in French philosophy that owes a great debt to Lévinas, as well as to Jacques Derrida and others.[11] There are significant differences between all these thinkers, and yet the fact that Marion also works out of a philosophical tradition is important, since it reminds us that all encounters with others are between people who are immersed in different traditions and cultures and that all encounter is an act of bridge-building.

BEING GIVEN

Being Given[12] is the second book in a trilogy in which Marion seeks to construct a phenomenology for today.[13] In this book, he sees himself as taking up questions left unanswered, certainly at a philosophical level, in his earlier work, *God Without Being*.[14] In that book, Marion had tried to show how it was possible to let God escape from the tyranny of Being. Thus God is not defined (quite literally, in the sense of limited) by a prior category, that of Being, of which God is the supreme exemplar. Rather, as he sums

---

8. Horner, *Jean-Luc Marion*, 11.

9. See Janicaud, *Le tournant théologique*, and Janicaud et al., *Phenomenology*.

10. Heidegger's relationship to Nazism is complex, but his refusal to apologise for his early involvement after Hitler's seizure of power was a source of much criticism. The initial case against Heidegger is made most starkly in Farias, *Heidegger and Nazism*. Among those who argue that Heidegger's political beliefs—whatever precisely they may have been—are not destructive of his philosophy; see, for example, Young, *Heidegger, Philosophy, Nazism*.

11. On this, see the essays in Jonkers and Welten, *God in France*, and Horner, "Gifted Self," who points out that Marion can be read in response (though not therefore in contradiction) to Derrida in terms of understanding the relationship between self and other.

12. Marion, *Being Given*. The French original is from 1997.

13. Marion comments on this in his preface to *Being Given*, ix–x.

14. Marion, *Being Given*.

his argument up in the preface to the English translation of *Being Given*, "God gives Himself to be known insofar as He gives Himself—according to the horizon of the gift itself. The gift constitutes at once the mode and the body of his revelation. In the end the gift gives only itself, but in this way it gives absolutely everything." Or, a few lines later, "To give pure giving to be thought—that, in retrospect it seems to me, is what is at stake in *God Without Being*."[15]

By the time he came to write *Being Given* Marion had moved from the language of gift to concentrate more on givenness (though he will still use "gift," but already in a more secondary sense), since it avoids the implication of a giver (and thus of being) into the phenomenon. But he is essentially asking how the phenomenon can be received as givenness. In order to understand what Marion is doing, and why it is of interest to me, it will be necessary first to pause and give a very brief summary of some basic principles of phenomenology.[16]

A Very Brief Guide to Phenomenology

What came to be known as phenomenology was first developed by Edmund Husserl (1859-1938). Rather than new content, it sought to outline a new approach to doing philosophy. Instead of applying pre-ordained categories to the world in order to understand it (for example, Platonic Forms, or Aristotelian Causes), phenomenology argued that, before being understood, objects presented themselves, and were experienced, and thus demanded the application of meaning.[17] Husserl sought to move philosophy to a reflection on the nature of consciousness, on what was grasped in order to be known.

In order to do this, Husserl posited a "phenomenological reduction" or *epoché*, a bracketing out of all that is extraneous to the question of the grasping of the phenomenon.[18] Primarily, this reduction for Husserl touches on existence. That is to say, when we grasp a thing, we grasp it without being able as such to make any claims about the real world. In this sense, it is similar to Kant's rejection of the *Ding an sich*, the thing in itself that we can never

---

15. Marion, *God Without Being*, xxiv and xxv.

16. For an excellent and accessible introduction to phenomenology, see Moran, *Introduction to Phenomenology*, though he completely ignores Marion. See also Dreyfus and Wrathall, *Companion to Phenomenology*.

17. See Moran, *Introduction to Phenomenology*, 4–5.

18. See Moran, *Introduction to Phenomenology*, 124–63. See also Føllesdal, "Husserl's Reductions."

know. Thus, for Husserl, all is reduced (he uses the word in its Latin sense of "to lead back") to what is present, or what presents itself. In developing and ultimately critiquing Husserl, his student Martin Heidegger (1889-1976) introduced another form of reduction. For Heidegger phenomena presented themselves in their "thereness" (*Dasein*), and thus all is reduced to existence. There is no way for us to get behind our being-in-the-world.[19]

What Marion sees himself as doing is introducing a third and ultimate reduction, namely that of givenness.[20] Thus, the fundamental principle of phenomenology becomes for him, "as [so] much reduction, as [so] much givenness."[21] That is to say, whatever it is that appears to us and however it appears to us, does so as and only as given. It is the ultimate principle because whether we have a Husserlian reduction to presence, recognizing phenomena simply as whatever presents itself to be intuited, or a Heideggerian reduction to *Dasein* and to the "thrownness" of all that appears, all is at the most fundamental level given.[22]

At this point, for the reader not steeped in the phenomenological tradition, it may be helpful to indicate already what this means for my argument, and where it will take me. Essentially, the argument runs as follows. The one who comes is as such a phenomenon in the strict sense, not an already known and interpreted reality, but one who appears and demands reception and understanding or at least intuiting.[23] That is to say, I do not and indeed cannot know the other prior to their appearance. Of course, I can know many other things (the language this other will speak, culture, geography, history, and so on), but the other as phenomenon can only be known in their condition of phenomenon that is given to me.

---

19. See Moran, *Introduction to Phenomenology*, 160.

20. On why it is the ultimate reduction and not a kind of Platonic Third Man argument, with an infinite regress of reductions, see Marion, *Being Given*, 53–61.

21. Marion, *Being Given*, 14, for example, where it is given as "so much reduction, so much givenness" (French: *d'autant plus de réduction, d'autant plus de donation*.) See also Horner, *Jean-Luc Marion*, 111, 111n13.

22. On these concepts, see Wrathall, *Heidegger's Being and Time*, beginning with Wrathall and Murphey, "Overview," here especially 1 and 15; for a fuller discussion of *Dasein*, see Martin, "Semantics of 'Dasein.'"

23. The intuition is what one might call the first point of contact between the phenomenon and its perceiver. The phenomenon is as it presents itself and it is this presentation that is engaged with. See Moran, *Introduction to Phenomenology*, 126–29.

The Primacy of Givenness

In order to establish the primacy or priority of givenness, Marion works with the example of a painting. He sets the scene of a minor Dutch work of the late seventeenth century[24] and sets out to show that it is not reducible to object or to Being (the Husserlian or Heideggerian reductions), but only to givenness. He chooses a painting precisely because it is phenomenologically uncomplicated (at least in comparison to abstract ideas)—the whole point of a painting, as he notes, is to appear, to be seen.

The specific argument as to why it is not reducible to object or Being need not detain us here; what is of interest is the final positive part of the argument. First, Marion claims that, like any phenomenon, the painting "comes forward into visibility."[25] The point being made here is that phenomena cannot be, as it were, pre-identified, but intuit[26] themselves, show themselves to us—we might say that we do not choose our phenomena but that our phenomena choose us. Moreover, even as present to us, the painting is not seen as "painting"; rather,

> [t]o see the painting, to the point where it is not confused with any other, amounts to seeing it reduced to its effect . . . What more does a painting give besides what it shows in showing itself as object and being? Its effect. What more does the painting offer besides its real component parts? Its effect. But this effect is not produced in the mode of an object, nor is it constituted or reconstituted in the mode of being. It gives itself . . . It appears as given in the effect that it gives . . . The painting is not visible; it makes visible.[27]

At this point in his book Marion is seeking to set up possibilities, and uses the example of a painting to secure at least a foothold for the argument he will develop.[28] The painting is something that seems to have a particularly vested interest in being seen, and thus is a good place for him to begin. His contention, though, is that the painting comes to us in two related ways, through its effect and through its capacity not so much to be seen as to make visible.

---

24. Marion, *Being Given*, 40.
25. Moran, *Introduction to Phenomenology*, 49.
26. For a brief introduction to intentionality, see, for example, Horner, *Jean-Luc Marion*, 27–28.
27. Marion, *Being Given*, 51–52.
28. Moran, *Introduction to Phenomenology*, 39–40.

In relation to the task of Christian mission, this claim makes two important points. The first is to do with the question of effect. Mission could be visualized as a triangular relationship, with God at the apex and the two base points consisting of the missionary and the one who in this work I am calling the *prosēlutos*, the one who comes, the one addressed in mission. There are thus three levels of relationship going on—between God and the missionary, between God and the *prosēlutos*, and between the missionary and the *prosēlutos*. The outcome of these relationships will be seen in their effects.

The second point is related to this first one. How does God make himself visible? First, in a unique way, in Jesus Christ, "the icon of the invisible God" (Col 1:15). But also through human beings, created in the image and likeness of this same God. The last thirty or forty years, as noted in chapter 2, have been dominated in missiology by the concept of *missio Dei*.[29] And, if God reveals himself as a God who desires to relate to his creation and to bestow his blessings on that creation, then human beings, created in his image and likeness, have the potential to participate in this desire too. Moreover, this applies not just to the missionary, since all of humankind is created by God. Alongside the *missio Dei*, but utterly dependent on it, there is a *missio hominum*, a mission to and of human beings.[30] The task of humanity is to make God visible, to enable the seeing of the invisible God in his invisibility.[31] This task is entrusted to all humanity, and thus the one who comes to us is not, to borrow from Marion's imagery, a blank canvas, but also one who comes to make God visible to us.

---

29. Because of its careful examination of the origins and development of the phrase and its acute criticisms of some of the problems that have arisen, the key work on this is, as already noted, Flett, *Witness of God*.

30. For some interesting comments around this topic, see German missiologist Theo Sundermeier in *"Missio Dei* Today," reflecting on fifty years since the International Missionary Council meeting at Willingen in 1952. This may be a good place to refer to Sundermeier's work on the notion of *Konvivenz* (a word that translates very poorly into English, though it is quite common in its Spanish and Portuguese forms (*convivencia*), from which Sundermeier takes it). See Sundermeier, *Konvivenz und Differenz*. This notion of "living together" is, I think, something of what I am trying to say here. As Sundermeier, "Konvivenz," 36, sums it up: "The idea of *Konvivenz* has three pillars: *we help each other, we learn from each other, we celebrate together*" (italics in original; I leave *Konvivenz* untranslated, offering "living together" as a paraphrase). See also Sundermeier, "My Pilgrimage in Mission"; Kolář, "Hermeneutická misiologie"; Kisskalt, "Mission as *Convivence*"; Becker and Feldtkeller, *Mit dem Anderen leben*. My approach differs in that I would want to try to start, not with how we can live with the other, but with the other and what she or he brings to us in our journey towards God.

31. See Marion, *Idol and Distance*, 8.

The Other as a Given Phenomenon

It is now necessary to do justice to what Marion is aiming at in *Being Given*. As already noted, he is writing from a rigorously phenomenological point of view, and is very careful not to become entangled in theology. His argument is precisely that "the phenomenon gives itself"[32] and in giving itself, it shows itself. In this sense, there is no "behind" to the phenomenon, no prior explanatory phenomenon without which this particular phenomenon that gives itself cannot be grasped or intuited. He will go on to show why, from a phenomenological perspective,[33] he is not re-introducing transcendence.[34] That is to say, the encounter with the other cannot limit that other to the status of "angel," of a mere announcer of a message from God. The other is always solidly other, within, as Marion would say, the fold of givenness.

A related point here is that the other cannot be seen, either, simply as a gift of God. She or he is not a gift *of God* for the reasons outlined earlier, in the sense that there is no "prior" to the phenomenon as phenomenon. But also the other cannot be seen as gift, for reasons that Marion explains with recourse to Jacques Derrida. The basic argument here is as follows: a gift can only be a gift if both the giver and the receiver (Marion prefers the neologism "givee" to keep the relationship to the semantic field of giving) do not recognize it as such. Otherwise, the gift is always secondary, to the giver, or to the "givee." So, he quotes Derrida: "At the very least, the gift as gift ought not to appear as gift either to the givee or to the giver" and "If he recognizes it as gift, if the gift appears to him as such, if the present is present to him as present, this simple recognition suffices to annul the gift."[35] The problem is that if a gift is appropriated, made mine, then it loses its quality as a gift, either because it enters into a system of exchange, or it becomes property.

The other side of this that Marion needs to explain, though, is that if the gift does not show itself, then it cannot be grasped in any sense, not even as gift. The way out of this dilemma is complex, but essentially Marion argues that the gift can remain gift as long as it is not reduced (in the

---

32. Marion, *Being Given*, 68.

33. To reiterate, Marion himself would have no problem with the use of theology. As he puts it, with some irony: "the notion of givenness has no need, since Husserl, of a theological passport to intervene in phenomenology. It is at play there from the outset—officially, permanently, and as if it were at home. But why then attempt to disqualify it by assigning it a theological origin (supposing of course that theology implies of itself a disqualification)?" (*Being Given*, 72).

34. Marion, *Being Given*, 71–74.

35. Derrida, *Given Time*, 24 and 14, cited in Marion, *Being Given*, 78.

Husserlian sense) to presence.[36] It may be felt that it is somewhat abstract and not much of a gift, but the point is somewhat different. Needless to say, an object can be given, and that object can be received. But the gift is not the object itself—gift is gift and as soon as we reduce it to the content of the gift, we lose the gift.[37]

Again, it may be good to draw out the consequences of this for my work. In the first place, I very much do want to see the other as a gift from God, and that seems commensurable with the biblical terms we examined in chapter 1. Nevertheless, even here, Marion's strictly phenomenological approach can be helpful. He reminds us that, as soon as we try to limit the other, the *prosēlutos*, to something else, we lose the gift, and hence, for reasons previously discussed, the givenness. In more biblical language, we might say that the encounter with the other happens on holy ground, because at some level it is an encounter with God, and the sandals that we are called to remove are what we use as protection against the immediate contact with the roughness or sheer givenness that gives itself to us.

In this respect, Marion's insistence on the importance of the enemy for the possibility of bracketing out the "givee" is fascinating. He points out that, in giving to a friend, it is almost impossible for the friend not to make the gift a product of exchange—precisely as token of friendship the gift deepens the friendship and elicits a response in kind, out of friendship maybe, but actually now within an economy of exchange.[38] The enemy on the other hand is the one who refuses even to accept the gift, let alone to repay it with gift. Here Marion points both to Luke 6:33–35[39] and to the fact that the supreme gift is that of love, and most dramatically love of the enemy.[40] This is because it is a gift that cannot and will not be repaid, a pure, disinterested gift.

---

36. See, for example, Marion, *Being Given*, 81.

37. This is what Marion argues when it comes to the bracketing of the gift itself; see *Being Given*, 102–6.

38. We saw an example of this in chapter 1, in the reading of the encounters with gentiles in Matthew's Gospel made by Anderson in "Healthy Economics."

39. The text reads, "If you do good to those who do good to you, what credit is that to you? For even sinners do the same. If you lend to those from whom you hope to receive, what credit is that to you? Even sinners lend to sinners, to receive as much again. But love your enemies, do good, and lend, expecting nothing in return."

40. Marion, *Being Given*, 88–89.

The Saturated Phenomenon

I now turn to one of Marion's key contributions to phenomenology, the idea of the saturated phenomenon.[41] For Marion, following Husserl, phenomena can be not merely physical objects, but words or ideas. So he notes that most phenomena are "poor in intuition, or defined by the ideal adequation of intuition to intention."[42] That is to say, in a very over-simplistic way, most things do not have that much to say to us, or, what you see is what you get.[43] However, saturated phenomena are those with "a surplus of intuition, therefore of givenness, over and above intention."[44]

A saturated phenomenon, then, is that which always contains more than we can grasp. It manages, we might say, despite all the reductions that we make, to burst through all of them, except the final reduction of givenness. For our purposes, we can turn briefly to a description Marion gives in the final book of the trilogy of which *Being Given* is the middle volume. In that work, *In Excess*, he writes:

> The face, saturated phenomenon according to modality, accomplishes the phenomenological operation of the call more, perhaps, than any other phenomenon (saturated or not): it happens (event), without cause or reason (incident/accident), when it decides so (arrival), and imposes the point of view from which to see it (anamorphosis) as a *fait accompli*. That is why what

---

41. On this topic, see also Horner, "Gifted Self," 121–22.

42. Marion, *Being Given*, 199.

43. For a more nuanced, but intelligible, explanation of "intention" (that to which I turn my consciousness) and "intuition" (that which comes to my consciousness) in Husserlian thought, see the excellent book by Benson, *Graven Ideologies*, 34–36.

44. Marion, *Being Given*, 199. For a robust critique of this concept, see Puntel, *Being and God*, especially 343–60, who argues that Marion remains, in fact, bound within phenomenality, which becomes a restraint (much as Marion had argued that Being was a "de-finition"). Personally, I find this argument unconvincing, because it seems to me to want to make phenomenology (or indeed phenomenality) another competing school, rather than a way of doing philosophy or engaging with the world. But by misappropriating the nature of the phenomenological enterprise, it is almost inevitable that attempts to apply it will be viewed critically. See the critical review of Puntel's book by Gschwandtner, Review of Puntel. See also Gschwandtner, *Reading Jean-Luc Marion*, for her own reading of Marion. Kearney, *Anatheism*, 198–99, also criticizes Marion, rather more circumspectly, because of the total passivity involved in the confrontation with the saturated phenomenon. There is, I think, some force to this criticism, though Marion could say, in response, that attraction to the givenness of the saturated phenomenon is also an action, and that passivity implies a "by whom" to the givenness that he precisely wants to avoid. The phenomenon presents itself, and up to that point, which is the point that Marion wants to take us to, there is only receptivity (perhaps a better word here than passivity). What comes next, of course, is another matter.

imposes its call must be defined not only as the other person of ethics (Lévinas), but more radically as the icon.⁴⁵

The language here is somewhat complex (essentially he is rehashing his argument in *Being Given* in one sentence), but several points need to be drawn out. First of all, the face (as, in Lévinasian terms, the other who comes to us in their alterity) is always a saturated phenomenon. The other, the *prosēlutos*, is always more than I can know, and the saturated phenomenon is icon.⁴⁶

To put this again in very simple terms, the saturated phenomenon does not need me in order for intuition to occur, so I am not doing it a favor. The other does not depend on my noticing her or him, the other is not sitting around waiting for me to turn up in order to exist. Rather, the saturated phenomenon (in this case, the other human being), draws me on beyond the limits of my intention, forces me to enter more deeply into the excess of intuition that is given to me. Thus, through contact with the other, it is not simply that I am able to engage in mission, but that I am brought more deeply into an understanding of what that mission involves, and what my task is in it, and perhaps most fundamentally of all, of who I am before God.

In extending the presence of this saturated phenomenon to mission, I am going far beyond what Marion has in mind in his phenomenological writings.⁴⁷ Nevertheless, once again, I think that his language has much to commend it. The advantage of philosophical language over biblical language is that it is less able to commandeer us, to make us accept it without reflection or thought. This is not to say that Marion is here in conflict with biblical language, although obviously the Bible will turn more to narrative language, to images and metaphors. But the language of *prosēlutos*, of the one who comes, is, I would say, expressing the same reality. The stranger as phenomenon shows herself or himself at different levels, as the one who demands our care, as the one who shares in our fate, as the one who is part of our world, but perhaps most importantly as an icon of God, as a constant and stark reminder of what God has done for us. And because what God has done for us, and is doing for us, and will do for us, is never-ending and what

---

45. Marion, *In Excess*, 118.

46. See also on this Welten, "Paradox of God's Appearance," 203 (see 198–203 more generally on the saturated phenomenon), and Marion, *Being Given*, 232–33. In *Being Given*, 229–31, Marion also speaks of the saturated phenomenon as idol. As his intention in these pages is to speak in terms of paradox, this is not surprising, though I am not sure that his typical careful use of language may not break down somewhat here.

47. Though as Horner writes: "[Marion] also has theological interests and these enable us to extend the phenomenological account" ("Gifted Self," 116).

we can take from it is inexhaustible, this icon is a saturated phenomenon, a call to enter more deeply into the mystery of God.

The Phenomenon of Revelation

It is in a sense to this aspect that Marion turns as the final example of what he means by saturated phenomenon when he discusses revelation, and—though he is at pains to point out again that he does so as a phenomenologist—most specially the revelation of Jesus Christ. It is worth reading what Marion has to say on this:

> the phenomenon of Christ gives itself intuitively as an event that is perfectly unforeseeable because radically heterogeneous to what it nevertheless completes (the prophecies). It arises as "the lightning comes from the East and shows itself [*phainetai*] as far as the West" (Matt 24:27), saturating the visible at one fell swoop. This character of event that happens is not added extrinsically to the figure Christ assumes, but by contrast determines its first aspect, since he comes intrinsically as "he who must come [*ho erkhomenos*]" (John 1:15 or 2:7). He arrives under the banner of advent and advances only his own advance, which counts as one of his names.[48]

For Marion, "Christ appears as an absolute phenomenon, one that annuls all relation because it saturates every possible horizon into which relation would introduce it."[49] Thus, Christ is the givenness of God, the phenomenon that gives itself and in giving itself shows itself. And this phenomenon is saturated, is always beyond what we can grasp of it, is outside any of the categories into which we might want to place it. Christ comes, appears (that is the sense of epiphany, of course), and offers more than we can ever understand.[50]

Although Marion is examining revelation from a phenomenological standpoint, his rich reading of the scriptures is itself highly indicative of the possibilities inherent in his approach. The move from phenomenology to transcendence is in some ways on a different plane, and one that phenomenology has avoided, since it tends to replace the coming into consciousness of the phenomenon with the very prior categorization that Husserl was

48. Marion, *Being Given*, 236–37.
49. Moran, *Introduction to Phenomenology*, 238.
50. This, one cannot help but note, is a good thing for theologians, who would otherwise have long run out of things to say. But the fact that they (we) have not is in itself an argument in favor of Marion's claims here.

seeking to overcome.[51] Theology, though, is different, not least because the transcendent God is also saturated phenomenon, God who comes to us as Father, Son, and Holy Spirit. But more importantly, phenomenology reminds us precisely that God does come to us, that God reveals himself to us as the first and last step, God is pure givenness, self-givenness of God's self.

In describing the phenomenality of Christ as icon,[52] Marion draws attention to our "condition of a witness."[53] He writes: "Christ appears as an irregardable phenomenon precisely because as icon he regards me in such a way that he constitutes me as his witness rather than some transcendental I constituting him to its own liking."[54] In other words, mission comes not so much from a choice I make as from the very gaze of Christ that turns me into witness, by the choice of Christ himself; "Christ constitutes his disciples as witnesses by electing them; he can do this legitimately only because he sees them first—before they see themselves ('He saw two brothers,' Matt 4:18)."[55]

Marion goes into this in somewhat more detail through a reading of the story of the rich young man in Mark 10:17–22. He points out that "the gaze is not cast indifferently on just anyone, but differently on this one or that one, each time another Other."[56] This is important—the gaze of Christ is not impersonal, like some kind of Masonic All-Seeing Eye, distant, implacable, relentless. The gaze that goes beyond any intuition is always the gaze of Christ on a person, a gaze "that does not objectify or reify since it ends up loving, therefore letting what it just posited be set forth by its own withdrawal."[57] In other words, the love of Christ for the young man is such that he sets him free even to reject the possibility offered to him. Finally, then, Marion declares that the "irreducible saturated phenomenon . . . transforms the I into a witness, into its witness."[58]

---

51. Though in his later work, Husserl would turn more and more to the world of ideas, undertaking what has been called a transcendental turn in his work: see Moran, *Introduction to Phenomenology*, 136–42.

52. Marion examines the saturated phenomenon under four headings: as event, as idol, as flesh, and as icon. For a perhaps more accessible summary, see his comments in conversation with Richard Kearney in Kearney, "Dialogue," 12.

53. The phrase is from the title of a book by the French Dominican Jean-Pierre Jossua, *The Condition of the Witness*. Jossua comes out of a similar philosophical background.

54. Marion, *Being Given*, 240. I have smoothed out the somewhat random capitalization of the third person singular pronoun in the English translation.

55. Moran, *Introduction to Phenomenology*.

56. Moran, *Introduction to Phenomenology*, 241.

57. Moran, *Introduction to Phenomenology*. The aspect of love is one I return to.

58. Moran, *Introduction to Phenomenology*, 241.

Marion does not really develop here the notion of the witness, though later in a response to criticisms of the concept of saturated phenomenon he returned in somewhat more detail to the idea.[59] His key point is that the witness is precisely the one who bears testimony to something that she or he has seen, or better, something that has given itself as saturated phenomenon, but that moment, that experience, is something that can never be returned to, and never presented in itself. There are never words enough to capture what has been experienced.[60]

It needs to be admitted at this point that Marion is giving us a language not so much to speak about the *prosēlutos*, the other who comes, but rather to speak of the missionary, of the one who seeks to recount an experience that always surpasses the ability to tell.[61] And yet here the threefold relationship between God, the one sent, and the one encountered is at its clearest. The relationship must involve all three, and to that degree to talk of one is to include the others. Even to talk of God is necessarily to include the speaker who is not God, who relates to God (whether positively or negatively, in belief or disbelief, does not materially affect the argument), and, as human being, relates to some other.

This is, I think, what lies behind the closing paragraph of *Being Given*. Marion is interested in the relationship of the I with the other, now based on what he calls intergivenness. This, he claims,

> would also perhaps authorize broaching what ethics cannot attain: the individuation of the Other. For I neither want nor should only face up to him as the universal and abstract pole of counter-intentionality where each and every one can take on the face of the face. I instead reach him in his unsubstitutable particularity, where he shows himself like no other Other can. This individuation has a name: love . . . phenomenology claims to make it its privileged theme—"Love, as basic *motive* for phenomenological understanding" (Heidegger). Could the phenomenology of givenness finally restore to it the dignity of a concept?[62]

59. Marion, "La banalité," in *Visible*, 142–82: on the witness, see 179–81.

60. In *Being Given*, 239, Marion refers to the two summary statements at the end of the Gospel of John (John 20:30–31 and 21:25), which make precisely this point. It is not simply a banal comment about lack of time and space, but a realization of the nature of the saturated phenomenon itself, of Jesus as the icon of God who cannot be reduced to words, images, or anything else.

61. The ways that missionaries sought to make sense of their experiences is the subject of Johnston, *Missionary Writing*, who is, however, more interested in the problematic nature of how the experiences were categorized and recounted.

62. Marion, *Being Given*, 324. The quotation is from Heidegger, *Grundprobleme der*

Marion had already treated in detail the concept of *agape* (love) in his earlier works.[63] But here love is placed at the service not only of overcoming the tyranny of Being, but also as a creative force that enables us to avoid a possible aporia in the Lévinasian approach.

Lévinas had, indeed, argued—for Marion, persuasively—that the other is always beyond, always irreducible to the I. As Lévinas puts it: "To approach the Other in conversation is to welcome his expression . . . it is therefore to *receive* from the Other beyond the capacity of the I, which means exactly to have the idea of infinity."[64] But for Lévinas this meant that ultimately even to speak of the Face of the other is never to speak of a particular face, since that would be a form of totality.[65] This, though, means that, if the other is the one who can enable my being, this other is still too undetermined, and this lack of determination, for all that it serves to prevent totality, can lead to the other losing any reality, and becoming, in phenomenological terms, outside of perception.

In order to prevent the other coming to serve still only as a way for the I to exist, and thus actually remaining subservient to the I, Marion suggests the encounter in love. Love is what allows, as he puts it here, the "individuation of the Other," the Other to be encountered in their particular givenness. Love is a response to givenness with givenness, not part of an economic exchange ("if you love me, I will love you"). Love reaches out to the other as she or he is, as other, welcoming and embracing and being transformed by the encounter. Love in this instance goes beyond all strategy, all planning, all belief, as the radical openness to the gift/givenness of the other as other, as "unsubstitutable particularity."

SUMMARY

I realize that for some the engagement with the thought of Jean-Luc Marion may seem of limited relevance for the subject of missionary encounter with the other.[66] His philosophical approach can appear to the non-specialist

---

Phänomenologie, 185.

63. Especially in *God Without Being*. This is developed in Marion, *Prolegomena to Charity* and in Marion, *Erotic Phenomenon*. See also Horner, *Jean-Luc Marion*, 135–46.

64. Lévinas, *Totality and Infinity*, 51. Italics in original. In this sense, the face is, for Lévinas (and Marion) a saturated phenomenon.

65. See Lévinas, *Ethics and Infinity*, 86: "The best way of encountering the Other is not even to notice the color of his eyes."

66. However, in a short talk in discussion with Jacques Derrida, Marion concludes his reflection on the "name" of God by pointing out that "The Name is not said, it calls," which may not be a bad starting point for mission. See Marion, "In the Name," 42. See

difficult and abstract. However, I have included this brief discussion here for two reasons. First, I think that Marion gives us a clear conceptual hermeneutical language for addressing both the problem of how mission relates to its other, to the one who comes, and of understanding who that other is and what the other can bring to mission. Marion helps us to see that there is a problem in many common understandings of the addressee of mission and what that problem is. In doing this, he helps to see why we will continue to fail to fulfil the command to make disciples of Christ, because at best we will be making the other follow us and our vision of who Christ is (and it does not entirely matter if that is a "correct" vision or not).

The second, related reason is that this clear conceptual language has, in my view, very immediate practical effects. First, to accept Christ, in Marion's language, as a saturated phenomenon, is to renounce any claim to be the only vessel for the proclamation of the fullness of Christ. We should indeed aim to proclaim the fullness of Christ, but no single person can do this fully. Second, the givenness of the other allows us to accept the other not as a target, a means to an end, but as a companion, as a co-traveler on the road to God. Gifts are not exchange—at least not at their most profound level—so it cannot even be that the other will give me something in exchange for the gospel that I share with them. But together, like the disciples at Emmaus,[67] our eyes will be opened and together we will become those who are called to witness—however inadequately—what we have received.

With this discussion of Marion I have come to the end of the first part of this work. Through reflection on Scripture, contemporary missiology, and philosophy, I have shown the importance of the other for any engagement in Christian mission. This other is the starting point as blessing and challenge, the one who keeps before us constantly all that our God has done for us and asks us to be bearers and receivers of Good News. Ultimately, the encounter in dialogue with this other, the attempt to learn their language, their way of seeing the world, can only be done in the love of God and love of the other. This love is not a form of escape or a rejection of mission, but a commitment to follow Christ in such a way that the other is able also to respond in love to the same call that has taken possession of the disciple.

In the second part of the book, I turn to three examples of how this has played out in practice. It would have been possible to work with issues facing mission today, and to have seen what the role of the other might be in them. However, I have chosen historical examples, and I have chosen a

---

also the contribution by Caputo, "Apostles of the Impossible."

67. Marion has an interesting reflection on this too: see Marion, "They Recognized Him." For critical engagement with this article, see Mackinlay, "Eyes Wide Shut."

more biographical approach. This is for two reasons. One is that mission is always ultimately about personal interaction. The second is that historical case studies remove the possibility of any current bias towards privileging the other. This, of course, is something I welcome, but I want to argue that in many instances this privilege has been afforded in Christian mission, at least implicitly or subconsciously.

The people I examine come from three different Christian traditions: Ignatius of Loyola, a Roman Catholic, William Carey, a Baptist, and Innocent Veniaminov, a Russian Orthodox. This is by design, since my argument is that this attention to allowing the other to transform the missionary is present in Christian practice, irrespective of the particular tradition. It is not, of course, to deny the differences in theology or practice of those traditions, but to show that this attention to the other is a uniting factor. It would have been possible to choose many other examples, but all three have an important place both within their own traditions[68] and more generally in Christian history and in the history of mission. Not surprisingly, none of them is a perfect example of everything I have argued for so far. But in their various ways they all sought to respond in love to the challenge of the other in their desire to share their own experience of God's love. In what follows then I will examine how the three men reacted to the givenness of the other in their lives and what effect, if any, this had on their understandings of mission.

---

68. Ignatius and Innocent are both saints, and if Baptists had saints, Carey would be one; anyway, he plays fundamentally the same kind of role in Baptist mythology as saints do in Roman Catholic and Russian Orthodox mythologies.

PART 2

The Missionary

4

Saint Ignatius of Loyola
Mission as Service of the Other in Love

In this chapter I turn to Saint Ignatius of Loyola (1491–1556), founder of the Society of Jesus, one of most influential Roman Catholic religious orders of the past five hundred years.[1] I will examine the experience of God that is systematized in Ignatius's *Spiritual Exercises* and then developed and articulated for a specific purpose in the *Constitutions of the Society of Jesus*,[2] and that serves as the basis for his understanding of the response in mission to the call of the king.[3] This response is ultimately to the God who works to sustain us in love.[4]

Then I will look at how Ignatius came to understand the priority of mission and how he sought to mold the new religious order at whose head he was placed as a group of men formed and ready to go out to encounter

---

1. Coupeau, "Five *personae*," shows how the person I am calling Ignatius can be approached in five different ways: "'Iñigo' (the Christian in his relationship with the Absolute), 'our Father Master Ignatius' (the friend for the group of his intimate and close colleagues), the 'Founder' (the leader for the Society of Jesus), 'Saint Ignatius' (the point of departure for a new spirituality), 'Loyola' (as known by the Encyclopedists and 'Counter-Reformation' historians)" (32), and how each of these readings employs a different hermeneutical key.

2. Hereafter referred to simply as *Constitutions*.

3. See *Spiritual Exercises* (*SpEx*), paras. 91–100. I will use the translation in Munitiz and Endean, *Saint Ignatius*, here 303–4. References to the *SpEx* are given using the standard paragraph numbers, as shown above.

4. See the "Contemplation for Attaining the Love of God," *SpEx*, paras. 230–37. I will discuss this in more detail later in this chapter.

the other and respond to that other. In doing this, I will be tracing how, in the words of one commentator, "Ignatius shifts from a spirituality where concern for his personal salvation is paramount, to an apostolic spirituality that centers on the commitment to do the Lord's work."[5]

THE EARLY LIFE OF IGNATIUS

Iñigo[6] López de Loyola was born in 1491 in the castle of Loyola to a fairly wealthy and influential aristocratic family in a remote part of the Basque country.[7] Loyola was in the Province of Guipúzcoa, at that time belonging to the Kingdom of Navarre. It was in the diocese of Pamplona, a place that would play an important role in Ignatius's life. Navarre came under the rule of King Ferdinand of Aragon in 1512. There was nothing particularly unusual about Ignatius's early life as a younger son in a noble family.[8] He served in various capacities in the court of the Viceroy of Navarre. In his *Autobiography*,[9] he sums up his early life in one short sentence: "Until the age of twenty-six[10] he was a man given up to vanities of the world, and his

---

5. Schineller, "Pilgrim Journey," 3.

6. The Castilian version of the Basque name "Enneko," a popular name in the region at the time, after Saint Ennecus, an eleventh-century abbot from Oña, some 150 kilometers southwest of Loyola. He seems to have adopted the name "Ignatius" at some point in the late 1530s. For the sake of convenience, I will use "Ignatius" at all times in this chapter.

7. The date is not known, and there are still discussions about even the precise year, but this is the most commonly agreed date. There are many biographies of Ignatius. See, for example, Dalmases, *Ignatius of Loyola*.

8. On Ignatius's background, see Homza, "Religious Milieu."

9. In fact, it is a text narrated not long before his death at the hands of the Portuguese Jesuit Fr. Luis Gonçalves da Câmara. In it, at the request of his companions, Ignatius reflects on the beginning of his own spiritual journey and how it led him to Rome. The Latin translation, *Acta quaedam Rdi. P. Ignatii*, and the fact that it ends with Ignatius arriving in Rome may well allude to Paul and the Acts of the Apostles. Further study of the links between the pilgrim Ignatius and the pilgrim Paul would be, I suspect, interesting. See the fascinating work by Boyle, *Loyola's Acts*, esp. the title and the link to the Acts of the Apostles, 3. Boyle looks at what she calls *Acta* (she does not, to my mind, convincingly explain a preference for the Latin version over earlier, though not original, Spanish and Italian manuscripts) as a work with a moral end, in order to warn of the dangers of vainglory.

10. Given that the injury he suffered during the siege in Pamplona that led to his conversion took place in 1521, this is wrong. For a good short introduction to Ignatius's life up to that point, see Zajícová, "Vlastní životopis," 201–7n32.

chief delight used to be in the exercise of arms, with a great and vain desire to gain honor."[11]

This largely unremarkable life began to change in 1521, when Ignatius's leg was broken[12] as he took part in the defense of Pamplona against an attack by French forces. His account of his life goes on to record his experience of conversion as he lay at home in the castle of Loyola recovering from the wounds. On at least one occasion he was very close to death, and when the initial wound had healed, he asked for the leg to be reset, because it had healed in an unsightly way.[13] This concern with his physical appearance indicates as clearly as anything else that conversion was in no way instantaneous.

For obvious reasons Ignatius found himself with a great deal of time on his hands and so he asked for some romances. But the castle had only two books, the *Vita Christi* of Ludolph of Saxony (died 1377) and the *Flos Sanctorum* of Jacopo of Varazze (1228-1298), a compilation of lives of the saints.[14] As he read these, he came to feel torn between serving "a certain lady" and serving God. Over the time of his convalescence he gradually came to understand the workings of the Spirit in his life, recognizing that the thoughts of service to the lady, however pleasing at the time, ultimately left him unsatisfied whilst the thoughts of following Christ, even when he was not directly concentrating on the idea, left him content. Thus he found himself drawn to a life of service to God, in the manner of the saints whose lives he had been reading.[15] After his recovery, he set out first to Montserrat, a pilgrimage site in Catalonia.

On his way there, he had what might be termed his first missionary encounter with the other and, it must be admitted, it was not a particularly successful one. As Ignatius himself put it in his *Autobiography*: "And on this journey something happened to him which it will be good to have written, so that people can understand how Our Lord used to deal with this soul: a soul that was still blind, though with great desires to serve him as far as its knowledge went."[16] As he was riding on his mule, he came across

---

11. See his *Autobiography*, para. 1. I use the translation (entitled "Reminiscences") in Munitiz and Endean, *Saint Ignatius*, 13–64 (p. 13 is quoted here). As with *SpEx*, the *Autobiography* has standardized paragraph numbers.

12. It is often said to have been caused by a cannonball, but may have been something lighter; see Munitiz and Endean, *Saint Ignatius*, 361 n6.

13. *Autobiography*, paras. 3–4; in Munitiz and Endean, *Saint Ignatius*, 13–14.

14. See Munitiz and Endean, *Saint Ignatius*, 361, endnote 6, and Zajícová, "Vlastní životopis," 209, endnote 39.

15. See *Autobiography*, paras. 6–10; in Munitiz and Endean, *Saint Ignatius*, 15–16.

16. *Autobiography*, paras. 14; in Munitiz and Endean, *Saint Ignatius*, 18.

a "Moor," a Spanish Muslim,[17] travelling in the same direction, and they fell into conversation. The topic turned to Our Lady, and the Moor, though happy to accept the virginal conception of Jesus, was not prepared to accept that Mary had remained a virgin after the birth of Jesus.

The Moor ended up riding on ahead of Ignatius, who came to feel that he had not defended the honor of Mary sufficiently, and he began to feel anger with his conversation partner. Ignatius was unsure whether to follow him and kill him or leave it be. He knew that the man was heading for a small village, just off the main road, so he decided eventually to let the mule decide, leaving the reins loose. If the mule kept on the main road, he would leave the man, if it went to the village, he would kill him. Fortunately for all concerned, "Our Lord willed that, though the town was little more than thirty or forty paces away, and the road leading to it very broad and very good, the mule took the main road, and left the one for the town behind."[18]

Although there is something rather comic about this story, Ignatius has a serious reason for telling it. Missionary zeal is good, but one cannot serve the Lord by destroying the other. Looking back from a distance of thirty years, Ignatius recognizes how he had failed to engage with the other as a bearer of the Good News. This is the start of his life as a pilgrim,[19] but he had yet to learn that the encounters on pilgrimage could not serve as occasions to use violence to enforce his beliefs on others. The fact that his failure to love the Moor stayed with him is a sign of how he would come to understand the nature of mission, both for himself and the Society of Jesus.

After his journey to Montserrat, where he spent a night in vigil, he moved to a small town nearby called Manresa, where he spent a year or so in prayer and ascetic practice. During this time, he noted, "God was dealing with him in the same way as a schoolmaster deals with a child, teaching him."[20] Here the initial experiences that would later, in part, be systematized into the *Spiritual Exercises* took place, and he came to have a clearer understanding of his own calling and of how God was constantly at work in his life. It was a growing experience of the love of God that drew him on and called him to respond that would inform his understanding of mission as service in love.

---

17. On Muslims in Spain at this point, still only some thirty years after the end of the Reconquista under Ferdinand and Isabella, see the brief comment in Zajícová, "Vlastní životopis," 213–14 n57.

18. *Autobiography*, para. 16; in Munitiz and Endean, *Saint Ignatius*, 19.

19. It is during this account that Ignatius first uses this term to describe himself. It would go on to become one of the foundational self-understandings for him and for the nascent Society of Jesus. See Schineller, "Pilgrim Journey," 6–8.

20. *Autobiography*, para. 27; in Munitiz and Endean, *Saint Ignatius*, 25.

THE *SPIRITUAL EXERCISES*: MISSION AS SERVICE IN LOVE

A key reason that I have chosen to focus on Ignatius is that he was probably the first to take the medieval use of the language of mission as an intratrinitarian term and apply it to the task of proclamation, in deed and word, of the gospel.[21] For him, this task was the crucial one of the Christian, and even more specifically of those who were his companions in Christ.[22] At the heart of this engagement was the need to serve in love. As one commentator on the *Spiritual Exercises* notes: "[l]ove is the subject of many texts in the *Exercises* where there is no mention of the word 'love.'"[23] Love, together with service, is at the heart of Ignatius's spiritual experience and vision.

It was this experience of the patient love of God that serves as the backdrop to all that Ignatius would come to understand over the following years. In talking of the love of God, it is important to remember that the genitive can be both objective and subjective, God's love for us and our love for God, and that both of these form an integral part of the experience of the *Spiritual Exercises*. However, though the distinction is important, it should not be made too divisive, since it is the experience of God's love for us that Ignatius sees as arousing our love for God, which is always a dynamic response in and of service.

Thus, a British Jesuit writer, Michael Ivens, notes, with reference to what is known as the "Principle and Foundation," the text towards the beginning of the *Spiritual Exercises* that acts as a kind of programmatic summary of the process to be undertaken: "The opening sentence of the Foundation,[24]

---

21. See Kollman, "At the Origins." Note also the comment by Mooney, "Ignatian Spirituality," 201, that the Jesuit understanding of mission was always much broader than what she calls mission *ad extra*, and thus included what we might today term foreign and home mission.

22. The Spanish name of the Society of Jesus, the religious order founded by Ignatius and his companions in 1540, is *Compañia de Jesus*, the Company of Jesus. The placing of the order under the banner of Christ was something that came to Ignatius in a vision at a small wayside chapel in a place called La Storta, just outside Rome, as he was going there to offer himself and his companions to the service of the church. On the vision of La Storta and its importance, see Rahner, *Vision of St. Ignatius*. A collection of essays by a former Superior General of the Society of Jesus, Fr. Peter-Hans Kolvenbach, bears witness to the ongoing importance of the vision: see Kolvenbach, *Road from La Storta*.

23. Ivens, *Keeping in Touch*, 151. Michael Ivens, SJ (1933–2005), was a leading figure in the renewal of the tradition of the giving of the *SpEx* in the English-speaking world and an important commentator on the text of the *SpEx*.

24. Namely, "The human person is created to praise, reverence, and serve God Our Lord, and by so doing to save his or her soul" (*SpEx*, para. 22; in Munitiz and Endean, *Saint Ignatius*, 289). For an excellent commentary on this, see Cusson, *Biblical*

for instance, is about love, which people of Ignatius's day would have found it natural to describe, even outside of a religious context, in terms such as 'praise, reverence, and service.'"[25]

For Ignatius, then, love and service go together, and although he does not enter into a detailed theological reflection, this would entail God's love for us made incarnate in Jesus Christ, the one who took on the form of a slave (Phil 2:7), as well as our response to this God. And it is here that love and mission come together. The *Spiritual Exercises* of Ignatius are divided into four segments, traditionally called Weeks.[26] In the First Week, "Ignatius . . . initiates us into the interplay, the sheerly incomprehensible contrast, between divine goodness and creaturely sinfulness."[27] It is the experience of God's love and our failure so often to respond to that love that gives rise to the threefold question "What have I done for Christ? What am I doing for Christ? What ought I to do for Christ?"[28]

Responding to the Call of the King

The Second Week of the *Spiritual Exercises* focuses on the life of Christ, from the Incarnation to Palm Sunday, and also is the time when the retreatant is called on to make a decision about a way of life.[29] This segment of the *Exercises* begins with the Call of the King.[30] Here the exercitant (the one who is making the *Spiritual Exercises*) is asked to consider the call of some great earthly king who wishes to embark on a kind of crusade. The language may not be very helpful today, though Ignatius was fully aware that this is an imaginative exercise, not a report on the reality of Christendom.[31] The

---

Theology, 63–75.

25. Ivens, *Keeping in Touch*, 151.

26. On the dynamic of the *SpEx*, see, for example, Fleming, *Like the Lightning*.

27. Endean, "Spiritual Exercises," 58.

28. *SpEx*, para. 53; in Munitiz and Endean, *Saint Ignatius*, 296.

29. This is in the full version of the *Spiritual Exercises* that is normally done over a period of some thirty days, and that for Ignatius was aimed at discerning how or in what state (for example, as a married person or a religious or cleric) one was called to follow Christ. Such life-changing and determining decisions will not, of course, be part of every experience of the *SpEx*, in their manifold different forms, as currently practiced.

30. In fact, this is a kind of interstitial exercise, linking the First and Second Weeks. On this exercise in much more detail, see Cusson, *Biblical Theology*, 173–213.

31. See Connolly, "Story of the Pilgrim King," 269, quoted in Ivens, *Understanding the Spiritual Exercises*, 184. For the (highly positive) attitude of the early Jesuits towards the institution of monarchy, see Höpfl, *Jesuit Political Thought*, 37–52.

temporal king serves to awake in the retreatant a sense of desire, always important for Ignatius, a dream-vision of all that most inspires them to action.

And, then, even more, they should feel the desire to give themselves over wholly to the King, Christ. Ignasi Salvat, a Catalan Jesuit, argues that behind these texts lies an appeal to 1 Cor 15:24–26[32] and to John 12:25–26.[33] With reference to the second of those verses Salvat writes: "We have to read these words within the overall context of the Gospel of John, which constantly presents us Jesus as "the One Sent" from the Father. The following of Jesus always carries with it the following of the One Sent, and thus, service to his mission."[34]

Thus, from the very beginning of the Second Week, the response to the inexhaustible and merciful love of God experienced in the First Week is a desire[35] to follow Christ, wherever he leads and to whatever he calls us. Salvat does not employ the phrase *missio Dei*,[36] but that may be a fair summary of what he is talking about here. The response to the mission of Christ is a desire to participate in that mission.[37] This is seen even more clearly in the *Spiritual Exercises* in the first contemplation of the Second Week, on the Incarnation and Annunciation, one of the key exercises that sets up the dynamic of the remaining days.

This exercise[38] envisages contemplating the Trinity, gazing down on "the whole round world,"[39] seeing people in all conditions, of joy and sor-

32. The text is: "Then comes the end, when he hands over the kingdom to God the Father, after he has destroyed every ruler and every authority and power. For he must reign until he has put all his enemies under his feet. The last enemy to be destroyed is death."

33. The text is: "Whoever serves me must follow me, and where I am, there will my servant be also. Whoever serves me, the Father will honor."

34. Salvat, *Servir en Misión Universal*, 43. The somewhat inelegant "the One Sent" is my translation of Salvat's "El Enviado."

35. Or, at least, the person should have the "desire for the desire," a phrase that comes from the *Constitutions*, where a prospective applicant to join the Society is asked if he desires to follow Christ poor, humiliated, and humble, and if he does not at the moment have those desires, whether he would desire to have them. See *Constitutions*, 46, para. 102.

36. Mooney, "Ignatian Spirituality," 201–4, uses the language of *missio Dei* to talk about Ignatius's understanding of mission, though without developing the idea.

37. Cusson points to the fact that the text deals both with the mission of Christ, and the response in mission to the call that is part of Christ's mission: see Cusson, *Biblical Theology*, 190–91 on Christ's salvific mission, and 193–96 on the human response to this mission.

38. *SpEx*, paras. 101–9; in Munitiz and Endean, *Saint Ignatius*, 305–6.

39. "Toda la haz y redondez de la tierra"; *SpEx*, para. 106. I quote the Spanish text as given in Ignacio de Loyola, *Ejercicios Espirituales*.

row, sickness and health, war and peace, and desiring to redeem the world. Salvat stresses the universality of this picture—the repetition of words like "all" or "the whole,"[40] in which the gaze and the sight of the Trinity[41] settles on the whole of human endeavor, on all humanity in its wondrous diversity. Out of this setting the Son is sent, for the universal mission of redemption. Ignatius is not interested here, either spiritually or theologically or philosophically, in questions of universal salvation, but he does understand the offer of redemption, the possibility of being redeemed, as something that is made to all of humankind—the Trinity say: "Let us bring about the redemption of the human race, etc."[42] And as the mission of Christ is to all humankind, so the mission of his followers must also be.

The ultimate aim of this particular exercise is set out in the third preamble,[43] which as always in the *Spiritual Exercises* sets out what is to be desired in the particular exercise. Here, it is "interior knowledge of the Lord who became human for me so that I may better love and follow Him."[44] From love of the Lord who comes down to be among us and to redeem us springs the desire to engage in mission, to take up our cross and follow wherever we are led, or, as Salvat writes, "Following has to be the concretization of love."[45] So, for Ignatius mission is something that always happens within a double context—the love of God (both God's love for us and our love for God),[46] and the sending of Christ. The exercise we have just considered reminds us that, although Ignatius is deeply Christocentric in his spirituality and in his life, he is also and relatedly deeply Trinitarian. The mission of the follower of Jesus is rooted in the mission of God, depends on it, works from it, and towards it.[47]

---

40. Salvat, *Servir en Misión Universal*, 48.

41. Salvat, *Servir en Misión Universal*, 45–46.

42. *SpEx*, para. 107. The "etc." in the *Spiritual Exercises* is a fascinating theme, which perhaps serves as one way that Ignatius tries to avoid over-prescribing what the exercitant should experience. It is a reminder that these are indicators and guides rather than a step-by-step strategy for spiritual fulfilment.

43. The text of each exercise consists of a short prayer (through which exercitants place themselves in the presence of God), a number of preparatory remarks called "Preambles," and then a varying number of "Points," which introduce the material of the prayer.

44. *SpEx*, para. 104; in Munitiz and Endean, *Saint Ignatius*, 305.

45. Salvat, *Servir en Misión Universal*, 48.

46. On this topic, see also Egan, *Spiritual Exercises*, 128–29, who speaks of the need for a response of "loving reverence and thankfulness."

47. In this sense, Ignatius, even if he does not use the phrase, has a much healthier understanding of *missio Dei* than many today.

Service under the Banner of Christ

The most radical concretization of the love of the disciple for his master Christ is found in the meditation on the Two Standards.[48] Ivens sums up its purpose as follows: "Essentially the Two Standards prepares the exercitant for a particular election because it invites him or her to the radical conversion of outlook and desire that constitutes the true life in Christ."[49] This meditation carries forward that of the Call of the King, and asks the retreatant to make a firm response to it. It is a thought-experiment, asking the person making the *Exercises* to consider two calls to engage on a universal mission. There are two great hosts, one led by Lucifer, the other by Christ, gathered respectively on plains around Babylon and Jerusalem.

The mission of Lucifer, "the mortal enemy of our human nature,"[50] involves sending his adherents through the whole world (since his too is a universal mission), tempting people "first to crave after riches (the enemy's usual tactic), so that they might come more readily to the empty honors of the world, and in the end to unbounded pride."[51] In counterpoint to this is placed the equally universal mission of Christ: "the Lord of all the world selects so many persons as apostles, disciples, etc., and sends them out over the whole world spreading His sacred doctrine among all people of every state and condition."[52] The repetition of the universality is almost excessive,[53] and yet it points to Ignatius's grasp of the centrality of the response to the gift of love as a joyous self-giving in mission.[54]

Those who go will seek to draw those they meet to poverty, spiritual, and if God so deigns, actual, which will lead to insults and contempt, thus bringing about humility.[55] This is the polar opposite of the tactic of Lucifer, but it is not to be seen as a desire for suffering as an end in itself, or some kind of false humility. It comes out of a particular social context, and its primary aim is not to promote actual poverty as some kind of moral good.[56]

---

48. See on the Two Standards in Cusson, *Biblical Theology*, 253–58.

49. Ivens, *Understanding the Spiritual Exercises*, 105.

50. Thus he is called in *SpEx*, para. 136, the introduction to the meditation. See Munitiz and Endean, *Saint Ignatius*, 310.

51. *SpEx*, para. 142; in Munitiz and Endean, *Saint Ignatius*, 311.

52. Munitiz and Endean, *Saint Ignatius*; *SpEx*, para. 145.

53. "Lord of *all* the world," "the *whole* world," "*all* people of *every* state and condition."

54. On Ignatius's insistence on mission as related to his Trinitarian vision of the world and the incarnation, see also Kollman, "At the Origins," 431–32.

55. See *SpEx*, para. 146; in Munitiz and Endean, *Saint Ignatius*, 311

56. This can be seen in the ways in which Ignatius sought to alleviate the poverty

Rather it sets out the radical nature of Christian discipleship, a following that demands all. To follow Christ is to side with Christ in all that he experienced, in all that he went through; it is for this reason that confirmation of choices made are to be sought in the Third and Fourth Week of the *Exercises* through attention to respectively the Crucifixion and Resurrection, since the way of discipleship must pass always to life through death.

Love for God Expressed in Service

Having followed this path, we come at the end of the *Exercises* to the Contemplation for Attaining the Love of God (often known as the *Contemplatio*), or, as the Latin translation of the text puts it more clearly, the Contemplation for arousing spiritual love in ourselves.[57] In other words, it is our love for God that is contemplated here, and, as Ivens notes, "the love sought here is a gift and incommensurate with our own endeavors."[58] By this stage of the *Exercises*, the exercitant should have been overwhelmed by the desire to follow Christ, and to participate, in whatever way she or he is called, in the universal mission of the One Sent, God's emissary, Jesus Christ, in the power of the Spirit.[59] The grace desired here is a deeper repetition of that sought in the contemplation of the incarnation: "to ask for interior knowledge of all the good that I have received so that acknowledging this with gratitude, I may be able to love and serve His Divine Majesty in everything."[60]

---

of those to whom the early Jesuits ministered, working in hospitals, for example, or finding refuges for women forced into prostitution, not to mention his insistence on the gratuity of ministries, refusing to accept money for celebrating sacraments or other priestly ministries. On this, see Ivens, *Understanding the Spiritual Exercises*, 110–11, and Endean, "Spiritual Exercises," 60. See also Kolvenbach, *Road from La Storta*, 253–65, especially on the praxis of the early Jesuits on pp. 254–57. Dean Brackley, an American Jesuit who worked for a number of years in El Salvador, writes the following: "Poverty and persecution are neither desirable in themselves nor infallible means to serve God and neighbor," though he also points out that we need "to be free to embrace the poverty and contempt that following Christ normally entails" (*Call to Discernment*, 84).

57. See Ivens, *Understanding the Spiritual Exercises*, 172. On this part of the *Spiritual Exercises*, see also Cusson, *Biblical Theology*, 312–32, and Fleming, *Like the Lightning*, 125–9, and Brackley, *Call to Discernment*, 212–22. The Latin translation, known as the Vulgate, was made in the late 1540s and was the first version of the *Spiritual Exercises* to appear in print. See the introduction in Ignacio de Loyola, *Ejercicios Espirituales*, 26–29, for a history of the Vulgate.

58. Ivens, *Understanding the Spiritual Exercises*, 172.

59. On the role of the Spirit in Ignatius's understanding of mission, see Salvat, *Servir en Misión Universal*, 162–64.

60. *SpEx*, para. 233; in Munitiz and Endean, *Saint Ignatius*, 329. The Spanish for "to

The first of the four points that Ignatius offers for our consideration is as follows:

> This is to bring to memory the benefits received—creation, redemption, and particular gifts—pondering with great affection how much God Our Lord has done for me, and how much He has given me of what He has, and further, how according to His divine plan, it is the Lord's wish, as far as He is able, to give me Himself; then to reflect on and consider within myself what, in all reason and justice, I ought for my part to offer and give to His Divine Majesty, that is to say, everything I have, and myself as well.[61]

It would be possible to take this as advocating a kind of exchange—to give in exchange for what I have received. However, to do this would be to misunderstand Ignatius. He lived at the very moment when the feudal system was beginning to disappear, and the new urban capitalist system was beginning to dominate,[62] and yet in his own worldview, despite his ability to catch the needs of his day, he remained a product of his own upbringing. He does not see the world in capitalist exchange terms, but in terms of relationships, of duties, of service. In this sense, God does what God does because of who he is—that is to say, not out of need, or out of calculation in order to gain the love of humanity. Human beings respond to the love of God for them—what Marion might call the "givenness" of God—by being human, by embracing the possibility of service freely and joyfully, not as obligation, but as expressive of what it is for us to be most fully human and most fully alive.[63]

To understand this better, it is helpful to go to the preliminary note that Ignatius puts at the head of this contemplation, and that again I will quote in full:

> (i) love ought to find its expression in deeds more than in words;
> (ii) love consists in mutual communication, i.e., the lover gives and communicates to the beloved whatever the lover has, or

---

love and serve in everything" is "en todo amar y servir," a very important phrase today for understanding the Ignatian mission.

61. *SpEx*, para. 234; in Munitiz and Endean, *Saint Ignatius*, 329.

62. On why Ignatius chose to base his ministries almost entirely in urban spaces, and moreover, at their very heart, see Noble, "Budování."

63. In this light, Karl Rahner's argument about anonymous Christians, briefly discussed in a footnote in chapter 2, makes more sense. The "anonymous Christian" is simply a human being, not acting out of reciprocity of exchange with God, but responding to the givenness of life with the givenness of her or his action. On the significant influence on Rahner's theology of Ignatian spirituality, see Endean, *Karl Rahner*, and esp. 231–32 with respect to "anonymous Christians."

something of what the lover has or is able to give, and the beloved in turn does the same for the lover. Thus, one who possesses knowledge will give it to the one without it, and similarly the possessor of honor or wealth shares with the one who lacks these, each giving to the other.[64]

There are several points to note here. The first is that love is a verb rather than a noun, seen in God's sending of his Son to the world for its redemption.[65] For Ignatius, the importance of deed over word is a recurring theme, as is perhaps well summed up in the description, by Jerome Nadal, of Ignatius as "a contemplative even while in action."[66] Both the discovery of God's love for us and the manifestation of our love for God happen more through action than words.

Moreover, love is a communicative action.[67] It demands communication between at least two parties, so that, strictly speaking, self-love is not possible. Only in loving one's neighbor is one truly loving oneself. There is a giving of whatever one has, or whatever one can share, and a reception of that which the other has to give, as gift, as given. And it is precisely in this intercommunication that love consists. It is not a sign or a token of love, but it is precisely in this free giving and receiving of all that one can give and receive that love is manifest.[68]

In an article on the *Contemplatio* an American Jesuit Michael Buckley notes that the roles of lover and beloved are also interchangeable: "In the *Contemplación*, the giving of God evokes the giving of man; and in this mutual surrender they become one in their love. They become interchangeably lover and beloved. Each point begins with God as lover and man as beloved; it develops as God becomes beloved and man the lover."[69] This interchangeability, this kind of perichoretic relationship, is what prevents love becoming

---

64. *SpEx*, paras. 230–31; in Munitiz and Endean, *Saint Ignatius*, 329.

65. This is most clearly seen in the Johannine writings. See, for example, Painter, *1, 2, and 3 John*, 268–69.

66. On this topic, see Buckley, "Contemplation," 96, with the quotation from Nadal in footnote 19. See also the comments on this in Bangert, *Nadal*, 214–15.

67. I am not exactly using this in a Habermasian sense, though there is some crossover. See Habermas, *Theorie des kommunikativen Handelns*. On the importance of the "*comunicar*," see Fleming, *Like the Lightning*, 125–26.

68. On this topic, see Buckley, "Contemplation," 99: "While the first note speaks of the general expressions of love, this second maintains that love not only expresses itself but actually consists in the activity of intercommunion." The relation to the discussion on Marion in the previous chapter is obvious.

69. Buckley, "Contemplation."

part of an economy of exchange,[70] since there is a fundamental unity that cannot be wholly divided.

Mission emerges out of this experience of loving and being loved, of giving and receiving, not in exchange, but in reaction to Christ, the one in whom there is always more than we can ever hope to grasp, and who for that very reason calls us on deeper into his mystery. The beginning of mission is an experience of the sheer unfathomable givenness of all. For Ignatius, then, mission is not so much response to a commandment of the Lord, (for example, to the Great Commission of Matthew 28), at least not if that is understood as a duty laid on Christ's followers, whether they like it or not. Rather it is something to be grasped as gift, as a possibility opened up by the profound experience of communion in love with God, Father, Son, and Spirit.

THE *CONSTITUTIONS*

Although the relationship between the experiences contained in the *Spiritual Exercises* and the *Constitutions* is complex, and other factors need to be taken into account when considering the latter work, most commentators agree that in the *Constitutions* Ignatius in some way sought to codify and put into practice some of what he had gained and what he hoped others would gain through the making of the *Spiritual Exercises*.[71] Thus, I turn to the treatment of mission in the *Constitutions*. Broadly speaking, in the *Constitutions* and more generally, "'mission' for the Jesuits referred quite broadly to 'being sent out (like the apostles) to do ministry.'"[72] How was this mission envisaged, and why was it so central?

The latter question does, almost certainly, receive its answer in the kind of experience we have seen that Ignatius found in his relationship with God and that he sought to articulate in the *Spiritual Exercises*. But it is also at the very beginning of the foundation documents of the Society of Jesus. The first, limited, approval for the nascent order came in 1540 with the Apostolic

---

70. I refer back to the discussion in the previous chapter on Marion.

71. As a noted commentator on the *Constitutions*, Aldama writes, "the Ignatian Constitutions are not mere ordinances. The prescription of what is to be done is ordinarily supported and given life by a spiritual motive, or the "spirit" with which it is to be observed" (*Introductory Commentary*, 15). See also the following classic work on Jesuit spirituality by de Guibert: "The *Constitutions of the Society of Jesus* . . . are fully in the same line as the *Spiritual Exercises*" (*Jesuits*, 139). For a particular example, see Garcia, "Ignatian Obedience."

72. Mooney, "Ignatian Spirituality," 201.

Letter of Paul III, *Regimini militantis Ecclesiae*. This document begins with the following declaration:

> Whoever wishes to serve as a soldier of God beneath the banner of the cross in our Society, which we desire to be designated by the name of Jesus, and to serve the Lord alone and his vicar on earth, should keep it in mind that once he has made a solemn vow of perpetual chastity he is a member of a community founded chiefly for this purpose: to strive especially for the progress of souls in Christian life and doctrine, and for the propagation of the faith by the ministry of the word, by spiritual exercises and works of charity, and specifically by the education of children and unlettered persons in Christianity.[73]

The words are repeated in much the same form in the definitive letter of approbation, *Exposcit debitum*, issued ten years later in July 1550 by Julius III. These two documents, known as the Formulas of the Institute, contain *in nuce* the vision that the early Jesuits, with Ignatius at their head, had of their mission and task. It is clear from this that from the outset Ignatius and his first companions[74] saw their work in terms of being sent, and that to enter the Company was to share in this enterprise.

The Fourth Vow in Regard to Mission

This attention to mission is reinforced by what was to become one of the defining characteristics of the new order, the special fourth vow its members made to the Roman Pontiff. This vow was already part of the original submission made by the first companions when they were seeking papal

---

73. The First Formula of the Institute, para. 1, which is quoted here, is found in *Constitutions*, 3.

74. Ignatius began to gather companions whilst still in Spain. His journey had taken him from Montserrat to Manresa, then on to Jerusalem; he then returned to Barcelona and began to study. He was in Alcalá and Salamanca, where he suffered harassment from the Inquisition, and in 1528 he moved to Paris. There he gathered six companions, and in 1534 they made private vows at a chapel in Montmartre. The six were Saint Pierre Favre (1506–1546); Saint Francis Xavier (1506–1552); Diego Laínez (1512–1565), who was Ignatius's successor as Superior General of the Order; Nicolás de Bobadilla (1509–1590); Simão Rodrigues (1510–1579); and Alfonso Salmerón (1515–1585). They were soon joined by three others: Claude Le Jay (1504–1552), Paschase Broët (1500–1562), and Jean Codure (1508–1541). This was the group who participated in the deliberations concerning the initial founding of the Society of Jesus in Rome in 1540. On the first Jesuits, see O'Malley, *First Jesuits*, and on Le Jay, Broët, and Codure in particular, see Padberg, "Forgotten Founders."

approval.[75] It was incorporated into both the first and second papal bulls of foundation and remains an important, if not always unproblematic, part of Jesuit life. The vow was understood thus in the letter of Julius III, stating that the fully professed[76] Jesuits should:

> ... in addition to that ordinary bond of the three vows, be bound by this special vow to carry out whatever the present and future Roman pontiffs may order which pertains to the progress of souls and the propagation of the faith; and to go at once without subterfuge or excuse, as far as in us lies, to whatsoever provinces they may choose to send [*mittere*] us—whether they decide to send us among the Turks or any other infidels, even those who live in the region called the Indies, or among any heretics whatever, or schismatics, or any of the faithful.

The precise wording is not so important,[77] but what stands out is the openness to mission. In the actual vow that fully professed Jesuits took and still take, the Jesuit vows "special obedience to the sovereign pontiff in regard to the missions, according to the same apostolic letters and the Constitutions."[78] As an American Jesuit, Kevin Flannery, notes, the translation makes more specific the original Latin phrase *circa missiones*, by introducing the definite article.[79] Thus, in the mind of Ignatius himself and his early companions, as the quotation from *Exposcit Dominum* indicates, mission was not only about going somewhere else, but was necessarily universal.[80]

To ask whether such obedience to the pope is a good idea would be completely to miss the point. Many of the popes of Ignatius's time were,

---

75. See Salvat, *Servir en Misión Universal*, 91. For more detailed coverage, see Aldama, *Formula of the Institute*, 55–65 and Gerhartz, "Fourth Vow."

76. For various historical reasons, Jesuits at the end of their training were fully incorporated into the Society as either fully professed or co-adjutors (helpers). Only the first group (all of whom were priests) took the fourth vow. See Salvat, *Servir en Misión Universal*, 87, who points out that this distinction was itself made for the purposes of more efficiently engaging in the universal mission of the church, since clearly some people were more suited to this task than others—this was not a distinction of class or of holiness (a number of Jesuit saints, and indeed some of the best loved, were not fully professed, or even necessarily priests), but of suitability for availability in mission. See also Gerhartz, "Fourth Vow," 93.

77. For a much fuller treatment, see O'Malley, "Fourth Vow."

78. The text is given in Flannery, "Circa missiones."

79. Flannery, "*Circa missiones*," 3.

80. As indicated by phrases such as "*whatsoever* provinces," "*any* heretics whatever*," "*any* of the faithful." This universality is a central point of Mooney, "Ignatian Spirituality."

to put it mildly, not above criticism, and he was aware of that. But he was also profoundly aware of two other factors—mission was at the service of God in the church, and the call to mission should not be restricted by the limitations or fears of himself or his early companions.[81] To put it positively, the "more," the *magis* or *más* that so characterizes the Ignatian *Spiritual Exercises*, was always pushing Ignatius and his companions beyond their own horizons, to find and accept new tasks of mission.[82]

One further point may be worth commenting on here. Kevin Flannery observes that, in the context of the fourth vow, "A mission is given by one person to another."[83] It would, I suspect, be going too far to suggest that Ignatius and his companions wanted to have the fourth vow in order to underline the givenness of mission, in terms of a Pauline compulsion.[84] Nevertheless, even if this was not in the mind of the original companions, or at least not in so many words,[85] there is an important sense in which the givenness of mission is an integral part of their vision. It is not an optional extra, one way among many, but it is the foundation of their existence.[86] And, ultimately, it is given, and it is a saturated phenomenon, since in mission there is always more to discover than we can possibly intend.

Mission in Part VII of the *Constitutions*

The way this vow was to be put into practice, and the additional criteria that would serve to help the Society decide how to concretely perform any task given to it by the pope for the greater good of the universal church are set out in much more detail in the *Constitutions*, and especially in Part VII. In terms of what I am arguing in this book, the title of this part is itself of interest: "The relations to their neighbor of those already incorporated into

---

81. See also Gerhartz, "Fourth Vow," 83–86.

82. See Salvat, *Servir en Misión Universal*, 92. This is also clear from the explanatory note (Declaration) in the *Constitutions* that comments on this vow—see *Constitutions*, 276–78, para. 605. The version of the *Constitutions* I use here has the text on one page and subsequent norms on the facing page.

83. Flannery, "*Circa missiones*," 9.

84. See 1 Cor 9:16.

85. O'Malley, "Fourth Vow," 25, and elsewhere (e.g., 9, 14, 43) points to what he sees as a very Pauline emphasis in the early Society on the ministry of the word.

86. In an early draft of the *Constitutions*, Ignatius wrote that the fourth vow was the Society's "Principle and principal Foundation," though this was omitted from the final version. On this topic, see Flannery, "*Circa missiones*," 3 and 8. The reference is found in the first draft of the *Constitutions* I:162 (found in O'Malley, "Fourth Vow," endnote 98 on page 58). Flannery thinks the absence in the final text is unimportant, whereas O'Malley, "Fourth Vow," 35, deems it significant.

the Society when they are dispersed into the vineyard of Christ our Lord."[87] Jesuit mission was seen by Ignatius as a relationship with one who is neighbor (which might be one way of translating *paroikos*).

This section is, for many commentators, at the heart of the *Constitutions*.[88] It may well be one of the first attempts consciously to work out the mission of a particular group of people within the church[89]—at least it provides a fascinating account of how one community saw its role. Of course, this is particular to the Society of Jesus, and in that sense the specific details are not meant to apply as they stand to all other Christians, and the subsequent history of the Society would amply demonstrate that there is not always a perfect match between vision and reality. Nevertheless, the attempt to articulate the vision is worth attention.

Part VII of the *Constitutions*[90] dealing with mission begins with further reflection on "Missions from the Supreme Pontiff," where the commitment to respond to the needs of the church expressed by the pope are reiterated, with certain provisos.[91] Here too the ample understanding of mission is made clear. It encompasses those

> who have been sent to some places or others by either the Supreme Pontiff or the superiors of the Society . . . or [who] themselves choose where and in what work they will labor, having been commissioned to travel to any place where they judge that greater service of God and the good of souls will follow, or [who] carry on their labor not by travelling but by residing steadily and continually in certain places where much fruit of glory and service to God is expected.[92]

---

87. Schineller, "Pilgrim Journey," looks at how the imagery in Ignatius about mission moves from soldier to pilgrim to laborer in the vineyard, which becomes the key image for Ignatius in his later years.

88. See Alphonso, *Placed with Christ the Son*, 76: "The Part of the *Constitutions* that deals specifically with 'mission' is Part VII. It is the peak and summit towards which the genetic structure and development of the *Constitutions* moves up." See also Amaladoss, "Sent on Mission," 327: "Mission is central to the spirituality of Ignatius and of the Society which he founded . . . Such centrality of mission in the life of Ignatius helps us to understand the centrality of Part VII in the Constitutions of the Society of Jesus."

89. Kollman, "At the Origins," 429–31.

90. Apparently one of the first to be written; see Aldama, *Missioning*, 1.

91. See, for example, *Constitutions*, 278, para. 607 where representations can be made to the pope, if it is judged that, if the pope knew the circumstances better, he would not send this particular person. See Aldama, *Missioning*, 46.

92. *Constitutions*, 276, para. 603.

Whenever any work is undertaken, those undertaking it should be made aware of what they are to do and how they are to do it, and they should strive for the *magis*, going beyond the narrow limits set down, always only if it is for the greater benefit of others.[93] People should be sent and chosen with a view to doing that "which is conducive to the greater service of God and the universal good."[94]

The *Constitutions* contain a lengthy set of criteria for choosing where a mission is to be carried out[95]—these, as is not uncommon with Ignatius, range from the more spiritual to the more pragmatic. These criteria are best summed up with the claim that the "more universal the good is, the more it is divine."[96] This, as should have become clear by now, is a fundamental Ignatian insight, where universal service and mission comes out of the mission of Christ and the Holy Spirit, sent to the whole world for the redemption of the whole world.

It is this insistence on universality that saves the Jesuit vision from becoming a purely utilitarian one. On the face of it, this is a danger, with the insistence on giving priority to work with the more influential members of society providing a well-known example.[97] But the universal good remains, in the words of the *Exercises*, "the praise, honor, and reverence of God our Lord," and so it is not purely for the good of the missionary or for the good of the missioned, but for the service of God our Lord, as Ignatius would phrase it so often. As one of the great twentieth-century commentators on Jesuit history and spirituality, Joseph de Guibert, puts it, in the material on mission we discover "the fundamental concept of Ignatius in the founding of the Society: to place at the disposal of the Holy See a group of apostles thoroughly formed by the tests in their training, provided with sound learning, and accustomed to deal with men, always ready to be off at a simple sign to wherever authority designates work to be accomplished."[98] It is also important to note that the *Constitutions* say that, if a choice has to be made between works bringing spiritual benefit and works of "corporal mercy," then the first should be chosen, all other things being equal.[99]

---

93. *Constitutions*, 278–81, paras. 609–16. I will return to how this was done in practice shortly.

94. *Constitutions*, 282, para. 618. See Alphonso, *Placed with Christ the Son*, 81.

95. *Constitutions*, 284–88, paras. 622–26. See Amaladoss, "Sent on Mission," 333–35 and Alphonso, *Placed with Christ the Son*, 81–83.

96. *Constitutions*, 286, para. 622.8. On the importance of the universal good, see also Aldama, *Missioning*, 80–84.

97. *Constitutions*, 286, para. 622.9.

98. De Guibert, *Jesuits*, 150.

99. *Constitutions*, 286, para. 623.3. The final phrase "when all other things are

The missions are not specified as such in great detail, since in principle and if inspired by the Holy Spirit, anything could be undertaken that was to the service of the universal good. But the kind of people, the kind of combinations of people, the length of time, the ways of choosing between the good and the better, are all laid out. A good summary of the attention to detail is found in a paragraph on whether people should be sent as beggars or with money and letters of recommendation: "the superior will consider the greater edification of the neighbor and the service of God our Lord and then decide what should be done."[100] Thus it is for the service[101] of these others—the other human and the Divine Other—that mission happens, and whatever benefits that service is good.

MISSION AT THE COUNCIL OF TRENT

What this entailed in practice can be seen in the instructions that Ignatius gave to three Jesuits[102] who had been appointed to act as *periti* (theological consultants) at the Council of Trent (1545-1563). He begins by instructing them on how to relate to people (and it would seem here especially in the first place to the Council Fathers). "Much," he says, "can be gained, if God is willing, for the spiritual health and benefit of others by having social relations and contact with many people."[103] They are to listen, to be slow to intervene, not to display too much knowledge, and they are to attempt to see the good in both sides of the argument.[104] Their main task is to pray and elicit prayers for the Council, not drawing attention to the points of conflict between Catholics and Protestants, but encouraging ever greater love of God. Specific ways in which this can be done are given:

---

equal" is, of course, important, and is central to Ignatius's method of discerning.

100. *Constitutions*, 291, para. 625.2.

101. On the idea of service in Ignatius, see Fleming, "Here I Am."

102. The three were all early companions. Claude Le Jay was present as an adviser to the Cardinal Bishop of Augsburg, whilst the other two, Diego Laínez and Alfonso Salmerón, had been appointed by Pope Paul III.

103. "Letter 14: Conduct at Trent," in Munitiz and Endean, *Saint Ignatius*, 164.

104. This latter point chimes with a very important text in the *Spiritual Exercises*, the "Presupposition," which states that "it must be presupposed that any good Christian has to be more ready to justify than to condemn a neighbor's statement. If no justification can be found, one should ask the neighbor in what sense it is to be taken, and if that sense is wrong, he or she should be corrected lovingly. Should this not be sufficient, one should seek all suitable means to justify it by understanding it in a good sense" (*SpEx*, para. 22; in Munitiz and Endean, *Saint Ignatius*, 289).

> Our main aim (to God's greater glory) during this undertaking at Trent is to put into practice (as a group that lives together in one appropriate place) preaching, confessions, and readings, teaching children, giving good example, visiting the poor in the hospitals, exhorting those around us, each of us according to the different talents he may happen to have, urging on as many as possible to greater piety and prayers. All of this is undertaken so that they and we may implore God Our Lord that His Divine Majesty kindly infuse His divine spirit into all those due to discuss the questions proper to such a lofty gathering, in order that that Holy Spirit may descend with greater abundance of gifts and graces on the Council.[105]

For Ignatius, mission is what would be called today "holistic,"[106] and the practice of the gospel is as important as its proclamation.[107] The time is to be spent at least as much in catechesis, tending to the sick and poor, giving the *Exercises*, as it is in attending sessions of the Council, and if they are to be slow in coming forward in the council chamber, when it comes to spiritual guidance, they are to be "eloquent and ready to talk, full of sympathy and affection."[108]

Thus, for Ignatius, any mission of the Society was really aimed at winning people for God, and whatever served that end best and was not in itself wrong was to be used. The mission was to be carried out in love. His words to Claude Le Jay and others in Germany on how to deal with the Protestants they encountered bear repeating:

> They should make efforts to make friends with the leaders of their opponents, as also with those who are most influential among the heretics . . . They must try to bring them back from their error by sensitive skill and signs of love . . . They should defend the Apostolic See and its authority, and attract people towards true obedience to it, in such a way as not to lose credibility, as 'papists', through ill-judged partisanship. On the contrary, their zeal in countering heresy must be of such a quality as

---

105. Munitiz and Endean, *Saint Ignatius*, 165.

106. For a recent discussion on holistic mission, see Hartropp and Ronsen, "Evangelism Lost?" Their plea for an "anticipation of evangelism" is one that would have fitted naturally into Ignatius's practice.

107. See *Constitutions*, 294, para. 637: "The first [way to help souls] is by giving the good example of a thoroughly upright life and of Christian virtue, striving to edify those with whom one deals no less, but rather even more, by good deeds than by words."

108. Munitiz and Endean, *Saint Ignatius*, 166.

to reveal love for the heretics themselves, and a compassionate desire for their salvation.[109]

SUMMARY

The love for the other, the urgent desire to help her or him to come to a deeper understanding of God at work in their lives, is fundamental.[110] For Ignatius, the universal call to mission could never be divorced from the overwhelming sense that God's love for the world, God's desire to redeem the world, knew no bounds, and that nothing was too much to bring the other to God. To do this required coming to know and love the other, not as already perfect, but as they were, so that together the journey to God could move ahead.

To see how this journey was attempted in another setting, very different to sixteenth-century Europe, I turn in the next chapter to William Carey. As I do so, it may be good to have as an underlying question the ways that the experience of the otherness of God, in prayer and in ecclesial life, impact on how the other is perceived in mission. For Ignatius, his understanding of how God had operated in his life had a profound influence on how he came to see the mission of the Christian, and more specifically the mission of the Society of Jesus. Carey came from another ecclesial tradition, with very different theological starting points and a different experience of prayer and even of God. How this influenced him will be one of the themes I examine in the next chapter.

---

109. Munitiz and Endean, *Saint Ignatius*, 234. See also Endean, "Ignatius in Lutheran Light."

110. I am not, if it needs to be said, condoning the use of the language of heresy. It is a product of its time. However, we should remember that, by definition, the heretic is the quintessential "other," and as we saw with Marion it is the other as "enemy" who most allows for the givenness of love to be expressed. The problem in the Reformation, and frequently since, has been that the need to hate one's enemy as a sign of one's own orthodoxy has been so prevalent, among Catholics and Protestants alike. Ignatius was not in fact very interested in Luther or Protestantism (see on this Mooney, "Ignatian Spirituality," 197–98).

5

William Carey
A Particularly Baptist Missionary

William Carey (1761–1834) is often claimed as one of the founding fathers of the modern missionary movement.[1] He called the Calvinist Particular Baptists[2] to engagement in mission, and as the first missionary of the newly formed Baptist Missionary Society in England, it was he himself who set off to India, where he would spend the last forty years of his life. His achievements were many, as were the difficulties he faced, and the problems associated with him and some of his early companions. On several occasions in his life—from his becoming a Baptist to his going to India to his break with the mission society he had helped form—he seems to have consciously chosen to be an outsider, and the encounters with the radical otherness of India formed him in many ways.

Before I begin an examination of Carey's life and missionary engagement, especially from the viewpoint of his encounters with the other, a few

---

1. To cite just two examples from the texts I referred to in chapter 2, see Bosch, *Transforming Mission*, 280, and Bevans and Schroeder, *Constants in Context*, 210–12. Note Bosch's proviso, which Bevans and Schroeder pick up—there were many others, too, but Carey is still centrally important. A similar comment is in Neill, *History of Christian Mission*, 222, who points out, however, that Carey's "work does represent a turning-point."

2. On the Particular Baptists in England, see, on their development, White, *English Baptists*, especially 58–92, and on the story which further describes the kind of Baptist community Carey was part of, see Brown, *English Baptists*, especially 115–41, which covers this period. The Particular and General Baptists only finally and fully came together in 1891. See Briggs, *English Baptists*, 96–157, for the history of this process. See also for brief accounts, Hayden, *English Baptist Heritage*, 44–64 and 90–96.

comments need to be made. Carey is a European male of the late eighteenth and early nineteenth centuries who came out of a very particular religious background. He had neither the concerns nor the language of the twenty-first century, and to try to force him into an alien framework would both do an injustice to him, and be against what I am trying to argue in this book. Carey is also an "other" for us. His language especially is not always easy, and the way he talks about the "others" he encountered may not be our choice.³ But that is, at least from one perspective, our problem, not his, and I think that it is necessary to read Carey—to let him draw near to us as *prosēlutos*—sympathetically and trying to put the best possible interpretation on what he says.⁴ This does not mean that we cannot be critical of him, but it does mean that we need to understand him as far as possible on his own terms,⁵ before criticizing him for not being like us. Thus, in what follows I try to let Carey speak to us, in order to learn from him.

THE EARLY LIFE OF WILLIAM CAREY⁶

William Carey was born in August 1761, in the village of Paulerspury in the southern part of Northamptonshire, some hundred kilometers (sixty miles) north of London. His father and grandfather had both been employed by the local Church of England parish, as parish clerk and schoolmaster. Carey received a basic education and began the process of teaching himself languages (including Latin and later New Testament Greek). His linguistic skills would later serve him well in India. As a young man, Carey suffered from some unspecified illness that, according to one of his early

---

3. See Middlebrook, *William Carey*, 101. This volume was written to commemorate the bicentenary of Carey's birth.

4. This is the principle noted in the previous chapter that is so important in the *Spiritual Exercises* of Saint Ignatius, that we should always strive to understand well what the other is trying to say, and come to some kind of common understanding with them.

5. The hermeneutical problems present in such an endeavor do not excuse us from embarking on the task.

6. There are many biographies of Carey. Two were written by his descendants, the first by his nephew Eustace in 1836, and the second by his great-great grandson, S. Pearce Carey, *William Carey*. A third was written by the son of Carey's fellow Serampore missionaries, Joshua and Hannah Marshman in *Story of Carey*. A more recent biography is George, *Faithful Witness*. I will work mainly with the book by Marshman, for two reasons. One is that it is closer to Carey's time, and thus uncontaminated by more recent ideas, and secondly because it covers also the lives of two key companions of Carey in Serampore, who were deeply influenced by him and can therefore serve as corroboration for what I write about Carey himself.

biographers, John Clark Marshman, "unfitted him for outdoor labor,"[7] so he became apprenticed to a cobbler.

It was whilst learning his trade under a Mr. Olds, and influenced by a fellow apprentice from his first apprenticeship,[8] that he became a Baptist, receiving baptism in the River Nene on 7 October 1783. He had already begun to preach,[9] and continued to do so. Although the congregation at the church was not greatly impressed with his capacity to be a pastor, his own pastor supported him, and he held a variety of pastorates, in Northamptonshire and Leicestershire. In the meantime, after the death of Mr. Olds, Carey took over his business and married Olds's sister-in-law, Dorothy Plackett,[10] someone whose sufferings form a backdrop to his early life in India. He was, as in so many other things in his life, not very successful at the business—Marshman remarks that "he was a very indifferent shoemaker."[11] He was generally hard up, and was not very good as a schoolteacher either, and though he seems to have been appreciated by his congregation, they were too small to be able to support him.

However, it was in this period that two events occurred that would be of importance in his missionary career. The first was his reading of the story of Captain Cook, who had been killed in 1779, and whose journals Carey, a voracious reader, came across at this point. It was reading the account of Cook's travels that led him, in Marshman's words, "to contemplate the moral and spiritual degradation of the heathen, and to form the design of communicating the Gospel to them. The idea took complete possession of his mind, and absorbed his thoughts."[12] The other factor was his getting to know Rev. Andrew Fuller (1754–1815),[13] the Baptist pastor in Kettering, another Northamptonshire town, who would be the first Secretary of the "Particular-Baptist Society for Propagating the Gospel among the Heathen," the first name for what would soon become the Baptist Missionary Society (BMS).[14]

7. Marshman, *Story of Carey*, 2.
8. See Middlebrook, *William Carey*, 14.
9. Unwillingly, according to Middlebrook, *William Carey*, 16.
10. We will return to the travails of life with Dorothy. Here is a biography of her: Beck, *Dorothy Carey*.
11. Marshman, *Story of Carey*, 6.
12. Marshman, *Story of Carey*, 7.
13. On Fuller, see Young, "Andrew Fuller," and more generally on Fuller's great contributions to all elements of Baptist life in eighteenth-century England, Morden, *Offering Christ*.
14. Stanley, *Baptist Missionary Society*, is the standard history of the BMS with a full account of its beginnings. For some links to early documentation, see http://www.

CAREY'S ENQUIRY

Carey's first attempt to broach the idea of engaging in foreign mission at a meeting of the Northamptonshire Association (a regional gathering of Baptist ministers) in 1786 was not entirely successful. One of those present, the father of Dr. Ryland, the minister who had baptized him, got up and told him: "Young man, sit down: when God pleases to convert the heathen, He will do it without your aid or mine."[15] It was this rebuttal that served as one of the inspirations for Carey to write his famous missionary manifesto, *An Enquiry into the Obligations of Christians, to Use Means for the Conversion of the Heathens, in which the Religious State of the Different Nations of the World, the Success of Former Undertakings, and the Practicability of Further Undertakings Are Considered.*[16]

Before examining the short book itself, the very title raises some interesting points. It is, I think, somewhat overlooked that it is precisely "an enquiry," a recognition of a challenge (as raised by the old Dr. Ryland), and a need to respond to that challenge. Moreover, it is an enquiry into obligations for mission, not simply into whether mission is permissible, or possible. And these obligations come from outside, in the sense that the mission is both a response to the call of God, as Carey will argue, but also a response to the needs of the "unconverted," those whom he calls "heathens." Thus, the work is framed, in its title, which is also its plan, in terms of response to the other, both divine and human.

Enquiry begins with a brief statement of both the necessity and neglect of mission, since "Some think little about it, others are unacquainted with the state of the world, and others love their wealth better than the souls of their fellow-creatures."[17] Most people ignore the Great Commission (Matt 28:18–20) and argue, Carey says, that "if God intends the salvation of the

---

wmcarey.edu/carey/bms/bms.htm.

15. Marshman, *Story of Carey*, 7. The exact circumstances of this event are much debated, but at least it may sum up something of the attitude that led Carey to write *Enquiry*. Around this time, Carey also preached a sermon on Isaiah 54:2–3, which is usually quoted as the source of his "missionary motto": "Expect great things (from God). Attempt great things (for God)." The words in brackets, though often assumed to have been part of the address, are missing from early accounts. On this topic, see Smith, "Spirit and Letter."

16. It was first published in Leicester by a woman publisher, Ann Ireland. Various facsimile editions exist, and it is also reprinted as an appendix in George, *Faithful Witness*. A facsimile is also available online at http://www.wmcarey.edu/carey/enquiry/anenquiry.pdf. For rather obvious reasons, I will not use the full title, and will refer to the pamphlet as *Enquiry*.

17. Carey, *Enquiry*, 5.

heathen, he will some way or other bring them to the gospel, or the gospel to them. It is thus that multitudes sit at ease, and give themselves no concern about the far greater part of their fellow-sinners, who to this day, are lost in ignorance and idolatry."[18]

Carey uses a kind of *reductio ad absurdum* to show that the command of Christ to go to all nations and make disciples is still relevant.[19] To claims that the command cannot be fulfilled, he counters that others (such as Catholics—or the popish, as he calls them—and Moravian Brethren) have engaged in mission, and indeed "have not English traders, for the sake of gain, surmounted all those things which have generally been counted insurmountable obstacles in the way of preaching the gospel? Witness the trade to Persia, the East-Indies, China, and Greenland, yea, even the accursed Slave-Trade on the coasts of Africa."[20] If even something as abominable as the slave trade (and Carey's opposition to it was uncompromising[21]) could be carried out, despite the hardships involved, surely it would not be so difficult to go to preach the gospel?

Finally, Carey argues for the need to preach the gospel, because "[p]ity therefore, humanity, and much more Christianity, call loudly for every possible exertion to introduce the gospel amongst them."[22] This is the second time in the opening pages[23] that he calls first on a shared humanity as a reason for engaging in mission. Of course, on both occasions he sees the call of Christ[24] as an even more compelling reason, but nevertheless, the other as fellow human being has a call on us that Carey recognized was fundamental. Thus, the starting point for Carey's missionary desire, as evinced by his response to reading Captain Cook's journals, is the felt need to respond to the other, who through the writings of Cook and other travelers and explorers was allowed to come to him and challenge him.

18. Carey, *Enquiry*, 8. He may have specifically had old Dr. Ryland in mind here, but others held the same opinion.

19. Carey, *Enquiry*, 8–12. On Carey and the Great Commission, see O'Brien, "Great Commission."

20. Carey, *Enquiry*, 11–12.

21. There are some indications of links between Carey and the radical movement of his time, occasioned by reports of the French Revolution and the writings of Thomas Paine. On this topic, see Alban et al, "Writings," 90.

22. Carey, *Enquiry*, 13.

23. See also Carey, *Enquiry*, 3 and 68.

24. For an interesting, if not entirely convincing, argument about the centrality of the kingdom as an organizing motif for Carey's work, see Myers, "Tracing a Theology." Myers may somewhat overstate his case, but I would agree with his careful reading of Carey on many points, and the attention he draws to the role of the kingdom is worth reflection. There is also a rich bibliography for further study.

The second section of *Enquiry* looks at what today we would call the history of mission. It contains a long re-telling of the Acts of the Apostles.[25] This is such a large section of the book (it is longer, for example, than the preceding section on the Great Commission), that it is perhaps worth considering why Carey felt the need to tell his readers something that, presumably, they knew. Although I very much doubt that Carey would have phrased it in exactly this way, one might say that for him the early church serves as a kind of "stranger," which draws near and challenges us to act differently. Especially as a dissenter, from a background that stressed the importance of the early New Testament images of the church, it is a reminder that this church was also missionary to its core. Thus the mission of the church in Acts is a challenge and an encouragement to the church of his day, to respond to the needs around them.

Carey moves rather seamlessly from the narrative of Acts to the legends about the apostles preaching even further afield, indeed even telling us that it is likely that Paul preached in Britain.[26] He then continues with a history of the mission of the early church, including figures such as Justin Martyr and Irenaeus.[27] As the story goes on, so Carey is torn between pointing to the success of Christian mission and his (for the time perfectly normal) distaste for what he nearly always calls "popery."

In outlining the way the gospel was preached in the early modern period, he writes "blind zeal, gross superstition, and infamous cruelties, so marked the appearances of religion all this time, that the professors of Christianity needed conversion, as much as the heathen world."[28] Clearly, there were some limits to Carey's openness to the other, though even here a sympathetic reading, looking behind the overtly hostile language, might note that Carey still thinks that in some sense the gospel is preached, even if the preachers themselves leave a lot to be desired.[29] At any rate, the point of

---

25. Carey, *Enquiry*, 14–28. This is almost one-sixth of the entire book and, ignoring the statistical tables, a much higher proportion of the written text.

26. Carey, *Enquiry*, 28.

27. Carey, *Enquiry*, 32. Where exactly Carey got his historical information from is not clear, though he apparently had many maps and books in his workshop: thus Marshman, *Story of Carey*, 7.

28. Carey, *Enquiry*, 34.

29. As one way of strengthening the work of missionaries, Carey proposed a coming-together of missionaries from different denominations. He wrote in a letter to Andrew Fuller on 15 May 1806: "The Cape of Good Hope is now in the hands of the English; should it continue so, would it be possible to have a general association of all denominations of Christians, from the four corners of the world, kept there once in about ten years? I earnestly recommend this plan, let the first meeting be in the Year 1810, or 1812 at furthest. I have no doubt but it would be attended with very

this section is to show that the gospel had been preached ever since the time of Christ, in an unbroken chain. The "obligation" to preach the gospel is one that the church has always acknowledged, and in essence Carey is offering an early "history of world mission."

Carey then moves on to give a statistical overview of the world of his day, listing territories, populations[30] and religious belonging, divided into four categories—the three major monotheistic religions, Christianity,[31] Judaism, and Islam, and everyone else categorized as "pagans." He suggests that there are 420 million people who have never had the gospel preached to them (as well as Muslims and Jews), and in conclusion he reflects: "It must undoubtedly strike every considerate mind, what a vast proportion of the sons of Adam there are, who yet remain in the most deplorable state of heathen darkness, without any means of knowing the true God, except what are afforded them by the works of nature; and utterly destitute of the knowledge of the gospel of Christ, or of any means of obtaining it."[32]

Moreover, despite the way in which they are often referred to, Carey argues that

> barbarous as these poor heathens are, they appear to be as capable of knowledge as we are; and in many places, at least, have discovered uncommon genius and tractableness; and I greatly question whether most of the barbarities practiced by them, have not originated in some real or supposed affront, and are therefore, more properly, acts of self-defense, than proofs of inhuman and blood-thirsty dispositions.[33]

Here again, we see that, beneath the language, Carey reacts to the other positively as one who is equal in all respects. He is, anyway, if anything more scathing about most of those to whom he gives the label "Christian," condemning most of the Orthodox in the Ottoman Empire, Catholics again,

---

important effects; we could understand one another better, and more entirely enter into one another's views by two hour conversation than by two or three years epistolary correspondence." I take the quotation from Yeh, "Tokyo 2010," 122, and 125n19.

30. Carey's estimate of the world population at 731 million is considerably less than the figure given by the United Nations, which estimates the population in 1800 to have been 978 million, and in 1750 to have been 791 million. See the United Nations publication "The World at Six Billion," http://www.un.org/esa/population/publications/sixbillion/sixbilpart1.pdf. The sources for the UN data are not given.

31. In fact, he does subdivide Christians in different countries into denominations, "Papists" (once or twice he calls them Catholics), Lutherans, Calvinists, the Greek (i.e., Orthodox) Church, Protestants, and sometimes also he mentions the Moravians.

32. Carey, *Enquiry*, 62–63.

33. Carey, *Enquiry*, 63–64.

the Church of England, and especially Danish Lutherans.[34] The purpose of all this is to show that Christians have the "obligation" to preach the gospel to the world.

Having outlined the need for Christian mission, Carey then goes on in the fourth section to consider some of the potential obstacles and hardships. In terms of his own life, perhaps the most striking section is his description of the expectations of the Christian minister, which is worth quoting, despite its length:

> A Christian minister is a person who in a peculiar sense is *not his own*; he is the *servant* of God, and therefore ought to be wholly devoted to him. By entering on that sacred office he solemnly undertakes to be always engaged, as much as possible, in the Lord's work, and not to chuse [sic] his own pleasure, or employment, or pursue the ministry as something that is to subserve his own ends, or interests, or as a kind of bye-work. He engages to go where God pleases, and to do, or endure what he sees fit to command, or call him to, in the exercise of his function. He virtually bids farewell to friends, pleasures, and comforts, and stands in readiness to endure the greatest sufferings in the work of his Lord, and Master. It is inconsistent for ministers to please themselves with thoughts of a numerous auditory, cordial friends, a civilized country, legal protection, affluence, splendor, or even a competency. The flights, and hatred of men, and even pretended friends, gloomy prisons, and tortures, the society of barbarians of uncouth speech, miserable accommodations in wretched wildernesses, hunger, and thirst, nakedness, weariness, and painfulness, hard work, and but little worldly encouragement, should rather be the objects of their expectation.[35]

Better than anything else, this quotation shows that Carey was not ignorant of the challenges of mission, and it could be seen in many ways as a fairly good summary of the way his own life would go in the 1790s. The missionary is at the service always of an "other," primarily of God, but a God who is encountered also in the other human being, and thus, Carey also suggests,

> [The missionaries'] first business must be to gain some acquaintance with the language of the natives, (for which purpose two would be better than one,) and by all lawful means to endeavor

---

34. See Carey, *Enquiry*, 65–66.

35. Carey, *Enquiry*, 72–73. Italics in original. On this topic, see also Walls, *Cross-Cultural Process*, 225–26.

to cultivate a friendship with them, and as soon as possible let them know the errand for which they were sent. They must endeavor to convince them that it was their good alone, which induced them to forsake their friends, and all the comforts of their native country. They must be very careful not to resent injuries which may be offered to them, nor to think highly of themselves, so as to despise the poor heathens, and by those means lay a foundation for their resentment, or rejection of the gospel. They must take every opportunity of doing them good, and laboring, and travelling, night and day, they must instruct, exhort, and rebuke, with all long suffering, and anxious desire for them, and, above all, must be instant in prayer for the effusion of the Holy Spirit upon the people of their charge.[36]

Most of all, they should hope that they gain some indigenous converts and "if God should bless their labors, for them to encourage any appearances of gifts amongst the people of their charge; if such should be raised up many advantages would be derived from their knowledge of the language, and customs of their countrymen; and their change of conduct would give great weight to their ministrations."[37]

These quotations, whilst lengthy, describe the fundamental attitude with which Carey embarked on his mission, and I would suggest that this attitude is one primarily of attention to the other, to God who is the source and end of all mission, and to the other to whom one is sent. There is no triumphalism in Carey, but simply a response to the dream of doing something for God, something that he finds mandated in the Scriptures, and to have been part of Christian life through the centuries.

PUTTING THE MISSIONARY VISION INTO PRACTICE

It was not long after the publication of *Enquiry*[38] that the occasion arose for Carey to set out to India. The background to the voyage and the history of the East India Company and its attitude towards missionaries need not detain us at great length here.[39] There was strong resistance at the time

---

36. Carey, *Enquiry*, 75–76. See also Middlebrook, *William Carey*, 107–8.

37. Carey, *Enquiry*, 76.

38. It does not seem to have had a great impact on its initial publication. It cost one shilling and sixpence, relatively expensive for such a short book: the sum was roughly equivalent to a day laborer's daily wage. Whatever the reason for its limited appeal, it was only reprinted in 1818 after Carey had become much better known. See Alban et al., "Writings," 90.

39. There is an account in Marshman, *Story of Carey*, 14–19. See also Carson, *East*

to the presence of Christian missionaries on the part of some, though not all, of the leading lights of the East India Company, not least because they feared that it would interfere with trade. Finally, however, after several abortive attempts, and in the company of a doctor, John Thomas (1757–1801),[40] Carey set sail for India on 13 June 1793, on a Danish ship, the *Kron Princesa Maria*, accompanied, only after much persuasion, by his wife, Dorothy, and their children.[41]

It was at this point that Carey began a journal, which he kept up somewhat irregularly for the next two years, until 14 June 1795.[42] Rather than give a chronological summary of the contents, I want to focus on four recurring themes. Above all, Carey's journal is a kind of spiritual diary, so I will begin with that element. Given the emphasis of this book, I will also look at the importance of language and translation, at his interaction with the local inhabitants, and finally at the importance of the church in his thoughts, since this is the way in which his attitudes are ultimately going to be institutionalized.

Spiritual Encounter

The most striking part of Carey's journal is its description of his spiritual state, as the reality of missionary life hit home, and he struggled to find a hearing for the gospel and a safe and healthy life for his family. Carey's awareness of his need for some consolation from the God whom he had given up everything to serve comes across time and again. Mission is indeed about the expectation and attempting of great things, but expectation is not event and attempt is not always success, and it is the gap between the possible and the actual that is recorded in at times almost painful detail in Carey's journal. And yet, Carey never complains of God, only of his own inconstancy and weakness in responding to the word of God in his life.

India Company, and Stanley, *Bible and Flag*, 98–100.

40. The most recent biography of John Thomas is *John Thomas*, by Kemm. An earlier biography was written by Chute, called *John Thomas*.

41. British subjects were not allowed to go on British ships to India without special permission from the East India Company. As missionaries (most especially as Baptist missionaries), they would not have been given permission, so they sailed on the Danish ship to the Danish colonies in India.

42. The next few pages draw substantially on Noble, "Swiss Train," 149–55. For the text of Carey's journals, I am using the printed version in Carter, *Journal*, 3–59 (hereafter with date of entry and page number in Carter's edition; Carter helpfully inserts the page numbers of the journal in his text, but I will not cite those here).

As they were drawing near to Calcutta (Kolkata), where they finally disembarked on 11 November 1793, Carey reflected on what the sea journey had taught him. He writes:

> I hope I have learned of the necessity of beating up in the things of God, against the Wind and Tide when there is occasion—as we have done in our voyage: We have had our Ports in view all along and there has been every attention paid to ascertain our situation by Solar, and Lunar Observations—no opportunity occurred that was neglected; O that I was but as attentive to the Evidence of my state as they to their situation—a Ship sails within Six Points of the Wind, that is if the wind blow from North a Ship will sail E. N. E. upon Tach, and W. N. W. upon the other if our course is North one must, therefore, go E. N. E. a considerable way then W. N. W. and if the Wind shifts a point the advantage is immediately taken now though this is tiresome work, and (especially if a Current sets against us) we scarce make any way. Nay sometimes in spite of all that we can do we go backwards instead of forwards, yet it is absolutely necessary to keep working up—if we ever mean to arrive at our port.—So in the Xn Life we often have to work against Wind & Current, but we must do it if we ever expect to make our Port.[43]

This image sums up in a telling way Carey's understanding of his mission and his relationship to God. There is a double sense of both activity and waiting, of doing everything to be ready but the realization that ultimately all depends on God, and the coming of the other.[44] There is above all the need for "a patient waiting for Christ."[45] At the same time, patient waiting was also a time for hard work, and Carey, long accustomed to working alongside his pastoral commitments, did not hesitate to seek out ways of earning his living.[46] In this sense, before the idea of the Three Selves church had been articulated,[47] Carey was already practicing it.

---

43. Carey, *Journal*, 9 November 1793, 7. Spelling and punctuation (not Carey's strongest point) are as transcribed in Carter's volume.

44. As a Particular Baptist, Calvin never lost his faith in the utter dependency of all things on God.

45. Carey, *Journal*, 17 January 1794, 9.

46. He did this first as manager of an indigo dye works, and later as a professor of languages for the East India Company.

47. The idea that churches outside Europe should be self-supporting, self-propagating, and self-governing was developed in the mid-nineteenth century by Henry Venn (1796–1873), secretary of the Church Missionary Society (CMS) in London, in conjunction with the American Rufus Anderson (1796–1880), secretary of the American Board of Commissioners for Foreign Missions. On this topic, see Williams, who indeed

And yet it would be false to Carey's experience as he faithfully records it to deny the sheer hardship and weariness of the task that frequently faced him. Initially let down by John Thomas,[48] his wife slowly breaking down,[49] without as much as the hint of a convert, it is perhaps not surprising that he was tempted almost to despair at times.[50] The beginning of February 1795 found him in a particularly hard space. On 1 February he noted that "Through the Day had not much enjoyment. Yet I bless God for any; my soul is prone to barrenness, and I have every day reason to mourn over the dreadful stupidity of my nature, and the wickedness of my Heart,"[51] and the next few days only got worse:

> "Had a miserable Day, sorely harassed from without, and very Cold and dead in my Soul." "This is indeed the Valley of the shadow of Death to me; except that my Soul is much more insensible than John Bunyan's Pilgrim." "I don't love to be always complaining—yet I always complain." "O what a Load is a barren Heart . . ." "I sometimes walk in my Garden and try to pray to God and if I pray at all, it is in the Solitude of a Walk." "O that this day could be consigned to Oblivion."[52]

---

notes that in terms of these themes, the "Serampore Trio [i.e., Carey, Joshua Marshman (1768-1837) and William Ward (1769-1823)] . . . certainly developed many of them—most significantly a commitment to indigenous ministry working through its own cultural heritage" (*Self-Governing Church*, 1). Of course, however well-meaning and perhaps essentially correct Venn's vision was, it was not always unproblematic in practice: see Neill, *History of Christian Mission*, 221. There is also an element of what is now termed tent-making mission (with reference to the Apostle Paul), where a missionary has a full-time job using whatever skills or talents they have, whilst carrying out mission both within that setting and elsewhere.

48. Thomas had returned to England, partly to seek help in engaging in Christian work, but also because he was in debt. An entry in Cathcart, *Baptist Encyclopedia*, II:1148, concludes with the following judgement of Thomas: "He was imprudent, but full of zeal for souls and full of faith in the triumph of the truth." Marshman, *Story of Carey*, 26-27, is the first reference to Thomas's love of luxury. Seeing Thomas living so well, whilst Carey strove to adopt a more Indian way of life, was one of the first things that annoyed Dorothy Carey.

49. Over time, and hardly surprisingly, given the shock of change and the death of one of her sons, Dorothy Carey seems to have become more and more delusional, convinced that her husband was having an affair. See Beck, "Dorothy's Devastating Delusions." She never recovered, and became increasingly mentally ill, dying in 1807.

50. One must, however, be wary of what has been called "the 'heart of darkness' trope" in much missionary literature of the period. The quotation is from Johnston, *Missionary Writing*, 64.

51. Carey, *Journal*, 1 February 1795, 51.

52. Carey, *Journal*, 2-7 February 1795, 51-52. Things picked up a bit on the following day!

No doubt some of this is in a sense formulaic, the kind of thing an eighteenth-century Calvinist like Carey would be expected to say of himself. But this kind of language reveals more than purely perfunctory phrases—this is a man struggling with God, struggling with his own sense of vocation, trying to make sense of what it is that God has called him to do. This is the sense of God as the other, but as the other who draws near in his own time and in his own way.

Language and Translation

Carey is probably best known for his translation work, and he was clearly a gifted linguist. But, even so, he had to struggle to learn not simply to understand the language well enough to translate into it,[53] but also, more importantly, to be able to communicate in it. One of the themes that turns up on several occasions in his journal is his effort to learn the languages of the people among whom he lived (first Bengali, but later others too).

As we saw, as a boy and young man Carey had already taught himself a number of languages, and seems to have had a natural aptitude for language learning, but even he faced difficulties, especially in communicating in a way that people could understand. But as in all else, language for him was a means to an end, an important means but only that. So, early on in his sea voyage to India, he notes, "I find some delight in reading, and in preparing for my Work by writing the Bengali—only however because it relates to my great Work."[54]

In his *Enquiry* Carey had already considered the need to learn languages, and pronounced that "the missionaries must have patience and mingle with the people, till they have learned so much of their language as to be able to communicate their ideas to them in it."[55] There are two important points being made here that impact on the way in which the missionary behaves and encounters the other. The first is the reiterated need for patience, the ability to focus on intermediate goals and aims in order to be

---

53. On Carey's translation work, see George, *Faithful Witness*, 137–43. See also Omanson, "Bible Translation," 13–14. Given the strictures that Omanson records on the accuracy of the translation work, one might feel tempted to claim that Carey's contribution was rather negligible, though it was perhaps the principle of translation and the recognition of is central role that is most important, rather than the works themselves.

54. Carey, *Journal*, 29 June 1795, 4.

55. Carey, *Enquiry*, 74. He goes on to add that "[i]t is well known to require no very extraordinary talents to learn, in the space of a year, or two at most, the language of any people upon earth."

able to do what one really wants, and perhaps also the humility to become almost mute and unable to communicate for a while.[56]

The second is the need to mingle with the people, to become part of the society, and to learn by listening, letting the other be the one in charge as teacher and the one at home in the language and culture. Carey spent a lot of time in this fashion engaging with people and trying to use the language, as well as having the assistance of Ram Ram Basu, a Brahmin who professed a love of Christianity and served as Carey's *munshi*, a kind of personal interpreter of language and custom, and to whom I return shortly.[57]

There were, of course, ups and downs in the language acquisition process, but he remained faithful to his belief that only with a feel for the language could he successfully communicate the gospel.[58] At times he was filled with greater hope,[59] but then there were moments when it felt like he had made no progress at all. In this regard, the entry for 7 July 1794 is worth quoting. He complains that the natives in Malda, where he had gone to manage an indigo works, spoke "a dialect which differs as much from true Bengali as Yorkshire [*this was then crossed out completely in the text and replaced with*] Lancashire does from true English—so that I have hard work to understand them and to make them understand me."[60]

The major contribution of Carey in terms of translation lies outside the time period of the journal and I will return to it in more detail. It has also been the subject of critical comment for its low standard,[61] and concerning its tendencies to over-Westernize the Christian message,[62] which necessarily tended to have a negative effect on the standard of the translation. Nevertheless, at the very least, Carey needs to be given due praise for realizing

---

56. It would be wrong to say like a child, since clearly children learn much faster, and indeed Carey's children were among his best teachers of language. See George, *Faithful Witness*, 138.

57. See George, *Faithful Witness*, 101–2.

58. See, for example, Carey, *Journal*, 10 March 1794, where he calls the "Study of Language . . . a Dull Work, yet . . . productive of Pleasure to me, because it is my Business, and necessary to my preaching in any useful manner."

59. On 2 April 1794, he is hoping to be able to preach within a few weeks; Carey, *Journal*, 26.

60. Carey, *Journal*, 37. The comment in italics is as noted by Carter in his transcription.

61. See Omanson, "Bible Translation," and Neill, *History of Christian Mission*, 223.

62. See Smith, *Serampore Mission Enterprise*, 191–95, and indeed throughout the book. Smith is in general critical of the Serampore mission for a number of reasons, some of which seem reasonable, and others of which seem more questionable, but his is an important check on over-hagiographical accounts of Carey and his companions.

that language and translation are, almost self-evidently, key elements of any attempt to allow the gospel to speak to people.

It is also, of course, as Lamin Sanneh so eloquently argued,[63] necessary for local people to be involved, and in this sense translation is always subversive. An Australian scholar of missionary writings, discussing the experience of London Missionary Society (LMS) missionaries in Polynesia, notes how "[l]anguage learning . . . brought about a crisis in European self-confidence and could threaten the previously impermeable boundaries between the missionary self and the heathen other."[64] Something similar was certainly true for Carey in India.

CAREY AND THE INDIANS

In the course of his journal entries, not surprisingly, Carey reports on his first interactions with local people. There are of course various ways in which these can be read. At one level, much of it is rather painful for our ears today, simply because of the kind of language he uses. Thus he can be read as a fairly typical colonial missionary with an innate belief in the superiority of Western civilization.[65] On the other hand, one can also see him as someone who from the start rejected the caste system, and refused to use violence to proclaim the gospel.

It is also noteworthy that at least at the beginning Carey was minded to live as the natives did.[66] In this he was both similar and different to earlier missionaries to India, such as the Jesuit Roberto de Nobili (1577–1656).[67] De Nobili, in his work among Tamils in southern India, adopted many of the customs of the Brahmins. In this sense he served as a model for inculturation, in which the local setting was to provide the backdrop for the gospel. However, both by his choice of the Brahmins as his conversation

---

63. See Sanneh, *Translating the Message*; for example, 202–11.

64. Johnston, *Missionary Writings*, 130.

65. In this context, one is irresistibly reminded of Gandhi's famous, if apocryphal, comment when asked what he thought of Western civilization: "I think it would be a very good idea," he replied. The relationship between Christianity and imperial India in Gandhi's time is treated in Studdert-Kennedy, *Providence*. On the failure of Carey and his companions to extricate themselves fully from involvement with the colonial structures, see Smith, *Serampore Mission Enterprise*, 161–229. See also Wilson, "Mission and Cultures," 21.

66. See Carey, *Journal*, 14 January 1794, 7, confirmed in Marshman, *Story of Carey*, 26. By this time, there was much less sympathy in general for this kind of behavior amongst the British in India. See Dalrymple, *White Mughals*, 46–50.

67. For a more complete account, see Bachman, *Roberto Nobili*; and, more briefly, see Neely, *Christian Mission*, 32–50.

partners, and more still by his refusal to insist on the abandonment of the caste system, de Nobili was very different to Carey.[68]

From the beginning, Carey was faced with the problem of what to do about the caste system. He mentions it in his description referred to earlier of his first encounter with Indians. The more time he spent in India, the more he became aware of the problems it raised. This is made explicit in his journal entry for 5 July 1794, when he records a conversation with Ram Ram Basu, who he says, "I hope will lose caste for the gospel."[69] He continues with an example of what attachment to caste entails, a story of a poor boy "of the Shoemaker Caste (which is the very lowest of all),"[70] who refused to join him as a servant for fear of losing caste. He concludes "and perhaps this is one of the Strangest Chains with which the Devil ever bound the Children of Men; This is my comfort that God can break it."[71]

Although there was a period when Carey questioned himself over the matter of caste, and came closer to de Nobili's acceptance of it as a social and cultural necessity,[72] it was the initial intuition that proved strongest, and it was one that he and his later companions at Serampore insisted on implementing in their churches. It is, of course, a question that has continued to trouble Christian churches in India, and whether Carey or de Nobili chose the best path may be the wrong question to ask. But at least we might feel that Carey's choice remained faithful to the dissenting tradition into which he had been baptized. He would not allow human social constructs to determine the nature of God's kingdom[73] and recognized the injustice of a system that made some people inherently inferior to others.

It is perhaps in this light that we should try to read Carey's intemperance with many of the local customs.[74] Here again he was often torn, between a desire to be open to the native culture, and a sense of repulsion.

---

68. On this topic, see Saulière, *His Star*, especially 150–53, pointing out that de Nobili's own position was not without its subtleties.

69. Carey, *Journal*, 36.

70. This fact may have given Carey the cobbler pause for thought, and perhaps even some joy.

71. Carey, *Journal*, 36.

72. See Smith, *Serampore Mission Enterprise*, 145–51, and 199–203.

73. In this, then, in line with Myers, "Tracing a Theology," he was also following his own earlier instincts.

74. His most successful attempt to change these is in reference to the practice of *sati*, when widows would throw themselves on to the funeral pyres of their deceased husbands. For a more positive reflection on this, see Stanley, *Bible and Flag*, 100–101, and Walls, *Cross-Cultural Process*, 23–25. For ideological reasons, Johnston, *Missionary Writings*, 74–75, is less willing to praise the missionaries. Stanley notes, however, that the missionaries operated out of basic humanity, not specifically for Christian reasons.

At least for Carey it was very clear that salvation was only through explicit profession of faith in Jesus, and thus though he could hardly fail to acknowledge that there was some good in the Hindu writings and in the Qur'an, nevertheless his final verdict on each was that they were like good bread that contained "a very little malignant Poison, which made the whole so poisonous that whoever should eat of it would die," and that "their Writings contained much good instruction mixed with deadly poison."[75] This poison he saw in many of the celebrations and festivities of the local people, both Hindu and Muslim, which he generally viewed as forms of idolatry.

Even here, though, he refused to use force or his authority as manager of the works to enforce his position. So, he notes that he had found a worker making a statue for a celebration of Sarasuati, the goddess of learning: "I might have used authority and forbad it, but thought this would be persecution; I therefore talked seriously with the Man to Day, & tried to convince him of the sinfulness of such a thing, as well as its foolishness."[76] Whatever the views on the particular case, Carey's approach is a vivid reminder of what we saw in the previous chapter—the need for the gospel to be preached in love. It is also, in line with the previous chapter, reminiscent of Ignatius's instructions to his companions in Trent and Germany.

Ram Ram Basu: Carey's Teacher

Having looked at the *Journals*, it is now time to examine some of the particular responses to Indian others that are recorded in letters or elsewhere in writings by or about Carey. Unfortunately, these tend to be one-sided, and we do not get to hear very often the voice of Carey's "other," but nevertheless, it is a worthwhile attempt. How did Carey learn from and respond to these others, those who became Christians and those who did not?

I have already briefly referred to Ram Ram Basu and we can begin with considering him and his relationship with Carey in somewhat greater detail. We first encounter Ram Ram Basu not long after Carey's arrival in India. In his first attempts at preaching and evangelizing Carey was utterly dependent on his interpreter.[77] Writing in August 1795 to the mission society, he records the help he was receiving, even whilst regretting the lack of progress made. "I don't see that disinterested Zeal which is so ornamental to a Christian in either of them; Yet they have good knowledge of the things of

---

75. Carey, *Journal*, 9 May 1795, 58.
76. Carey, *Journal*, 1–15 January 1795, 47.
77. See Marshman, *Story of Carey*, 27.

God considering their disadvantages; with their help we have Divine Worship twice on the Lord's Day in Bengali."[78]

Ram Ram Basu was somewhat older than Carey,[79] and had already served as *munshi* for John Thomas in his previous stay in Calcutta. One of Carey's nineteenth-century biographers says of him that at the time of his early engagement with Carey "Ram Basu was himself in debt, was indeed all along a self-interested inquirer."[80] But this seems somewhat harsh, and the description of the relationship between Carey and Ram Basu as a love-hate one may be nearer the mark.[81] For the first three years of his time in India, Ram Basu was Carey's almost constant companion, and the one who taught him the language and the culture of India.

He was then dismissed by Carey because of his alleged adultery, but when the college at Serampore was opened, he was employed again as a teacher of Bengali, and is credited with having written the first work of Bengali prose. Although he remained a Hindu until his death in 1813, he also wrote several works on Christianity in Bengali. As a nineteenth-century writer George Smith put it in his biography of Carey: "He [Carey] had produced the first edition of the New Testament. He had reduced the language to literary form, with the help of Ram Basu, who to the last did everything for the propagation of the new faith except give up himself."[82]

A glimpse of Carey's feelings for Ram Basu are to be found in a letter that he wrote to Andrew Fuller back in England in 1796, shortly after the dismissal: "The discouragement arising from this circumstance is not small as he is a man of the very best natural abilities that I have ever found among the Natives and being well acquainted with the Phraseology of Scripture was peculiarly fitted to assist in the Translation—but I have no hope of him."[83] But the fact that he reappointed him to teach at Serampore indicates the value Carey attached to Ram Basu.

---

78 Carter, *Journal*, 84 (letter from Carey to the Society, 13 August 1795: the spelling and punctuation are as in Carter, who generally transcribes Carey's own very idiosyncratic writing). The other person (hence "them") referred to here is someone Carey calls Mohund Chund.

79. The date generally given for his birth is around 1757. See Murshid, "Ramram Basu."

80. Smith, *Life of William Carey*, 84.

81. This is the phrase used by Ghulam Murshid in the encyclopedia article "Ramram Basu."

82. Smith, *Life of William Carey*, 132. See also 218 and 275.

83. Carter, *Journal*, 106 (letter from Carey to Fuller, 17 June 1796). See earlier remarks, however, recording his initial impressions in Dec 1793, in Carter, *Journal*, 115.

As often seems to be the case with Carey, one has to go behind the often rather stereotypical language and look at what he actually did in order to get some idea of how he reacted to these others who surrounded him. Certainly his encouragement of Ram Basu to write, and in general his desire to further the languages of India and give them written form is impressive,[84] and in this at least he had something in common with Roberto de Nobili, often considered one of the most important figures in the development of literary forms of Tamil.[85]

Krishna Pal: Carey's First Indian Convert

Another figure of major importance is Carey's first native-born Indian convert, Krishna Pal. It took seven years for Carey to baptize his first Indian convert,[86] though there had been moments of hope before. It would appear that the first major interest seems to have come from Muslims, though in general Carey did not regard his mission as being to them.[87] Krishna Pal first encountered the Christians through Carey's fellow-missionary John Thomas, in the latter's capacity as a doctor. Krishna Pal was a carpenter, and had broken his arm. At the time he was around thirty-six (a similar age to Carey himself).[88]

Krishna Pal, in common with various other early converts,[89] had previously been an adherent of one of the *bhakti* movements, which had begun as a kind of Hindu spiritual revival in the eleventh or twelfth centuries.[90] He had joined this movement (more specifically the *Kharta Bhoja*, a Hindu group that began in the eighteenth century and did not practice within its

---

84. On this, see Brockington, "William Carey's Significance."

85. Apart from the references previously given, see also Lorance, "Cultural Relevance." See also Clooney, "Roberto de Nobili." This article is particularly insightful on why de Nobili (and I would suggest Carey too) cannot be read in contemporary terms, since they are asking different questions, but also showing how in fact he was influenced deeply by the culture in which he lived.

86. The first convert in fact seems to have been a man of Portuguese descent, Ignatius Fernandez (1757–1830). See Carter, *Journal*, 104–5 (letter from Carey to his sisters, 21 Feb 1831) for Carey's reaction to his death, and see also Jackson, "From Krishna Pal."

87. See Johnson, "Carey's Muslim Encounters."

88. There exists an early biography of Krishna Pal, by an unnamed author, *The First Hindoo Convert*. The encounter is told on 9–10.

89. See Jackson, "From Krishna Pal," 174.

90. See Smith, *Life of William Carey*, 133. On the *bhakti* movements, see Schomer and McLeod, *Sants*, and Werner, *Love Divine*.

own confines the caste system), and had been an itinerant for a number of years.

He had turned to the Hindu religious movements because of sickness, from which he was cured. However, when Thomas had set Krishna Pal's arm, he also began to speak of Christianity. Krishna Pal obviously showed some interest, since the next day Carey visited him. Not much more than a month later, on 28 December 1800, he was baptized, something that gave great pleasure to Carey, not least because of the clear affection he felt for Krishna. In a letter to John Ryland, written a month after the baptism, he says that "Krishna walks so as to give us all great satisfaction—and by his simple affectionate conversation with others is likely to be of great use."[91] And indeed, soon after, Krishna's wife and other members of his family were also baptized.

Whether the fact that it took Carey seven years to gain his first Indian convert is a sign of success or failure is, of course, an open question. At least it seems to suggest that he was prepared to wait, and that he was not prepared to set aside some of the principles that he had come to regard as fundamental, for example, in relation to the caste system. "Colonial" Christianity (so leaving aside the indigenous Syro-Malabar Church) has generally adapted one of two approaches to this question. Either it has approved of it, and sought to find converts among the highest and most influential castes, or it has rejected it, or, which was much the same thing, worked with the so-called *Dalit*, those excluded by other castes.

Carey and the early Baptists rejected caste, and at least in the early days managed to attract people of different castes to live together in Christian villages, following what Christopher Smith has called a "'reduction-like' policy."[92] Nevertheless, as Eleanor Jackson, author of a study of early Indian converts, points out, it is a "striking fact that as far as can be discerned from available biographies of church workers, none of the converts who became pastors or evangelists on a permanent basis were drawn from untouchable groups or unclean professions."[93]

CAREY'S LATER REFLECTIONS ON MISSION

Attracting people to live in Christian compounds was one of the ways in which Carey, and his companions William Ward (1769–1823), and Joshua

---

91. Carter, *Journal*, 150.
92. See Smith, "Mythology and Missiology," 463.
93. Jackson, "From Krishna Pal," 171.

Marshman (1768–1837) and his wife, Hannah Marshman (1767–1847)[94] carried out their mission. Other approaches can be seen in some of Carey's letters and reports to the Baptist Missionary Society and his family and friends in Britain.[95] In 1814, Carey's fourth son, Jabez (1793–1862), set off to be a missionary in Amboyna in the Moluccas (now Ambon, Indonesia).[96] As he was setting off, his father gave him some advice, born out of twenty years of experience on the mission field. Much of it is what one might expect from a father to his son, and especially from a man like Carey.

He begins by encouraging his son to "[l]ive a life of prayer and devotedness to God."[97] He also urged him not simply to conduct himself "towards your wife with propriety. Let love to her be the spring of your conduct towards her."[98] This is more than just conventional platitude. In part, it is a sign of the happiness of his second marriage in 1808 to a Danish aristocrat Charlotte Rumohr. Dorothy had died in 1807, having suffered for most of her time in India from increasingly severe mental illness, and finally with Charlotte he seemed to have found peace and understanding in his married life.[99] It may also be that he had had cause to reflect on the demands he had placed on Dorothy, bringing her to India, where one of their sons had died, and where she had had, at least initially, to put up with similar material privations to those they had experienced in England, without any of the support networks that would have been available to her there. In that sense, at least, Dorothy is always one of Carey's most demanding "others."[100]

---

94. Apart from the biography by the Marshmans' son (Marshman, *Story of Carey*), see also Smith, "Legacy of William Ward."

95. These do need to be treated with some reserve, though. As Jackson, "From Krishna Pal," 175, points out, there was a certain amount of censorship, and "[a]ccounts critical of Indian society and religion were highlighted, showing how dark things were without the Gospel [whilst c]omments commending aspects of Hindu, Sikh or Muslim practices were often excised." Therefore, at least from the perspective from which I am arguing here, the surviving documentation is probably even more skewed against the "other" than the practice itself.

96. For a brief biographical note, see Savage, "Jabez Carey." Jabez was born just before Carey left for India. When the Dutch retook the islands, he eventually returned to India, serving as a school inspector and judge, as well as being involved in various churches.

97. Carter, *Journal*, 130 (letter from Carey to his son Jabez, 24 January 1814).

98. Carter, *Journal*, 130.

99. See Tucker, "Family Life." Charlotte was the same age as Carey. She died in 1821 and in 1823 he married for a final time a widow, Grace Hughes, who cared for him in his old age. In his will he asked to be buried alongside Charlotte.

100. A hint of this is heard in a letter to the mission society in 1796 when he reflects on the kind of wife required by a missionary. They should be full of missionary spirit, and of prudence and "not afraid of hardship, but if they are otherwise, they will prove

He commends Jabez to make the acquaintance of the authorities on the island[101] and to make sure that he could hold his own in society. These are, at one level, rather strange suggestions, especially from Carey, and yet by this time Carey was employed (and relatively well-paid) by the colonial administration in India as a language teacher,[102] and arguably, despite his evident and sincere concerns for those most disadvantaged by the caste system in India, he was unable to escape some of the trappings of colonialism.[103] But he also recommends that Jabez finds himself an interpreter, again perhaps recalling how important Ram Ram Basu had been to him. Through the aid of this person, Carey encourages his son to "become a perfect master of the Malay language."[104]

The way he suggests to do this is worth quoting:

> associate with the natives, walk about with them, ask the name of everything you see and note it down. Visit their homes especially when any of them are sick . . . try to talk as soon as you get a few words and be as soon as possible one of them. A course of kind and attentive conduct will gain their esteem and confidence and give you an opportunity of doing much good.[105]

This is perhaps one of the clearest statements of Carey's own practice, or at least how he wanted to practice. To some extent, in his early days, as manager of an indigo works,[106] he had been almost forced into this, if he wanted even to do his day job, let alone preach and translate. But his reflection also showed him the value of this way of behaving. Again we see how, simply through the act of learning the language, power roles are reversed. Normally in these situations it was the white colonial who had the power, but in these settings it is the native speaker of the language who is in control, who has the knowledge that the colonial lacks. In this sense, there is an important

---

a far greater Burden than you can well conceive of as many things will occur that will feed a discounted mind as full as it can well be." Carter, *Journal*, 133, letter of Carey to Society, 28 December 1796.

101. Jabez went as superintendent of schools, so was part of the colonial civil service.

102. He has been appointed first tutor and then professor in Bengali, Sanskrit, and Marathi at Fort William College, the administrative college of the East India Company. See Brockington, "William Carey's Significance," 82–83.

103. See Wilson, "Mission and Cultures," and see also, for a view of Carey's "orientalism," and especially for the practice of science in Serampore, Sivasundaram, "'A Christian Benares.'"

104. Carter, *Journal*, 131.

105. Carter, *Journal*.

106. On the importance of indigo dyeing in India at this time and later, see Kumar, *Indigo Plantations*.

kenotic element to language learning, a giving up on what one knows and possesses in order to be able to receive the gift of another language.

Another feature is the importance of visiting, especially the sick. As we saw, Krishna Pal was converted as a result of contact established by the giving of simple medical assistance. It would be anachronistic to force Carey into the debate between action and proclamation, but clearly he saw the need for both, and especially for care of the sick. It is "kind and attentive conduct" that will enable good to be done. This is not pure pragmatism, treating kindness as a means of entrapment, but something about the attitude to the other that must precede any form of evangelism.

It is not, of course, that Carey does not think the latter important. Indeed, he is eager that as soon as Jabez has learnt sufficient of the language, he should start to explain from the Scriptures why infant baptism is wrong.[107] But even here, it is not the first thing to be done: "You must say little till you know something of the Language and then prove to them from Scripture what is the right mode of Baptism and who are the proper persons to be baptized."[108] In other words, in order even to preach about one of the core Baptist convictions, it was necessary to wait, to learn the language, and, by extension, the mind of the other, in order to be able to speak. And here too, the aim is as soon as possible to find indigenous ministers: "as soon as you see any fit to preach to others call them to the ministry and settle them with the churches."[109]

Early on in his stay in India, Carey reflected to Ryland on the missionary calling, especially as a European in India. "A Missionary must be one of the companions, and equals of the people to whom he is sent and many dangers and temptations will be in his way."[110] The sentence can be read in two ways, either as encouraging inculturation, or, more probably, as admitting that in India, the European missionary will have to engage also with other Europeans. But that is something to be wary of, since to speak with Europeans is to listen to people complaining about the Indians, and to find "[p]eople treating him [i.e., the missionary] with the greatest kindness but whom he must be entirely different from, in his life, his appearance and

---

107. Carter, *Journal*, 131.

108. Carter, *Journal*. In a remark to Fuller, Carey compared himself to his fellow missionary, Joshua Marshman, saying "In point of zeal, he is Luther, I am Erasmus." Quoting this, Smith, "Legacy of William Carey," 4, says that this "corroborates other evidence picturing Carey as a pious, irenic, hard-working, low-key leader . . . a more meditative person who preferred to 'sit on the fence' in times of strife." See also Smith, "Tale," 484.

109. Carter, *Journal*, 131.

110. Carter, *Journal*, 132 (letter from Carter to Ryland, 26 December 1793).

everything."[111] The temptation to be like the other Europeans was one that was constantly present in the mission—it was one of the weaknesses of John Thomas, for example, but it was something that crops up on several occasions in Carey's correspondence.[112]

CAREY'S REACTION TO HINDUISM AND ISLAM

For Carey, on the other hand, the important thing was to try and learn the native culture. Again, it must be admitted that, as a child of his time, Carey's language is often somewhat intemperate, especially when it comes to treating Hindu and Muslim beliefs and practices. Nevertheless, he was also capable of appreciating some of the riches of Indian culture that he encountered. The two features are present in his reaction to the great Hindu classic, the *Mahabharata*, contained in the letter to Ryland that has been already cited. He says that it is

> written in the most beautiful Language; and much upon a par with Homer. And was it like his Iliad only considered as a great effort of human genius, I should think it one of the first productions in the world, but alas! It is the ground of Faith to Millions of sinful sons of men, and as such must be held in the utmost abhorrence.[113]

This ambivalence remained with Carey for the rest of his life in India. Like so many others, he could not fail to be deeply impressed by the wealth and depth of Indian culture, and the literary power of the great Sanskrit epics, but at the same time, he rejected almost completely everything to do with Hindu religious practices and beliefs.

It is worth pausing to reflect on this, since the encounter with the religion of the other is clearly such a fundamental part of mission, and in this aspect, it might well be fair to say that Carey did not adopt the attitude I am arguing for in this book.[114] But before I look in more detail at the at-

---

111. Carter, *Journal*.

112. See, for example, Carter, *Journal*, 133 (letter to Fuller, 4 October 1809), 134 (letters to Fuller and Sutcliffe, 2 August 1811, and 18 August 1812).

113. Carter, *Journal*, 143 (letter from Carey to Ryland, 26 December 1793).

114. In this, I think, he differs significantly from a later Baptist missionary, Timothy Richard (1845–1919), though both were suspected by the Baptist Missionary Society (or at least parts of it) of spending too little time on matters of evangelism, and relations with the Society broke down in both cases, later to be re-established (the two cases are different, though, and complex, and with both there are points to be made on either side). Richard was a missionary in China who opted for the route of inculturation in a

titude to Hinduism of Carey and his fellow missionaries, two points can be made. The first is that there was a certain element of censorship involved in reporting missionary activity. This censorship, though, may not only be from the side of mission agencies, but also from the side of the missionaries themselves. The very complex relationship between missionary and sending agency needs to be borne in mind[115] and there is, even apart from that, a self-image of the Christian missionary that is hard to shake off.

The second point is that Carey may not always have been so combative as he makes out, at least judging from some of his comments. In 1813 there was a renewal of the charter of the East India Company, which included debates on whether Christian missions should be allowed, and in which there were attacks on Carey and the other Baptist ministers by lobbyists for the Company.[116] The missionaries were alleged to have made remarks concerning the Hindus that were "infamous and unfounded libels."[117] Carey responded to accounts of these attacks in a letter in early 1814, denying some specific accusations about his having preached on the streets of Calcutta and having created disturbances that almost led to riots. He admitted though that "I should perhaps have acted more like a Missionary, if I had often preached in Calcutta Streets, and if I had asserted that they would go to Hell if they did not leave Idolatry."[118]

Nevertheless, there is no doubt that Carey and his companions did regard Hinduism[119] as something essentially wrong. The clearest expression of this is in the work of Carey's Serampore colleague, William Ward, whose four volume work *A View of the History, Literature and Mythology of the Hindoos* was first published in 1811, under a slightly different title. Although the work is generally very negatively disposed towards Hindu practices, it is perhaps not quite right to see Ward as utterly condemnatory of Hinduism. As Christopher Smith notes, he did at one point also say that "the Hindoos

---

very similar way to that adopted by Matteo Ricci some three hundred years earlier. On Richard, see Cracknell, *Justice*, 120–32, and on Ricci see Hsia, *Matteo Ricci*. On both Ricci and Richard, see Treadgold, *West in Russia and China*: on Ricci and the Jesuits in China till 1774, 1–34, and on Timothy Richard, 56–65. A more critical view of the Jesuit (Riccian) position is to be found in Cummins, *Question of Rites*.

115. Bonk, *Missions and Money*, is important on this, and on the equally difficult question of the status relationships of missionaries to those to whom they are sent.

116. See Marshman, *Story of Carey*, 187–205, for a full account of this episode.

117. Marshman, *Story of Carey*, 199.

118. Carter, *Journal*, 152 (Letter of Carey to Burls, 22 February 1814).

119. On whether "Hinduism" is a religion, see Sweetman, "'Hinduism.'" His argument is that to deny that there is a religion called Hinduism is dependent on particular ways (Protestant Christians ones specifically) of understanding what a religion is.

themselves, amidst much that is positively evil, have precepts in their books which a Christian would not be dishonoured by observing."[120]

But the general tone of the work is undoubtedly negative, and the space of the other is largely denied. The Hindus are defined in terms of what they are not or do not have.[121] As Sharada Sugirtharajah puts it, for Ward, "Hinduism lacks what Protestant Christianity affirms."[122] Although Sugirtharajah has her own ideological points to make, it must be admitted that there is a lot of force in what she argues. Ward writes to demonstrate the inferiority of Hinduism against the alleged superiority of Christianity, but often in such a way as to destroy any possibility of accepting Christianity. There is a kind of colonial demeaning of the other going on here that is, for modern ears, unacceptable.

However, it should also be noted that the very severity (and injustice) of attacks of the kind that Ward launched against Hinduism were in part responsible for the Hindu revival movements that began in the early nineteenth century.[123] Moreover, as was noted previously, many of the (relatively few) Indian converts made through the mission at Serampore had been involved in forms of *bhakti* devotions that were already somewhat iconoclastic.[124] Thus we may have to conclude that in attacking what they perceived as "Hinduism," the missionaries were actually contributing to its revival, and anyway were to a large extent failing to engage with most of those around them, and that in fact their success came mostly either with other Europeans or with people who felt themselves on the margins of Hindu life and practice.

---

120. Smith, "Legacy of William Ward," 126. Smith also points out that Ward argued in favor of creating a pantheon of Hindu images and sculptures in Calcutta, or, perhaps, in London. See Smith, "Legacy of William Ward," and also in more detail, Smith, "Mythology and missiology," 457–58.

121. I am drawing here on Sugirtharajah, "Virtuous Christians," 197–99.

122. Sugirtharajah, "Virtuous Christians," 201.

123. See Pennington, *Was Hinduism Invented*, who views modern Hinduism as a construct of Calcutta at roughly the time that Carey was there. For a similar work, see Oddie, *Imagined Hinduism*. See also Aghamkar, "Traditional Hindu Views," and on Rammohan Roy, who had at one stage close connections with Carey, see Zastoupil, "Defining Christians."

124. For a fuller account, see Frazier, "Bhakti in Hindu Cultures," and Dutta, "Bhakti Movement."

SUMMARY

The last section of this chapter may seem to indicate that we will have to discount Carey when it comes to a reflection on the role of the other in mission. But I think that is too hasty. There are other episodes that I could have quoted that show how in limit situations he was far more nuanced in his reaction to the other. Particularly moving in this respect is the narrative of the death of his son Peter, at a time when he himself was just recovering from illness. At first none of the Hindus or Muslims around the indigo factory where he was superintendent would bury the boy, because of fears of rejection, the Hindus on account of caste and the Muslims because of strict rules on contact with non-Muslims. Eventually, four poor Muslims agreed to bury the boy. But the next day they came to see Carey, having been cast out of their village. Carey persuaded the local village head to re-integrate them into the community, blaming the episode on caste.[125] Here Carey was dependent on and deeply grateful to the other who had risked everything for him, and, in a move that was very unusual for him, even threatened to report the village head to the local British colonial authorities if he did not accept the men back.

This episode seems to me to show that at some levels Carey did have the ability to transcend his prejudices and beliefs to engage with the other who came to him, those who dwelt near to him (*paroikoi*). I think that this is also evident at least in the way he wanted to do mission, in his initial desire to be one with the people, and his commitment to learning languages, and even to some extent to befriending people like Ram Ram Basu. The advice he gives to his son would seem to back this up too, where the stress is on getting to know the people, on opening oneself up to them. The story quoted previously might seem to suggest that it was when he truly learned to be non-possessive, in moments of the greatest crisis, that he acted in the most missionary way, allowing himself to be served and helped by those around him, responding, in Marion's terms, to their givenness.

I think that we can see this as the "ideal" Carey. Writers such as Christopher Smith have helped to show that there is always a danger of creating Carey and the Serampore missionaries in our own image and likeness, either negatively, as with Sugirtharajah, or far too uncritically.[126] This latter image is the "ideal" Carey, the kind of missionary who was engaged with the

---

125. See his journal entry of October 1794, in Carter, *Journal*, and also Johnson, "Carey's Muslim Encounters," 104–5.

126. Many of the works cited in this chapter are perhaps guilty of this. See also Watts, "Baptists."

culture of the other, and acted like a good anthropologically-trained twenty-first-century missionary would (or at least should).

There is, of course, much to admire in Carey. There was what one might call a "non-religious" Carey, the one who introduced science into Serampore, who was a great botanist and observer of the natural world around him,[127] and someone who had a curiosity about and sympathy with the otherness of the other. This Carey was able to see the good around him, in people and ideas. He was also able to separate the religious from the customary, which is part of the strength of his campaign against *sati*, the practice of self-immolation practiced by widows. He was often at pains to argue that *sati* was even contrary to the practices of the Vedas.

But there was also the "religious" Carey, the Particular Baptist who had given up his security and culture for the gospel, and who was simply incapable of seeing the religious practices of the other as anything else than evil. The few examples we have of Carey's preaching and engagement with Indians do not offer much encouragement here. With typical Evangelical fervor, he wants to convict them of their sin, so that they will accept the gospel, without even considering if the language he uses even begins to meet their concepts for understanding the spiritual life. There is a complete failure to engage with the beliefs and customs of the other, a sure sense of possessing the gospel, the answers to questions that his listeners do not have the language to ask, even if they wanted to.

There are two responses to this. Either we can use it to dismiss Carey—and given that something similar can probably be said about a lot of mission practice, the very idea of mission—or we can accept even this "dispraxis" as a kind of gift, a suggestion to us to reflect on our own possessiveness. It is too simplistic to dismiss Carey completely though, and I would suggest that his "theoretical" approach is something that helps us to see how to react to and engage with the other. Even his "religious" approach may give pause for thought. Is there a dividing line between firm belief (faith or conviction, we could call it) and ideology, and if so where, how and by whom is it to be drawn? Perhaps the best epitaph and summary of Carey's life and engagement as a missionary can be found in the remarks made by one of the others whom Carey touched, an Indian who was not a Christian, and who described Carey as "a rare spirit crossing barriers of national prejudice."[128]

In the next chapter, I will turn to Innocent Veniaminov, another missionary, though in a very different setting, to see if he can take us any further.

---

127. As detailed in Sivasundaram, "Christian Benares."

128. See Middlebrook, *William Carey*, 107. Unfortunately, no further reference is given.

The question that persists is how to respond to the beliefs and practices of those who dwell among us. Carey, in religious matters at least, could not really see in Hindu or Muslim beliefs and practices the *logoi spermatikoi*. For him, there was only one gospel, and his Bible translation was indicative of where he saw that truth to be expressed. Yet, as Sanneh has pointed out,[129] the very act of standardizing and printing the language—Bengali in the first place, but other Indian languages too—was subversive of his intentions, since it transformed the way in which people saw themselves and their culture. With Innocent we will see something similar, but we will also see how this subversion can be, if not intended, at least welcomed and how it can become a tool for resistance and opposition.

---

129. See Sanneh, *Translating the Message*, 149, on the subversive results of translation.

6

Bishop Innocent Veniaminov and Russian Orthodox Mission in Alaska

In this second part I have looked so far at Saint Ignatius of Loyola and William Carey. With Ignatius we saw that the development of a commitment to service in love underlaid his attention to the centrality of mission in the life of the new religious order he helped to found. It was the love for the other and for God that drove his desire to engage in mission. However, though with Ignatius love is central, it is an attitude that is taken to the encounter with the other. Although coming from a very different ecclesial tradition, something similar could be seen with William Carey. However, unlike Ignatius, whose mission in his final years was one of governance, Carey was also a missionary in India, and his experiences of the other who drew near had an impact on his deepening reflection on mission.

In this chapter I examine another missionary who moved to a different setting, a Russian Orthodox priest, later bishop, and finally Metropolitan of Moscow, Saint Innocent Veniaminov. Innocent's move across the Bering Straits was less dramatic than Carey's across the oceans to India, and, according to the geo-political realities of the time, he was in the same country. He did not have any background—or, as we will see, initially any particular interest—in mission. So with him we will see someone learning to be a missionary mainly by doing, with few preconceptions about what such activity should entail. How did his encounters with others in Alaska shape his missionary endeavor?

THE BEGINNINGS OF THE RUSSIAN ORTHODOX MISSION IN ALASKA

With some justification, the nineteenth century has been termed "the Great Century" for Orthodox mission.[1] As the Russian Empire spread eastwards, it is hardly surprising that Russian Orthodoxy moved with it. The story of this migration and its engagement with the native populations that were encountered is mixed,[2] but there were always those who were able to transcend the limitations of their time and the pressures to make Christianization and Russification coincide. There were also Russian missions beyond the boundaries of Russia, most notably perhaps that to Japan.[3] However, despite the similarities that undoubtedly exist with Western imperial missions, there are differences, and these are especially marked in the case of the mission to Alaska, to which I now turn.[4]

The traditional starting date for the Russian Orthodox mission in Alaska is 24 September 1794, ten months after Carey landed in India.[5] Ten Russians (a mixture of priests, monks, and others) arrived, having set out on 25 December 1793 from the monastery of Valaam[6] on the Finnish-Russian border, north of Saint Petersburg.[7] Because of the role of Valaam in support-

---

1. Bevans and Schroeder, *Constants in Context*, 227.

2. See, for example, Johnstone, "Czarist Missionary," and Kan, "Russian Orthodox Missionaries."

3. See for a brief history of this mission, Ushimaru, "Japanese Orthodoxy." See also Pospielovsky, *Orthodox Church*, 166–70, which points to the influence of Bishop Innocent Veniaminov on the then Archimandrite, and later Bishop Nicholas, who was the most significant leader in the establishment of the Japanese Orthodox Church.

4. Although I am writing this chapter specifically for this book, I have already dealt with the Russian Orthodox mission to Alaska elsewhere, and there will inevitably be overlaps. See Noble et al., *Ways of Orthodoxy*, 105–24; Noble, "Rights of Indigenous Peoples"; Noble, "Pathway."

5. It should be noted, however, that there was already a Russian Orthodox presence. On this subject, see Skedros, Review of *The Orthodox Church*, 727–28, and on the pre-history of the Unalaska parish, see the introduction in Mousalimas, *Journals*, xvii–xxvii.

6. Oleksa, "Orthodoxy," 246, says that some of the missionaries (whom he calls "willing volunteers") were from the monastery of Konevitsa.

7. Ann Elizabeth Williams gives the names of the monks who first came to Alaska from Valaam as Archimandrite Iosaf, Hieromonks Iuvenalii, Afanasii, Nektarii, Makarii, and Stephan, Monks Iosaph and Herman, and two acolytes. Some of them died in Alaska or in a shipwreck, while others later returned to Russia. See Williams, "Father Herman," 23. According to the earlier work of Frank Golder, author of the first English life of Saint Herman, based on notes taken from the Valaam Monastery during a visit in 1914, among the ten names mentioned, it is stated that Nektarii and Stefan were deacons and Dimitrii and Nikita were the two acolytes. See Golder, *Father Herman*, 22.

ing the revival of the type of hesychast life initiated by Saint Nil Sorsky, with its emphasis on non-possession, a brief comment on the monastery at this time is in order.

THE MONASTERY OF VALAAM

Valaam lies on the eponymous island in Lake Ladoga, the largest lake in Europe, part of the disputed territory of Karelia, ruled over at various times by Finns, Swedes, and Russians.[8] The monastery was most probably founded around the end of the fourteenth or beginning of the fifteenth centuries, though legend attributed its foundation to two monks, Sergei and Herman, from an earlier period. Under Swedish rule in the seventeenth century, the monastery had closed, and only re-opened at the beginning of the eighteenth century through monks coming from the Kyrillo-Belozerskij Monastery.[9]

This monastery had played an important role in the late fourteenth and fifteenth centuries in the establishment of Russian monastic life, in the form in which it was developed by Saint Sergius of Radonezh (1314–1392), who was the spiritual father of Saint Kyrill and the monastery's founder.[10] Shortly after Saint Kyrill's death in 1427, Nil Sorsky had entered the monastery, and eventually his influence would be felt by Saint Paisius Velichkovsky, the great eighteenth-century compiler of the *Dobrotolyubie* (the Slavonic version of the *Philokalia*).[11] The *Dobrotolyubie* was first published in 1793, and one of its sponsors was the *Igumen* (or Abbot) of Valaam, Nazarii, who had been appointed by Metropolitan Gabriel of Saint Petersburg to oversee the publication.[12]

Nazarii had become the *igumen* of the monastery in the early 1780s, and helped to revitalize it. Its relative closeness to Saint Petersburg made it a popular place of pilgrimage, partly because its restoration had been decreed earlier in the century by Peter the Great. This was despite his otherwise somewhat complex relationship to the church,[13] but, as one writer

---

8. The following articles both contain good background information about Valaam, its history, and its present status: Mikula, "Island Monastery," esp. 16, and Parppei, "Pagans of Darkness," esp. 137, on the early history.

9. See Parppei, "Pagans of Darkness," 139.

10. On hesychasm in Russia, see Noble et al., *Wrestling with the Mind*, 79–119. See also Meyendorff, *St Gregory Palamas*, 143–46, and Treadgold, *West in Russia and China*, 1:xxxvi.

11. On Saint Paisius, see McGuckin, "St Paisius Velichkovsky." See also Louth, "Influence of the *Philokalia*," 53–54.

12. This despite apparently being illiterate. See Nazarius, "St. Herman's Elder."

13. See Cracraft, *Church Reform*.

on the topic puts it, perhaps "the decision-makers were visionary enough to appreciate any attempts to consolidate the ideological grip of Russia in the regained areas—even more so, when the foundation of the new capital had brought the borderland area of Ladoga closer to the center of the imperium."[14]

Whatever the reasons, Valaam was an important place by this period. One of the books that the best-known of the first missionaries, Saint Herman, took with him to Alaska was a copy—presumably a first edition—of the *Dobrotolyubie*.[15] He would also call his hermitage on Spruce Island "New Valaam," and there seems little doubt that the two worlds were close for him. In versions of the history of Valaam published a century after Herman, there are descriptions of peaceful co-existence between Sergei, the alleged missionary founder of the monastery, and the local "pagans" that sound very similar to the stories told about the monk in Alaska. As Kati Parppei, a Finnish historian, puts it:

> In some of the later versions of the story, it is described how Sergej first taught Christianity on the shores of Ladoga and was advised by the local pagans to go to Valaam, where resided "the most mighty power of their religion" and to talk to the elders about the issues concerning gods and religion. Sergej travelled to Valaam and settled down armed only with the holy cross. Unlike in *Skazanie* written three centuries earlier, Sergej's co-existence with the "harsh and wild pagans" is described as a relatively smooth one, and the monastery established by him gradually acquired new inhabitants.[16]

Given that this story was written when accounts of Herman's life had already come to Valaam, it is of course a moot point as to who influenced who, but clearly Herman and the Alaska mission is placed in a tradition of peaceful co-existence with the other, which also tends to give a fairly high value to indigenous traditions.

This also makes clear that the narratives of the early Alaskan mission are, like those of Carey's mission in India, not always entirely free of ideological import. However, as before, what is of interest is the kind of ideology that is being supported. With Carey it was often one that sought to downplay

---

14. Parppei, "Pagans of Darkness," 139.

15. This is what is claimed in Nazarius, "St. Herman's Elder." Although I have not found separate corroboration of this, in a biography of Saint Herman (Korsun and Black, *Herman*), the authors claim that Herman had a substantial library.

16. Parppei, "Pagans of Darkness," 141. The *Skazanie* was a sixteenth-century document.

the religiosity of the native populations, but this is not so much the case with the Alaskan myth. There may be various reasons for this. Although the relationship between the early missionaries and the Russian American Company was not much better than that between the Baptist missionaries and the East India Company, it was not, certainly at first, identical. Indeed, Grigorii Shelikov (1747–1795), the main figure behind the Russian American Company, had basically inveigled the monks into going with him, partly through offering shares in his company to them, as a way of currying official favor.[17]

FIRST ENCOUNTERS IN THE ALASKAN MISSION

Thus, the monks were, at least in theory, present with official backing, and, as already noted, they came to a setting where some rudimentary form of Christian life already existed. The first baptism in what became the Unalaska[18] parish took place in 1762, and a strong lay-led community was in place by the time Fr. Ioann Veniaminov (Saint Innocent) arrived in 1824.[19] Part of this was brought about by alliances across the islands, where village leaders (called *"toions"* by the Russians) established partnerships with hunters. This, combined with intermarriage, led to the growth of family groups who took on some of the Russian customs and habits, especially that of being baptized, and at least basic elements of Christian life.[20] The *toions* also managed both to adopt the faith and adapt it, so that they gained a good deal of autonomy and were able to maintain their people's lifestyles at least to some degree, despite the often tyrannical behavior of the Russian American Company in the early years.[21] The editor of Veniaminov's journals sums it

---

17. See Hardwick, *Russian Refuge*, 54–55; and Oleksa, *Orthodox Alaska*, 89–93. Shelikov was not altogether successful, as the company only gained its monopoly in 1799. See also Oleksa, "Orthodoxy," 246–48; and Nikitin, "Russian America," 229.

18. Although I speak most commonly of the Alaskan mission, for most of the initial period, strictly speaking, the mission was to the eastern Aleutian Islands off what is now mainland Alaska (most specifically Unalaska, where the early missionaries landed), followed by Kodiak Island, and later Sitka (on what is now Baranof Island), further to the east (from a Russian perspective), in the Alexander Archipelago. Settlements on the mainland began earlier, but tended to remain along the coast.

19. Mousalimas, *Journals*, xix. However, as Nikitin, "Russian America," 230–31, notes, there was a considerable hiatus after the first missionary group arrived, with only one priest for much of the first fifteen years of the nineteenth century.

20. See Mousalimas, *Journals*, xx–xxi.

21. See Mousalimas, *Journals*, xxii–xiv.

up like this: "Russian Orthodoxy thus merged with the people's own leadership, with their own struggle, with their destiny."[22]

Unlike in India, then, the Russian Orthodox missionaries to Alaska entered into a situation where they were both generally welcomed by the indigenous population and where they had the power—moral and to some extent even legal—to do something about the way in which the Russian American Company was behaving.[23] Under the local manager, Alexander Baranov (1747–1819),[24] the company was exploiting the local people in order to gain the most it could from the animal furs that it traded. As this involved hunting populations to extinction and then moving on over hostile seas to other islands, this was very dangerous for the people, and, moreover, the time devoted to finding furs could not be devoted to hunting for food, so there was grave danger of starvation.[25] Even if there was also an element of enlightened self-interest—since the missionaries themselves found that Shelikov had been somewhat carefree in the accuracy of his promises[26]—the Valaam monks were certainly moved by the plight of those around them, and this response to the needs of the other, and to the fundamental goodness of the other, became an integral part of the mission to Alaska.

The mission itself was also not established without difficulties. The original group was diminished by the martyrdom of one of the monks, Father Iuvenalii, on the mainland, and the shipwreck and death of the mission leader, Archimandrite Iosaph (who had been consecrated the first bishop), and two others as they returned to the islands. Others, shaken by assassination attempts, often by their fellow Russians, returned to Russia.[27] Eventually Herman moved to Spruce Island, a small island just off Kodiak Island, to his New Valaam hermitage, where he spent the rest of his life, dying in 1837.

I will develop in more detail the theological presuppositions that seemed to have helped the first monks in their encounter with the indigenous

22. Mousalimas, *Journals*, xxv.

23. I have dealt with this at much greater length in Noble, "Rights of Indigenous Peoples," so I will not repeat that material here at any length.

24. On Baranov, see, for example, Rochcau, "St Herman," esp. 22–23. For much more on the first Russian settlers in Alaska, including Baranov and Shelikov, see the informative article by Grinëv, "First Russian Settlers," which includes a list of early settlers, though it does not touch at all on the missionaries.

25. On this, the first letters of the missionaries back to Igumen Nazarii in Valaam, and to Shelikov are highly revealing. See, for example, letter from Archimandrite Iosaph to Gregory Shelikov, 18 May 1795, in Oleksa, *Alaskan Missionary Spirituality*, 58–63.

26. Oleksa, *Orthodox Alaska*, 89, remarks rather nicely that "[h]onesty was not one of Shelikov's virtues," though he tempers this by going on to say that, nevertheless, "he comes through his own writings as an almost likeable and certainly charming rogue."

27. See Oleksa, "Orthodox Church," 283.

populations. Here it is necessary to make only a few brief comments. It is perhaps somewhat iniquitous to compare too closely the situations encountered by Carey and the Alaskan missionaries, especially if such a comparison would seek to denigrate Carey's approach. The principle of response to the other has to be maintained here. Nevertheless, the different circumstances in which the Alaskan missionaries found themselves, and the background from which they came, made it possible for them to respond in a particular way that tended to have a much more positive view of indigenous religiosity and to see in it a starting point for encounter.

Like Carey, though, they were disturbed by the social injustices they met with, and did their best to campaign against them, and to work—with limited success—for a more humane regime on the islands. But arguably they were just as unable to criticize the principle of colonization and to be really aware of the dangers inherent in it.[28] In addition, they were as likely to be just as paternalistic in their view of those they lived amongst as the Serampore missionaries, and sometimes even more so.

THE BEGINNINGS OF THE STORY OF SAINT INNOCENT[29]

With Baranov's replacement as manager in 1818, relationships between the church and the Russian American Company improved,[30] and a new drive for missionaries began. One of the first to respond to this was a young priest from Irkutsk, Ivan Veniaminov. He was born Ivan Popov in 1797 in a small village called Anginskoye, not far from Lake Balyal, in eastern Siberia.[31] One writer has made the intriguing suggestion that he may even have had indigenous roots himself.[32] Ivan's father was a chanter in the church, and

28. I think that this is the implication of remarks by Mousalimas, *Journals*, xxvi–xxvii.

29. As will become clear, it is rather hard to determine what particular name to give this person. Ivan (or John), Ioann (the priestly version of Ivan), Innokentii, and Innocent are all possible, and all have their advantages and disadvantages. Because I am talking about him mainly in relation to America, I will use the English form Innocent or the name Ivan for his earlier life until he became a monk and later bishop.

30. A new charter was issued in 1821, which required the Company to see to it that there were enough clergy in the region. See Garrett, *St Innocent*, 32.

31. Garrett, *St Innocent*, gives the date, according to the parish register, as 26 August; Innocent later said it was 11 September (dates in Old Style, according to the Julian calendar: the dates are 6 September and 22 September respectively in the Gregorian calendar).

32. Mousalimas, *Journals*, xxxi, though I have found no corroborating evidence for this. However, Shishigin, "Prelate Innokentii," 597, notes that Innocent himself claimed

his uncle was the parish deacon, and thus it was always likely that he would himself come to participate in the church. From a very young age, his father began to teach him to read, but unfortunately, following bouts of ill-health, his father died in 1803, and it was his uncle who continued his education.

Following repeated pleas by his mother, he was finally accepted for the seminary in Irkutsk in 1806, where he was joined by his uncle, who, on the death of his wife, became a monk in a local Irkutsk monastery.[33] His education was a mixed bag, with a secular content influenced by the Enlightenment, and of course a theological education,[34] though one still subject to what the noted Russian Orthodox thinker Fr. Georges Florovsky would call in the twentieth century "the Western captivity."[35] However, it had two definite advantages. It gave him a practical and scientific bent,[36] and at a later stage in his career, his knowledge of Latin enabled him to engage in conversation in that language with Spanish Franciscans in California. Because there were so many boys with the surname Popov, and in part because of his prowess at study, in 1814 Innocent was given the surname Veniaminov, in honor of the recently deceased bishop of Irkutsk, Veniamin. He finished the seminary in 1817, and, having got married, he was ordained deacon that same year. He had to wait until 1821 for an opening as a priest, and thus for the possibility of ordination, but he was finally ordained in May 1821.[37] He began his priestly ministry at a church in Irkutsk, where he seems to have been well-liked, and where he supplemented his meagre income from the church by making clocks and barrel organs.

At around this time, Bishop Mikhail of Irkutsk was looking for clergy to go to Alaska, and sent around a circular letter to all the clergy, asking them to go, and demanding that they should give him any reasons why they should not accede to the request. Fr. Veniaminov's first response was decidedly negative, saying he did not want to go because of the distance, and the very practical reason of what would happen to his wife if anything should

---

to know well the Yakuts and Evenks, among whom he had grown up.

33. Garrett, *St Innocent*, 19.

34. On this topic, see Garrett, *St Innocent*, 19–21; and, more generally, on education in this period, see Arzhanukhin, "Greek Patristics in Russia," and Deicha, "Patristics in Russia."

35. On this topic, see Noble et al., *Wrestling with the Mind*, 32. See also Louth, "Patristic Revival," 188–89.

36. In this he was certainly very similar to Carey.

37. See Garrett, *St Innocent*, 25. On ordination he took Ioann, the more common church form of Ivan, as his name, hence the second of the three first names by which he is identified.

befall him.[38] At this period he also became spiritual father to a veteran of the fur trade in Alaska, who tried, for a long time in vain, to win him for the mission.

The final breakthrough came when, purely by chance, Veniaminov and the fur trader happened to meet at the Bishop's house, and Fr. Ioann began to feel himself consumed by a desire to go to Alaska.[39] He thus asked the bishop to allow him to go, but the bishop had decided that he wanted his instructions to be obeyed. He found that four of the clergy had insufficient reasons not to go, so he decided to draw lots, including Ioann's name. The lot fell on another clergyman, who however declared that he would rather join the army than go to America,[40] so finally Bishop Mikhail accepted Fr. Ioann's offer, though his family was, perhaps understandably, not so positive.[41]

They set off in mid-1823, arriving finally in Sitka in October 1823. Just over a week after his arrival, he preached his first sermon (presumably on the Sermon on the Mount), in which he urged his listeners to: "love your enemies and return good for evil, not only without bearing any grudges but with love. This is the highest and most useful Christian virtue, a Christian's distinguishing trait, and so forth."[42] As a principle that would guide and govern his missionary activity this serves very well, and perhaps displays the kind of person he was. With an attitude of love towards the other (and a kind and forgiving love), it is possible to encounter the good of the other and to welcome them, and this is, I think, what marks Innocent's mission in Alaska and beyond.[43]

As with Carey in India, the first thing that the new arrival set about doing was to learn the local language,[44] Fox (or Unangan) Aleut.[45] Although he

38. Garnett, *St Innocent*, 32.

39. Garnett, *St Innocent*, 33–34.

40. Apparently he did so.

41. Garnett, *St Innocent*, 34–36. It should be noted that Veniaminov's family also suffered a fair amount, though eventually his wife seems to have adapted better than Carey's, no doubt in part because the cultural differences were not so vast.

42. Mousalimas, *Journals*, 28 October 1823, 4. This is not the text of the sermon, but his journal entry about it, hence the concluding "and so forth"!

43. On this subject, though from a slightly different perspective (more in keeping with Justin Martyr), see Ware, "Light."

44. For an excellent overview of this, see the very important MDiv thesis of Eliel, "Russian Icons." This thesis is critical of the mission's failure to engage with the indigenous artistic tradition, but for that reason, in part, its appreciation of the linguistic attention to the other is noteworthy.

45. Names of peoples and languages in this region are complex and changeable, depending on sources and place. For a fascinating examination of this by an anthropologist who is well-versed in the region, and whose work on orthodoxy there I have

never felt entirely comfortable with using it without an interpreter, he nevertheless made good progress, and would later learn several other languages too, in order to work on translation and general communication with his parishioners.[46] The idea of writing some kind of short catechetical work seems to have come to Innocent fairly early on in his time on the island of Unalaska,[47] and it was already complete by May 1826 when it was given its first reading.[48] However, it is important to note here that, just as William Carey relied heavily on his *pandits*, so Fr. Ioann relied on help from native speakers.[49] Indeed, he was always very careful to acknowledge the assistance given him by Ivan Pan'kov, a local village chief, who had been baptized by one of the original missionaries, Fr. Makarii, on his visit to the island in the mid-1790s.[50]

VIEWS OF INDIGENOUS RELIGIOUS BELIEFS AND PRACTICES

At this point, it is worth considering the view of indigenous religion that the missionaries seem to have held. Because it is so profoundly different to the views held by Carey and his companions of Hinduism and Islam, it may be said to constitute the major division between their approaches to the religiously diverse other whom they encountered and who encountered them. It is, of course, important not to make simplistic judgements here. An integral part of my argument in this book is to recognize the otherness of the other as a gift, but of course the otherness of the other cannot be reduced to totality. Hinduism and Islam are neither similar to each other, nor to Alaskan native religion, and there is less evidence for how Orthodox

---

drawn on elsewhere, see DeHass, "Ethnonyms," with reference to Innocent and other early missionaries on p. 9 and elsewhere. Generally, Aleut (*Alutiiq*) is a Russian import, whereas the original term the people used to describe themselves was *Sugpiaq* ("the real people"), but what they use today still varies somewhat.

46. On this topic, see also Nikitin, "Russian America," 232–33.

47. The parish covered the whole island and several neighboring islands too, as far away as the Pribiloff Islands. See Mousalimas, *Journals*, xiv.

48. See Mousalimas, *Journals*, xxviii.

49. This reliance was there from the beginning, with Joseph Prianisshnikov, son of a Russian trader and a local Kodiak woman, acting as the linguistic and cultural interpreter for the first missionaries: see Oleksa, "Orthodoxy," 252–53.

50. See Oleksa, *Alaskan Missionary Spirituality*, 57; also on Pan'kov, see Black, "Ivan Pan'kov."

missionaries would engage with Hinduism, especially the particular kinds of Hinduism that Carey encountered.[51]

One of the main sources for understanding how the native religion was viewed is found in a document that was published by Valaam Monastery, as part of the centennial celebrations of the beginning of the mission.[52] The peoples who lived on the various islands[53] no doubt had slightly different expressions of belief, but there was presumably some overlap too. The first thing that is noted is that they have a belief in the afterlife, and some kind of bodily resurrection. They also had a creation myth, referring to a wise man who began to blow on a straw, and as he kept blowing, in a roughly similar way to the creation story of Genesis 1, the earth and everything in it was created.[54] This, the document from Valaam says, "is all we know about the religion of the Aleuts and Kadiaks [sic]."[55] It is also suggested that there were many customs and superstitions, though, with one exception,[56] they do not appear to have been viewed negatively.

There was, where possible, an attempt to find harmony between native religion and Christianity, even if the language in which this was done was often quite patronizing. So, the document turns to some of the religious ideas of the Aleuts and Alutiiq and says that their "concepts and laws have sometimes a very distant and sometimes a very close similarity to the message preached in the Holy Scripture."[57] Perhaps the most interesting part of

---

51. There was, however, Orthodox mission among Muslims in the Tatar region. See comments in Johnstone, "Czarist Missionary Contact," esp. 67–69 on Archimandrite Makarii Glukharev (1792–1847) and Nikolai Ilminskii (1822–1891). On Ilminskii, see also Johnson, "Imperial Commission"; on Glukharev, see Kharlampovich, *Archimandrite Makarii Glukharev*. On the ongoing question of Russia and its Muslim territories, as well as an overview of the history, see Cousins, "Russian Orthodox Church." For a contemporary reflection on Orthodox relations with people of other faiths, see Garvey, *Seed of the Word*, taking—as the title suggests—the line of Justin Martyr.

52. I follow the text as printed in Oleksa, *Alaskan Missionary Spirituality*, 68–72.

53. The Sugpiaq/Alutiiq, who lived on Kodiak Island, and who are described in the translation in Oleksa as "Kadiak," are different from the Unangan Aleuts (or Unangan as they called themselves) who lived on Unalaska.

54. Oleksa, *Alaskan Missionary Spirituality*, 69.

55. Oleksa, *Alaskan Missionary Spirituality*.

56. The exception is the allegation that slaves are killed over the graves of their masters. Just as Carey opposed *sati*, the missionaries were, obviously, not in favor of this practice. It should also be noted that the word "*kalga*" used in the text is a Tlingit word, and the Tlingit seem to have been practitioners of slavery, and were known to kill slaves (but also to release them) so that they could serve their masters in the afterlife. Thus, this practice was probably not strictly speaking an Aleut or Alutiiq one, but a part of Tlingit culture.

57. Oleksa, *Alaskan Missionary Spirituality*, 69.

that sentence is that even those ideas that are "very distant" are nevertheless connected to Holy Scripture. The document shows the belief in a kind of pre-lapsarian world into which "need and enmity" came, though through natural causes, rather than because of human sinfulness.

Similarly, in returning to the creation myth outlined previously, the document is keen to find parallels, and perhaps not surprisingly, finds them in the idea of breath, though interestingly for an Orthodox reading of this story, there is no mention of the Holy Spirit.[58] This is despite the fact that the document, compiled as it was at the end of the nineteenth century, shows distinct signs of the patristic revival that had already begun to have a deep effect on Russian theology.[59] Thus, the document wants to argue that "the pure and elevated moral ideas of the Aleuts and Kadiaks and their religious views are in essence similar to the Bible stories, although they are fragmented and obscured by the continuing moral condition of these peoples," and that they "were not completely bereft of God's Grace, as a result of which there remained with them a sense of morality which prevented them from falling into ultimate sin."[60] This latter comment is both Pauline and patristic, and it is also indicative of the attitude to the indigenous people that marks the mission, one that is both appreciative of and at times rather patronizing towards the other.

Alongside the biblical and patristic references, there is a more "modernist" approach that appeals also to the findings of the then new science of anthropology.[61] This science, "directed to studying various peoples from a psychological point of view, cannot now but recognize that 'the basic traits of human psychology appear to be similar in people with different colored skins.'"[62] Whether, though, the appeal is to the Scriptures, the Fathers, or to

---

58. Oleksa, *Alaskan Missionary Spirituality*, 70.

59. There is one direct reference to Justin Martyr, and several indirect ones. On nineteenth-century theological education, I refer back to the article cited earlier, Deicha, "Patristics in Russia." In an earlier article, Mousalimas, "Patristics in Missionary Work," argued that Ivan Veniaminov was using patristic ideas in his missionary work. However, he does not return to this, and I suspect rightly realised that it was going to be very hard to argue convincingly that this was the case.

60. Oleksa, *Alaskan Missionary Spirituality*, 71.

61. Edward Tylor (1832–1917) had published his *Primitive Culture* in 1871, and had been appointed as the first lecturer (Reader) in anthropology at Oxford University in 1884, becoming professor in 1896. The first edition of James Frazer (1854–1941), *The Golden Bough*, with its fascination with myth and ritual, was published in 1890. A Russian translation of Tylor's work had already appeared by the time of the second English edition in 1873. I have not found any record of a Russian translation of Frazer prior to the early 1920s, but it may have been available to interested readers in other languages.

62. Oleksa, *Alaskan Missionary Spirituality*, 71. The source of the quotation within this sentence is not given, and may be a general rather than specific summary of the idea.

modern science, the upshot is the same. In reading the religious and moral behavior of the indigenous people of the islands, the predisposition is to see the other in a favorable light. However, a note of caution should also be sounded.

First, this can sometimes veer towards another form of reductionism, what we might call the "Noble Savage" tendency. This concept is almost as old as the first encounters between Europeans and the indigenous peoples of the Americas.[63] However, despite its frequent association with Jean-Jacques Rousseau, it probably reached its peak in the nineteenth century,[64] and it is certainly part of the response to the indigenous peoples of Alaska recorded by the Valaam document. Second, the situation in Alaska, it must be reiterated, cannot be read in the same light as that of Carey in India. This document was compiled almost thirty years after the sale of Alaska to the United States in 1867, and thus it has at least a double polemical purpose. As we will see, the treatment of indigenous Orthodox believers by the new American government was a denial of all the missionaries had sought to do, and thus the document is one of the items of supporting evidence for their mission. In addition, it reflects a situation where the people had long accepted Christianity, and it also serves as a defense of the people themselves, as having a long tradition of morally elevated behavior that was given final and definitive shape by their acceptance of Christianity.

VENIAMINOV AND IVAN SMIRENNIKOV

We can now turn to a particular instance of the encounter with the other, one of the best-known episodes in Innocent's missionary life. In April 1828 Fr. Ioann was on a pastoral visit to some of the outlying islands to the east of Unalaska.[65] When he arrived, he found that he was expected because his

---

The quotation given here continues "True science only confirms the Holy Scriptures."

63. See, for example, Cro, *Noble Savage*. He argues that the first to give a picture of indigenous peoples free from the burdens of property, etc., was Lombard humanist Peter Martyr (c. 1457–1526) in his book *De Orbe Novo* (first published in 1504). This book, Cro maintains, influenced the French essayist Michel de Montaigne (1533–1592), one of the first to use the phrase "*bon sauvage.*" On the translation of this idea into English, and the differences between "*sauvage*" and "savage," see Franks, "In Search."

64. On the development of the concept (including a firm rebuttal of any direct association with Rousseau), see Ellingson, *Myth*. For a provocative but interesting essay arguing that much post-development (and, I would argue, post-colonial) discourse has an underlying reliance on something like a "noble savage" myth, see Kiely, "Last Refuge."

65. On this trip, see Mousalimas, *Journals*, 12–24 April 1828, 75–78. Veniaminov says that Akun was 120 *versts* (approximately 125 kilometres) distant from Unalaska.

visit had been foretold by a local man, Ivan Smirennikov.[66] According to Innocent, Smirennikov was at this time around sixty years old, and lived some distance from the main settlement on the island of Akun.[67] Garrett suggests that the old man was upset with the priest for not engaging in conversation with him to find out if he was indeed a *shaman*, something that Smirennikov was accused of but anxious to deny, either for pragmatic or for religious reasons.[68] Eventually, they arranged a meeting and the priest and the old man began their conversation.

There were already indications of his special powers, which Fr. Ioann only recounts, having reminded his bishop that "I am very far from believing various superstitions and still less inclined to invent false miracles."[69] But he had heard stories of an apparently miraculous healing, of how Smirennikov had told the villagers where to go to find a fresh whale carcass in a time of great hunger, and how he had known that the priest's voyage, initially planned for early autumn, would be postponed till the following spring.[70] Intrigued by these stories, Veniaminov wanted to find out more. In itself this is not insignificant, since it shows that his first reaction was not to assume that Smirennikov was possessed by some kind of dubious spirit.

Smirrenikov had been baptised by Hieromonk Makarii, presumably in the course of his visit to these islands in 1795 and 1796. Since then, as we have seen, there had been very little clerical contact with the Unalaska parish as it came to be established, and probably none at all with the people on Akun Island.[71] According to the report prepared for the Synod

> Soon after he was baptized by Hieromonk Makary, there appeared to him, unseen by anyone else, first one spirit, and then a second, in human form, white-faced and clothed in white garments that, according to his description, looked like deacon's

---

66. Thus Garrett, *St Innocent*, 77, based on a report written to the Holy Synod, which can be found in "Angels of Akun." Veniaminov also wrote a letter to his bishop in June 1828, which was printed in Oleksa, *Alaskan Missionary Spirituality*, 132–35. The letter is somewhat confusingly dated by Oleksa as November 1829, presumably when it was deposited in the Episcopal archives in Tobolsk.

67. The island no longer has a permanent population, and presumably did not have a large one even then—he refers to the chrismation of 46 people, which was probably the majority of those present at the time.

68. See Garrett, *St Innocent*, 78, and "Angels of Akun," 22.

69. Oleksa, *Alaskan Missionary Spirituality*, 132.

70. Mousalimas, "Patristics in Missionary Work," 329, points out that these in fact correspond to the three main tasks of the southern Alaskan shaman as healer, hunting facilitator, and seer.

71. The list given in Mousalimas, *Journals*, xviii, does not indicate anyone who is likely to have travelled to Akun, or indeed to any of the other islands of Unalaska itself.

vestments trimmed with rose-colored bands. They told him that God had sent them to instruct, teach, and protect him. For thirty years, they had appeared to him almost daily in the daytime or late afternoon, but never at night. They instructed him in Christian teaching and in the mysteries of the Faith; also, they rendered him help in illnesses, and at his request, others (though rarely).[72]

Thus, in the intervening period the spirits had guided Ivan Smirennikov and led him to an obvious understanding of Christian faith, despite the absence of any formal teaching. Smirennikov, who did not want to be considered a shaman, had asked them—obviously unsuccessfully—to leave him in peace.[73]

Fr. Ioann was both struck and perplexed by the knowledge that Smirennikov (who was also illiterate) had acquired, since even Ivan Pan'kov was somewhat afraid of him, and tried to dissuade others from approaching him with requests.[74] The conversation, however, deeply reassured Veniaminov, since, although "[d]emons may assume the image of Angels of Light . . . [this is] never for the purpose of instruction, teaching, and salvation of human beings."[75] The priest also turned down the possibility of seeing the spirits himself,[76] since he first wanted to gain his archbishop's[77] permission. By the time this had been received and he next visited Akun, Smirennikov had already died, so the opportunity never arose.

What can be taken from this encounter? It would be wrong to assume that Innocent was open to shamanism in general,[78] and anyway we may have to take Smirennikov's word that he was not—or did not consider himself

---

72. The translation is as given in "Angels of Akun," 23 and 25 (p. 24 is a full page photograph).

73. Oleksa, *Alaskan Missionary Spirituality*, 133.

74. Oleksa, *Alaskan Missionary Spirituality*, 134.

75. Oleksa, *Alaskan Missionary Spirituality*. Note the similarity to the rules of discernment in the Ignatian *Spiritual Exercises*.

76. There is something rather charming about the spirits' response when Smirennikov asked if Fr. Ioann could speak to them. Apparently they replied, "What does he want? Does he consider us demons? If he insists, he can see and converse with us" (Oleksa, *Alaskan Missionary Spirituality*, 134).

77. Irkutsk had been raised to an archdiocese in 1826.

78. Mousalimas, "Patristics in Missionary Work," 330–31, points out that he reacted differently to others whom he suspected of being shamans elsewhere.

to be—a shaman.[79] But, whatever description we give Smirennikov,[80] it is clear that in the first place Innocent was prepared to meet him as he was, and to put aside his natural curiosity for the sake of both obedience and also, perhaps, respect. He can recognize the goodness in the other that coincides with Christian teaching, and yet is clearly not a simple by-product of a pious imagination. Makarii's strategy had been to baptize and move on, not spending any time instructing the people in their new faith, so its roots would have, in theory, been fairly weak.[81] But Innocent met in Ivan Smirennikov someone who he saw was in touch with the transcendent in a special way, and he was ready to accept that, even if he could not altogether understand how.

What is perhaps most impressive in this encounter is that Innocent allowed his own flaws to show, whether by design or not. He was and even to some extent remained a little suspicious of visions and spirits, mainly because of his own education and character rather than on purely religious grounds. That also means that he managed to avoid the approach of the kind sometimes present in accounts of Western encounters with Eastern religions, where the local authority is elevated to an almost semi-divine status. In addition, he did not seek to generalize out of this encounter, which thus allows the other to be other. It is not that all who claim powers of healing and clairvoyance are to be admired and accepted, but each case, or better each person, is encountered in their fullness.

SITKA AND BEYOND

After spending ten years on Unalaska, in 1834 Veniaminov moved to become parish priest at Sitka, on what is now Baranof Island, though at the time the island too was known as Sitka. Sitka had been the headquarters of the Russian American Company since 1808,[82] and with 1300 inhabitants was one of the largest conglomerations in the region.[83] Here he also encountered another indigenous people, the Tlingit, who lived in a state

79. Moreover, on the day of his encounter with Smirennikov, Fr. Ioann noted, "I conversed with one of the local elders, Ivan Smirennikov, who is considered a shaman in these parts. I found the facts quite to the contrary" (Mousalimas, *Journals*, April 23, 1828, 78).

80. He is now on the path to canonization in the Orthodox Church of America. See "Blessed John Smirennikov."

81. See Mousalimas, "Patristics in Missionary Work," 329–30, and "Angels of Akun," 21–22.

82. See Grinëv, "First Russian Settlers," 460.

83. Garrett, *St Innocent*, 105.

Bishop Innocent Veniaminov and Russian Orthodox Mission in Alaska 161

of some animosity with the Russians.[84] For this reason, and because the Tlingit refused to be cowed by the Russians, the colonizers did not have a very favorable opinion of the local people.[85] Moreover, an absence of qualified and competent interpreters made it difficult to establish contact.[86] The outbreak of a virulent smallpox epidemic in 1836 allowed for the first real encounter with the local Tlingit. The attempts by the local shamans to cure the sickness were unsuccessful, whilst the vaccines administered by the Russians were seen to offer sound protection against the sickness.[87] As many of the shamans were also older and thus even more susceptible to the disease, most of them died, and this combined with their obvious ineffectiveness at combating the smallpox gave a point of entry for Veniaminov.[88]

From the very beginning, he was interested in understanding and learning from the Tlingit beliefs and customs. The way in which he seems to have transcribed the name of the creator in the Tlingit creation stories—Raven, or *Yeil* in Tlingit—led him to wonder if there were connections to the Hebrew "El."[89] However, Veniaminov's further comment should be noted: "their traditions are but a mixture of lies and fabrications, even so . . . in their mythology can be seen traces of true history, as for example in their tradition of the flood."[90]

This somewhat negative assessment bears out a point made by an American scholar, Michael McNally, who argues that, even in the more positive examples of the Russian Orthodox mission that I am considering here, "most missionaries agreed that Christianity was an all-embracing system of belief, the integrity of which relied on its exclusive claims to truth."[91] In

---

84. The settlement at Sitka had been destroyed in 1802, and retaken in 1804, and the Tlingit culture of resistance was more advanced than among the Alutiiq-Sugpiaq. See Grinëv, "First Russian Settlers," 459; for interesting competing accounts of the first contact between Tlingit and Russians, see Russell, "Cultures in Collision," 232–33.

85. Garrett, *St Innocent*, 105.

86. See Kan, "Russian Orthodox Brotherhoods," 198.

87. See Garrett, *St Innocent*, 106–7; Kan, "Russian Orthodox Brotherhoods," 198; and Kan, "Shamanism and Christianity," 366.

88. Garrett, *St Innocent*, 107.

89. Garrett, *St Innocent*, 109. Fr. Ioann—at least as reported by Garrett—transcribed this word as "El," also. If a soft Russian "e" is used, this would give something like "*yeil.*" For an interesting comparison (especially because of its rather patronizing nature), see an account of the Jesuit missions to Alaska, written around 1925 by Pieta, *Land of the Midnight Sun*, esp. 4–5 on the Tlingit (spelt here Thinklet).

90. Garrett, *St Innocent*, 109n.

91. McNally, "Practice," 846. I will return later to McNally's argument that it is in the encounter of practices that the most interesting adoption and adaptation of Christianity to native beliefs is to be found.

other words, for all his openness to the other, Innocent still read the native beliefs and stories as more or less close to the Christian story as he understood it, and thus shared to some extent Carey's attitude of superiority to the native religions. The obvious danger is that a sense of religious superiority leads to a sense of human superiority, and though I think it is fair to say that both men were aware of the danger, it is also true that they did not always manage to avoid succumbing to the temptation.

But, at the same time, Fr. Ioann was patient, and even with the opportunity offered by the illness, and the subsequent greater willingness of the Tlingit to listen, he did not seek to enforce faith on them. At one point he noted: "The Tlingit are not today what they were a year ago, and even if they will not soon become Christian, they are at least at the point of listening—or at the *very* least of *beginning* to listen—to the Word of Salvation."[92] And, indeed, this seems to have been the case for most of his time in Sitka, and later. Sergei Kan, an anthropologist who has worked extensively with the Tlingit, points out that, even by the time of the sale of Alaska in 1867,[93] less than half of the Tlingit population of Sitka was even baptized, let alone greatly invested in their Orthodox faith.[94]

In November 1838 Fr. Ioann left Sitka to return to Russia, travelling halfway round the world by ship to Saint Petersburg to make a presentation to the Holy Synod.[95] Whilst he was in Saint Petersburg, he received news of the death of his wife, Katerina, who had returned with their children to Irkutsk. After some indecision, to do with his wish to look after his children and his commitment to the missionary lifestyle that he feared was incommensurate with monasticism, he was finally tonsured as a monk by Metropolitan Philaret (Drozdov) of Moscow (1782–1867)[96] in November 1840.[97] He took the name Innocent (Innokentii in Russian) in honor of the first bishop of Irkutsk.[98] A few days later, he had a meeting with the Tsar, Nicho-

92. Garrett, *St Innocent*, 109. Italics in original.

93. On Tlingit reactions to this, see Russell, "Cultures in Collision," 234–38.

94. Kan, "Shamanism and Christianity," 366, and Kan, "Russian Orthodox Brotherhoods," 198.

95. The Patriarchate was suppressed by Tsar Peter the Great in 1721 (he had left the office unfilled since the death of Patriarch Adrian in 1700, appointing only a *locum tenens*) and replaced with a body called the Holy Synod, which effectively governed the church, and was closely linked to the state. See Cracraft, *Church Reform*, and Pospielovsky, *Orthodox Church*, 105–12.

96. See Tsurikov, *Philaret*.

97. See Garrett, *St Innocent*, 135–36.

98. For a brief comment on Saint Innocent of Irkutsk (c. 1680–1731), see Ganaba, "Response," 326. Originally destined to be a missionary in China, Innocent became known as the Apostle of Siberia. On the Orthodox Church in China, see Yaokum and

las 1,[99] who decided to appoint him to a newly established see, as Bishop of Kamchatka, the Kuril, and Aleutian Islands.[100]

On 25 September 1841 (forty-seven years almost to the day since the arrival of the first Valaam missionaries), the new Bishop landed at Sitka, which would be his base for the next twelve years.[101] In 1850 he was made archbishop, and the Yakut region in eastern Russia was added to his responsibilities. In 1853 he finally left Alaska to take up residence in Yakutsk. There he would learn further languages, and become a member of the Holy Synod. Following the death of his friend Metropolitan Philaret, he was appointed Metropolitan of Moscow in 1867, a position he held until his own death on Holy (or Great) Saturday, 1879. In all this time, he remained at heart a missionary, seen, among other things, by his establishment of a fund to support mission during his time as Metropolitan in Moscow.[102]

MISSIONARY INSTRUCTIONS

In looking at Ignatius, we saw how he sought to prepare his fellow-Jesuits for mission, and we saw with Carey how he, too, wrote to his son on the task of being a missionary. In 1853 Innocent also wrote a set of instructions to a new missionary who was about to take up duties in Alaska, the Hieromonk Theophan.[103] As with Carey, these instructions serve as a distillation of his

---

Chen, "Beyond the Great Wall," and Pozdnyaev, "Pearl of Great Price."

99. The relationship between the church and Nicholas I was not altogether straightforward. See, for example, Nichols, "Metropolitan Filaret."

100. See Garrett, *St Innocent*, 137–38

101. For more on Innocent's work as bishop, see Nordlander, "Innokentii Veniaminov."

102. I have not looked here at another very important initiative that Innocent started whilst in Alaska, namely the establishment of a seminary (the All-Colonial School) for training indigenous clergy. Though in Alaska, in its initial foundation, it was fairly short-lived, it helped to maintain the Orthodox faith alive even after the sale of Alaska to the United States. See Oleksa, *Orthodox Alaska*, 134. A similar desire for educating native clergy was present among at least some of the early Jesuits (though not all). Writing in 1919, the then-Jesuit General Fr. Wlodomir Ledochowski had this to say: "That a native clergy sufficiently numerous, well selected and solidly established contributes profoundly to the spread of the Gospel: that it is even indispensable if the Christian communities are to receive their definitive form and a lasting prosperity: that the effects and cooperation of all should be directed to this end—all this is something which cannot be doubted" (Ledochowski, *Choice and Formation*, 2).

103. The instructions are printed in Oleksa, *Alaskan Missionary Spirituality*, 238–51, to which I refer here. On these instructions, see also Senyk, "Search for Holiness," 268–69. Senyk is somewhat inaccurate when she describes these instructions as having been written shortly after Innocent became a bishop—she is referring to his translation

own reflection on his missionary career, and offer an invaluable insight into what he thought was most important for the missionary. In reading this material, two slightly different interpretations can be made, which display a distinction to which I shall return in the conclusion. The *Instructions* can be read as suggesting a form of inculturation *avant la lettre*, and in itself that would be both commendable and perhaps even surprising. But I think that more than simply accommodating to the local customs and rites,[104] there is a sense in which these can be seen as opening up new possibilities that had not been thought of before, so that it becomes possible for Innocent to distinguish the essential from the inessential.[105] This in turn leads to a new way of being Christian that may outwardly appear very similar, but in fact, in subtle but increasingly important ways, is different.

Mission as Enlightenment

The instruction begins with a reminder of what, arguably, is one of the key Orthodox contributions to mission, the idea of the missionary as "enlightener."[106] This term is applied in Orthodox hagiography to those who are responsible for bringing the gospel to a particular region or territory,[107] and indeed is one of the honorifics given to Saint Innocent. But what is being referred to is made clear in the opening words of Archbishop Innocent's instructions:

> To leave one's native country and seek places remote, wild, devoid of many of the comforts of life, for the sake of turning to the path of truth men who are still wandering in the darkness

---

to Yakutsk. However, in general, this is a very rich article, with helpful references to Russian sources.

104. Nikitin, "Russian America," 231, points to this attention to the life and customs of the other as a strong characteristic of Innocent's missionary work.

105. It is hard to find a good language for this, since I do not want to imply, in a Harnackian way, that there is some essence (*Wesen des Christentums*) that can be isolated out. All Christian living is culturally rooted (perhaps most of all when it seeks to be counter-cultural), just as all life is, and it seems a waste of time to worry about that. Perhaps what I am arguing is more to do with what Vatican II called "the hierarchy of truths."

106. In Greek, *phōtistes*, and in Slavonic, *prosvetitel*. I have dealt with this topic at greater length in Noble, "Mission as Encounter." Note the title of a short essay on Innocent by a Russian scholar, Oleg Dmitrievich Yakimov, "Enlightener." At one point in this essay, Yakimov writes, "we should speak not only about the influence of a parish priest at Unalaska on the American Natives, but also about a mutual influence" (626–27). Nikitin, "Russian America," 240, also refers to Innocent as an enlightener.

107. On this subject in relation to Innocent, see also Ware, "Light."

of ignorance, and of illuming with the light of the Gospel them that have not yet beheld this saving light—this is an act truly holy and apostolic. Blessed be he whom the Lord selects and appoints to such a ministry. But doubly blessed he who labors with undivided zeal, sincerity, and love in the work of conversion and enlightenment, enduring the hardships and suffering which he encounters in the course of his ministry, for 'his reward is great in heaven'.[108]

At one level, this may sound rather negative, at least in terms of what I am trying to argue for in this book. The missionary here is the one who goes to the "wild" places,[109] devoid of home comforts, to help those who live in darkness to see the light (the echo of Isaiah 9:1–2, as quoted in Matt 4:15–16 is certainly intentional). It must be admitted that this is a part of what is going on here, and that there is a clear sense that the missionary is the one who knows, and the addressee of mission is the one who is in ignorance.

However, as we read through the document, another interpretation is possible, one that at least recognizes the missionary's own dependence. For, ultimately, it is the light of the gospel that enlightens, not the missionary. Innocent does not say that the missionary is the enlightener, but the one who works for enlightenment. This is a small but crucial distinction. The missionary and the one whom mission addresses are both involved in this work, one bearing the light, the other seeing it and coming to it. Thus the symbiotic relationship between the two is enhanced and a form of synergy established. The work of mission and enlightenment is never one-sided, but always part of a triangular partnership, in which the missionary and her or his addressee are accompanied and guided by the Holy Spirit.

That this may be a possible reading of what Innocent understands is borne out by the fact that he goes on to remind Theophan of the dangers, recorded in Matthew 23:15, of making life even worse for the converts (the proselytes).[110] Moreover, he begins the list of fifty-two specific instructions by saying, in words that Ignatius and Carey would have welcomed, that the "first and most efficient preparation is prayer" (1).[111] In this sense, any work of mission is ultimately gift. And the second instruction continues in the same vein, with its stress that "the conversion of a sinner or a heathen to the

---

108. Oleksa, *Alaskan Missionary Spirituality*, 238.

109. Among the "sauvages," in the terms described so well in the article mentioned previously: Franks, "In Search."

110. Oleksa, *Alaskan Missionary Spirituality*, 238.

111. Oleksa, *Alaskan Missionary Spirituality*, 239. Numbers in parenthesis in the body of the text—as here, "(1)"—will refer to the number of the instructions as given in Oleksa, and footnotes will reference the page in his book.

right path comes not from us or from our skill, but directly and solely from God" (2).[112] The work is God's work (4),[113] and thus the missionary's role is greatly relativized. Although Innocent does not say as much himself, this makes it easier for the missionary to appreciate and learn from the other, since any true encounter will be directed by God, and what is of God can be discerned in it.

Perhaps the single most important element for Innocent is one that echoes the words of his first sermon, preached on his arrival in Alaska almost thirty years previously.[114] The instruction reads: "Remember always that if the preacher has not within himself love to his work and to them to whom he is preaching, the very best and most eloquent expounding of the doctrine may remain absolutely without effect, for love alone creates—therefore strive to cultivate within yourself the spirit of holy love."[115] If there is one characteristic that marks Innocent, it is this insistence on the centrality of love, something that is at times evident in his journals, too.[116] Mission can only happen in the context of the creative power of love. In this, as in other things, there is a deep agreement between Ignatius and Innocent. This context of love is expressed in practical ways, such as beginning a visit with a time of teaching rather than launching straight into liturgy (6), and being ready either to let the other come to where the missionary is, or for the missionary to go to where they are, depending on what is more appropriate (7 and 8).[117] And special attention should be given to work with the interpreter, who needs to understand what is being translated (9).[118]

At one level, this is of course practical and apparently commonsensical advice, and it follows earlier Orthodox advice against too rapid baptism.[119] But it is also a way of respecting the other, and of loving the other. It does not impose, it makes the missionary open to the needs and possibilities of

---

112 Oleksa, *Alaskan Missionary Spirituality*, 239.

113. Oleksa, *Alaskan Missionary Spirituality*.

114. See earlier discussion on this subject, as well as the reference to the journal entry in footnote 42.

115. Oleksa, *Alaskan Missionary Spirituality*, 240. The translation in Oleksa, for some bizarre reason, uses archaic forms, including "thou" and other second person singular forms, and so I have slightly altered it to more modern and readable English.

116. As one example, see the entry for 30 May 1832 in Mousalimas, *Journals*, 180–81.

117. Oleksa, *Alaskan Missionary Spirituality*, 240.

118. Oleksa, *Alaskan Missionary Spirituality*.

119. See the *Ukaz* (instruction from the bishop or Holy Synod) of 1777 that Innocent quotes in this instruction to Theophan in Oleksa, *Alaskan Missionary Spirituality*, 239.

Part 2: The Missionary

It is only when the groundwork has been done—a kind of natural theology—that the preaching of the gospel should begin. Here there is, perhaps surprisingly, a strong overlap with Carey, since, in slightly different terms, what Innocent enjoins is the need to convict people of their sins (12 d)[126] so that they will feel the need for repentance and contrition. The ultimate aim of this preaching, which should not contain too many words, is to instill in the hearts of the listeners "the entire doctrine of Christ . . . *that we repent, believe in Him, and have towards Him and all men a feeling of pure, disinterested love*" (13).[127]

At this point, it is necessary to reiterate that, for all the attentiveness to the other, and for all that the other is central to a proper and fuller understanding of the gospel, in the end, the missionary is also beholden to God and to the proclamation, in deed and word, of the good news. Thus, I would say that Innocent is right to stress the need for the call to *metanoia*, even if the idea of convicting people of their sinfulness seems to me to be only part (though an important part) of that conversion.[128] In defense of Innocent, it should also be stressed that he does not think that people should be allowed to become Christians purely out of fear—it is only after telling them about the joy and hope that people have found in Christ and the promise of both present and future salvation that they should be asked if they would like to join the body of believers (12 f).[129]

Conditions for Baptism

Four conditions are laid on those who wish to be baptized: the renunciation of former beliefs, at least those that are contrary to Christianity, and an agreement to abide by all that is demanded by the new Christian faith that the person wants to adopt, and finally the confession of sins (13 a).[130] As already noted in discussing Innocent's meeting with Ivan Smirennikov, he was generally opposed to shamanism,[131] probably recognizing it as the

---

126. Oleksa, *Alaskan Missionary Spirituality*, 242.

127. Oleksa, *Alaskan Missionary Spirituality*, 243; italics in original.

128. As an image of this, consider the character Christian in John Bunyan's *The Pilgrim's Progress*. Christian is heading in the right direction, but is often tempted to go off the right track. The missionary's task could then be seen as going to people who are also heading in the right direction, but have not yet found that there is a more secure path for them to follow—I refer back to the discussion of Bevans and Schroeder in chapter 2, and their image of the trail-guide.

129. Oleksa, *Alaskan Missionary Spirituality*, 243.

130. Oleksa, *Alaskan Missionary Spirituality*.

131. On Tlingit shamanism, see Kan, "Shamanism and Christianity," 365, and more

most powerful expression of the religious other in the islands. Thus, he was insistent on the complete rejection of former beliefs,[132] but, and this is worth stressing, only in so far as they were inconsistent with Christianity. So any custom (and presumably anything that the shamans did) that was not contrary to Christianity is permitted.[133] Obviously in practice this will allow for a certain amount of creative tension, in which the elasticity of Christian and native beliefs is tested to the full, thus allowing both to expand their horizons and their recognition of the other.

In terms of how to live the Christian life, it is interesting to note that Innocent suggests that it is not necessary initially to go into too much detail—the one example he gives (again reminiscent of his first sermon in Alaska) is that "Jesus Christ forgave his enemies, and we should do likewise" (14 c).[134] Although Innocent refers in (16) to the neophytes as infants in the faith, it is also clear from his journal entries and other writings that he recognized that there was already a strong moral sense present, and that the people could be more or less trusted to live a good and honest life, even without detailed instructions. And it is here that, for the first time, the Holy Spirit is mentioned, as the one who gives assistance and who comes in response to prayer (15).[135]

Some Practical Considerations

After discoursing on the nature of the kergymatic proclamation, Innocent turns to somewhat more practical matters. This is arguably the most striking part, with constant attention to the needs and possibilities of the indigenous peoples, and a willingness to, if not break, at least bend the rules, "partly in consideration of local conditions, partly in expectation of their growing firmer in the faith and the new mode of life" (17).[136] Here I address these criteria briefly, but they would repay closer study.[137]

---

generally on how modern Tlingit have sought to reconcile their shamanic past with their more Orthodox Christian present.

132. I refer back to McNally, "Practice."

133. Or, at least, as he goes on to say in (21), Oleksa, *Alaskan Missionary Spirituality*, 246, "tolerated." For an overall judgement on this, see also Oleksa, "Orthodoxy," 257–58, noting how the mission "'sanctified' and 'endorsed' the people's personality."

134. Oleksa, *Alaskan Missionary Spirituality*, 244.

135. Oleksa, *Alaskan Missionary Spirituality*.

136. Oleksa, *Alaskan Missionary Spirituality*, 245.

137. As far as I am aware, there is no single study devoted to these instructions, though they are of course mentioned in much of the literature quoted in the preceding footnotes, and I have drawn attention to some of these aspects as well in my work (see

He begins with some remarks on fasting, where he insists that the nature of the land means that people cannot be expected to adopt a vegan diet during the times of fasting, and that rather they should be called on to reflect on the amount and the time when they eat (18).[138] He also says that, apart from the liturgy, the kind of requirements for church attendance expected in towns in Russia should not be required here—partly no doubt because people had to be out hunting, and also because, despite the occasional use of native languages in the liturgy, most of it was in Slavonic, which they would not understand anyway (19).[139] Even when it comes to marriage, there is to be no blind application of rules, even if "departures from the strictness of existing rules can be permitted only for the most cogent of reasons" (20).[140] But even this suggests that there may indeed be cogent reasons, and Innocent goes on to add that it would not be advisable to over-extend the degrees of consanguinity, given the smallness of the populations in some parts.

The advice to Theophan continues in the same tenor with regard to participation in liturgy, where everyone is permitted to attend the whole of the Divine Liturgy because, although "it is against church rules to allow their [i.e., the non-baptized] presence at the Liturgy of the Faithful, [s]till as the envoys of Saint Vladimir in Constantinople were permitted, though they were heathens, to remain during the entire Liturgy, to the unspeakable benefit of all Russia—you may also grant the same favor, in the hope that the sacred act may have a salutary effect on hearts as yet unenlightened" (22).[141] The equation of the indigenous population with the envoys of Rus may be unintentional, but it may also indicate that Innocent did indeed view the peoples he worked amongst as, in principle, equal to those of his home nation, especially in the period leading up to its conversion. At least this shows that for him church rules are never an absolute, and exist for the service of mission.

The rest of the instructions can be placed in four broad categories, to do with marriage, economics, and relationship to, respectively, the state authorities, and the local people. In terms of marriage, apart from the permission of closer ties than was the case elsewhere, it is also stressed that

---

Noble, "Pathway," and Noble, "Rights of Indigenous Peoples").

138. Oleksa, *Alaskan Missionary Spirituality*, 245.

139. Oleksa, *Alaskan Missionary Spirituality*.

140. Oleksa, *Alaskan Missionary Spirituality*.

141. Oleksa, *Alaskan Missionary Spirituality*, 246. The reference is to the legend of the conversion of Vladimir in 988, which recounts how he sent envoys to different places, and it was the splendor of the liturgy at Hagia Sophia in Constantinople that decided him on accepting Orthodoxy. See Noble et al., *Ways of Orthodoxy*, 37–41, for a brief overview of this legend and what most likely happened.

marriages that had been entered into should be acknowledged and not seen as a hindrance to baptism (23).[142] Where polygamy is encountered—which Innocent says is mainly among the rich and powerful—although it is the duty of the missionary to incline them to monogamy, this should be done carefully "so as not to anger or embitter them" (38).[143]

On several occasions, attention is given to economic matters. First, Innocent is very clear that the newly baptized, or those interested in baptism, should be given no presents at all, lest they associate the rite with material benefit in any form (24).[144] This is almost the polar opposite of the so-called "rice Christians," where material benefits were an inducement to conversion. And in a later paragraph (29) he reinforces this, by instructing Theophan not to attempt to increase the number of baptisms by inducements such as bribes, or promises (for example, of tax exemption).[145] Moreover, just as no gifts should be given, none shall be required: "you shall not on any account whatsoever demand contributions or donations for the church or any good work" (39).[146] On the other hand, no offer of a gift is to be turned down, though it is necessary to explain what use it will be put to and to make sure that the giver does not think they can buy salvation. Finally, in this regard, Innocent instructs the missionary always to try to visit the villages and settlements at times when people are not engaged in hunting or fishing expeditions, so that they will not lose time or money, for themselves or the Russian American Company (42).[147]

In relation to the latter organization, and to the authorities in general, the missionary should never claim to represent them (31), nor however should he seek to belittle the authorities. However, if there are examples of abuse, he should report them to the bishop or other senior official with all the details, so that action can be taken (46).[148] This latter bears testimony to the memories of Baranov still no doubt present among the native peoples, and is something that the mission always took very seriously.[149]

Perhaps the greatest amount of time is spent on detailing the nature of the relationship to the people. Here, it is interesting, in the light of our

---

142. Oleksa, *Alaskan Missionary Spirituality*, 246.
143. Oleksa, *Alaskan Missionary Spirituality*, 248.
144. Oleksa, *Alaskan Missionary Spirituality*, 246.
145. Oleksa, *Alaskan Missionary Spirituality*, 247.
146. Oleksa, *Alaskan Missionary Spirituality*, 248.
147. Oleksa, *Alaskan Missionary Spirituality*.
148. Oleksa, *Alaskan Missionary Spirituality*, 249.
149. See Noble, "Rights of Indigenous Peoples," including the continuation of this stream of the mission after the sale to the United States.

earlier discussion on the *gēr*, that Innocent suggests that the missionary should go among the people "in the guise of a poor wanderer, a sincere well-wisher to his fellow-men, who has come for the single purpose of showing them the means to attain prosperity and, as far as possible, guiding them in their quest" (31).[150] The missionary is the stranger, the one who comes from outside, who must treat the other always with respect and kindness and attention (32–36, 45), even those who do not wish to accept baptism (37).[151]

What stands out throughout nearly all the Instruction is Innocent's attention to the other. No doubt some of this can be dismissed (or welcomed) as purely pragmatic or strategic, but the whole tone of his writings here and elsewhere suggests that this is not the case for most of what he writes. However patronizing the language can be, the Russian Orthodox Church never had the kind of debates held at Valladolid between Sepúlveda and Las Casas in the mid-sixteenth century over the "humanity" of the inhabitants of the new world.[152] Thus, Innocent never doubts the essential humanity of his hearers, and is therefore always disposed to find the presence of God amongst them. To what degree this is a conscious drawing on patristic sources[153] and to what degree it comes more out of who Innocent was, is, at this distance, hard to say, but he was someone who for the most part tried to find the best in the other, and to do mission based on the premise that the other already had some knowledge of God.

SUMMARY

As with Carey and his colleagues at Serampore, it would be possible and instructive to prolong the investigation of Bishop Innocent and the Alaskan mission, both in the subsequent remaining years of Russian rule and after the sale to the United States, when the influx of various forms of Protestant mission threatened to undo much of what the Orthodox mission had stood for, with an insistence on everyone speaking English and a very particular view of what constituted belonging. Innocent's own further missions

---

150. Oleksa, *Alaskan Missionary Spirituality*, 247. I have not had access to the Russian text of Innocent's *Instructions*, but the poor wanderer (*strannik*) is the figure found also in *The Way of the Pilgrim*, the popular nineteenth-century work that probably set out to defend and promote the rediscovered hesychast tradition. See Noble, "Writ Good Guide."

151. See Oleksa, *Alaskan Missionary Spirituality*, 247–49.

152. See, for example, Brunstetter, "Sepulveda, Las Casas," which offers an interesting look at the complexity of the issue. On Las Casas, see Gutiérrez, *Las Casas*.

153. Apart from Justin Martyr, Oleksa, *Orthodox Alaska*, 52–61, also mentions Origen, Saint Gregory of Nyssa, and Saint Maximus the Confessor.

in Eastern Siberia, especially in Yakutia,[154] could also be considered, and the important foundations he left for the establishment of the Orthodox Church on more secure grounds in the rest of the United States, not least through the financial help provided through the mission society that he formed when he became Metropolitan of Moscow.

However, I hope that this relatively short overview of the life of Saint Innocent and his work as part of the early Russian Orthodox mission to Alaska has served to give some picture of how these "poor wanderers" aimed at bringing the gospel to the indigenous peoples. The setting was very different to that experienced by Carey in India, or indeed Ignatius in early Renaissance Europe.[155] A substantial if inchoate missionary activity had already taken place, there was a greater receptivity, and the Russian American Company had at least to pretend to tolerate and even support the church. There was no existing literary culture at all, and thus no competing written material. And the climate, of course, posed its own particular challenges.

Thus, while it is clearly true that Innocent appears to have had a different attitude towards those he met than Carey, the two were not in identical—or even necessarily comparable—conditions, so to attempt to compare them would be both unwise and unjust. Having said that, it is still, of course, possible to offer a critical assessment of Innocent and his mission. Innocent comes across as someone who had a genuine interest in and attentiveness to the people among whom he worked. At times, admittedly, he can be rather condescending and look down on them, but at the same time, he responds to them also with genuine love and affection. I would imagine that when your life is in people's hands as they paddle you across dangerous seas, it is not hard to come to appreciate them and to trust them at a very deep level, and this is certainly reflected in his missionary approach. To what extent he was able to let the other change his own views of things is open to question, but from the evidence I have presented here, I would argue that to some extent it did. He was able to see the world—and the role of God in it—in a different way because he was taught to do so by the other around him.

---

154. See Shishigin, "Prelate Innokentii."

155. Hempton, *Long Eighteenth Century*, 188, argues that Innocent displayed an "almost Jesuitical" approach. I think that he is using the word "Jesuitical" neutrally, though it often has a pejorative ring. In the neutral sense, I would agree.

Conclusion

In this book, I have set out to examine what mission looks like when its other is taken into consideration as subject and not just as object. I have sought to show that mission is a three-way task, involving the missionary, the addressee of mission, and God. In practice, missiological writing has focused more on the first of these, the missionary, with some attention given to the role of God, certainly in theologies of mission.[1] There has been very little attention given to the third of these partners, a gap I have tried to remedy. In this conclusion, I will draw together the diverse strands of the book and suggest a few ways forward, aiming at including the other in the task of mission without destroying either the other's alterity or the possibility of mission.

I began the book by looking at one way in which the other is presented in the Bible, namely as "stranger" or "resident alien"—*gēr* in Hebrew, most commonly translated as *prosēlutos* in the Septuagint. The *gēr*, we saw, evokes two contrasting responses, with a third implicit in the very existence of the legislation. On the one hand, she or he is a challenge, indubitably present, and yet exterior to Israel, and demanding some form of—admittedly limited—incorporation. They thus posed a question to Israel: where do these people stand in relation to us? But at the same time, the legislators sought to use the *gēr* as a kind of teaching tool for Israel, reminding the people of their own experiences in Egypt, and thus, and more importantly, of the way in which the Lord had treated them, setting this forth as the paradigm for how the other should be encountered. Implicitly, however, both this way of dealing with the *gēr* and the very existence of legislation suggest that the

---

1. The attention to God is perhaps less than one might expect. I refer again to Flett, *Witness of God*, which spells out the practical dangers of some prevalent ways of using the *missio Dei* trope in modern missiological writing and thought. It is probably the case that the majority of works on mission concentrate most on missionaries, a criticism that could well be raised against my work, and to which I respond momentarily.

Conclusion

175

other was not in fact always well-treated and was perceived more as a threat (to ritual purity, if nothing else)[2] than as a blessing.

The choice by the Septuagint translators of *prosēlutos* as the main term for rendering *gēr* is an intriguing one. Long held to be a coinage of the translators themselves, I noted that more recent evidence[3] has indicated that it may have been an Alexandrian term for "in-comers" or "new arrivals," those who had migrated to the city from outside. Whatever the precise origin of the word, I have argued that its root meaning of "the one who comes" or "the approaching one" is very rich and suggestive for a consideration of the place of the other in mission.

One reason for this is that it acts as a useful critique of the idea of the missionary as the one who is sent out to convert the non-believer. Although such a view has both justification and validity, it does clearly tend to favor the person of the missionary (with the passive connivance of God—the one by whom the missionary is sent) as being at the center of the missionary endeavor. The *prosēlutos*, though, is the one who comes or draws near—from where we do not know—and encounters the missionary, and without that drawing near the sending of the missionary is incomplete.

The *prosēlutos* may also be a particularly helpful image for mission today, with the increased mobility of much of the world's population and the re-centering of mission, so that Western Europe and North America are no longer the main points from which missionaries go out, but mission is "from everywhere to everyone."[4] This, I think, is also a reminder that the missionary is always already both the one sent but also *prosēlutos*, the one drawing near, coming also from outside, and thus irrevocably transforming the place in which she or he arrives. In this sense, then, mission can be seen as a form of convergence, of *prosēlutoi* drawing near to a given point of encounter on holy ground. Seen like this, none of the human conversation partners can claim superiority, but all are subject to the commands of God to remember where they meet, treating the encounter with circumspection.

The Septuagint, I also argued, while very unusual in Bible translation,[5] was a key step in the process of deciding that the Scriptures could be translated and brought to the other in a form that was comprehensible, rather than forcing the other to learn a particular language. This was to become especially important in the New Testament world, where the lingua franca

2. On this topic, for example, see Goodman, *Mission and Conversion*.
3. I draw here on Moffitt and Butera, "New Evidence."
4. Escobar, *New Global Mission*.
5. In that it is a translation from a minority to a majority language—on this, see Bellos, *Fish in Your Ear*, 171–86 (the chapter is entitled "Bibles and Bananas: The Vertical Axis of Translation Relations").

of the Mediterranean, *Koinē* Greek, was chosen as the means of recording the life, death, and resurrection of Jesus of Nazareth, and the reflections on him of his first followers. They, as we saw, chose to see themselves as *paroikoi*, reveling in their outsider status. Theirs, then, truly was mission from the margin.[6] With their home only in Christ, they were on the edge of society, but also free to welcome the other who drew near, regardless of race, gender, or social status.

This openness to the other was, of course, primarily based on the memory of Jesus. In encounters with people like the Roman centurion, and even more the Canaanite (Syro-Phoenician) woman, we saw how Jesus had his core convictions about the addressees of his mission transformed.[7] He came to realize that his mission was to whichever other came to him with hope and in need,[8] and that none were to be turned away who sought him with open and loving heart. It was the experience of mission and of the other who comes near in mission that helped teach Jesus what his mission was.

Contemporary missiologists have also started more and more to reflect on the impact of mission's other. I examined in particular how Stephen Bevans and Roger Schroeder have focused increasingly on an understanding of mission as "prophetic dialogue." It is only through (*dia*) speaking together that we can even begin to engage in a mission that moves from a kind of divine courier service to a joint exploration of what it means to be a follower of Jesus Christ today. The mission remains prophetic, though, because to learn more about what we believe through dialogue is not to deny that we start with some belief, some faith that we wish to share. That faith contains—though is not limited to or even mainly defined by—an ethical demand and a view of human life that is simply incompatible with certain sorts of behavior and that no amount of dialogue will make us accept. So

---

6. I draw here on Wilbert Shenk, who has spoken of Anabaptist mission as being mission from the margins. See Shenk, "Mission and Marginality," especially the comments on 241, where Shenk details how the missionary as outsider encounters people, often on the margins of their own cultures, in a "creative encounter."

7. I realize some people may be upset with the idea that Jesus could have changed his mind. But, the alternative explanation is that he knew all along, but pretended to be focused on Israel alone so that his disciples could be gradually brought to understand the importance of the gentile mission. To prefer a Jesus who, for whatever reasons, deceived his disciples over one who grew in his understanding of his mission seems, to me, to be rather odd, but even if this is true, the point I am making here still stands.

8. In Mark and in the story of the Final Judgement in Matt 25:31–46, it is only need (and response to it) that matters, not even faith. Or perhaps, it is better to say that the evidence of faith is in the response to the one who draws near in faith, not in verbal proclamation of the Lordship of Jesus.

there are times when it is necessary to speak out against elements of the culture around us. How we do this, and how we go about finding remedies will demand dialogue, encounter, listening, trying to understand, and searching for any good that might have gotten lost behind the particular elements, but in the end there is a need for a prophetic voice that also hears the prophetic voice of the other.

In the third chapter I turned to Jean-Luc Marion. The first reason was to find a language on which to construct and base a missional hermeneutic that takes the other seriously. Second, I appealed to Marion's concept of givenness as a central term in constructing a contemporary phenomenology. For Marion the other and the other's situation are phenomena to which we respond and to which we seek to give meaning. But the starting point is in this other who appears, coming to us from we know not where, a reminder of the uniqueness and preciousness of each encounter. The other is always, if encountered as givenness, iconic, another key concept for Marion. Faced by this iconicity, the temptations to make our own articulations of our beliefs into idols are constantly being broken down because the other forces us to journey more deeply into what we proclaim. Marion sees the most radical form of givenness in revelation, and the ultimate term for this encounter with the iconic givenness of the other is love, the open-hearted and open-minded acceptance of the fullness of the other in their alterity. And it is in the relationship of love between self and other that I come to understand who I am.

The aim of the first part of the book was to introduce a reflection on the other as necessary for mission. It is only because of the other, approached and welcomed in love, that Christian mission can even begin. Thus, the other is not a kind of problem to be overcome in mission, but a constant reminder of all the good that God has done and of the need to tread carefully with the other because she or he bears the image of God. When the other draws near, God draws near with them, and we are on holy ground. In mission, in the first place, God must speak to God, and as human participants in the conversation it is our task to allow this to happen, acknowledging the presence of God already there before us wherever we go.

In the second part of the book, I turned to three examples of how leading figures in the history of mission have tried, more or less sucessfully, to incarnate this approach to mission. First I examined Saint Ignatius of Loyola and his vision of Christian mission. He was among the first in modern times to expound a notion of mission *ad extra*, whilst also recognizing that a person (and therefore necessarily a member of a community) could grasp their own mission only by deep reflection on their life and calling. As I just noted, at the heart of any mission is God, and Ignatius never lost sight of this. The constant challenge, then, for him, was to respond to the call of Christ, to go where Christ goes, in poverty and humility, ready to accept whatever Christ gives. In all this, love should be central, a love that speaks more by actions than words, and that is at all times deeply attentive to the other.

This vision encapsulated in various key moments in the *Spiritual Exercises* is also present in the Jesuit *Constitutions*. In these Ignatius looked at how to transform the inspiring but somewhat general call of the *Spiritual Exercises* to follow Christ into a more programmatic approach for a nascent religious order. The chief criteria for Ignatius were dependent on the other—of course first on God, but on the church, and especially on the needs of those among whom the "missionary" would live. Ignatius saw mission as service in love of God and the other, and that service necessitated immersing oneself in both God and the life of the other.[9]

Ignatius was not alone in his approach, and so I looked also at the Baptist William Carey and the Russian Orthodox Saint Innocent Veniaminov. Both demonstrated how missionaries in fact strove, despite all their limitations, to do mission with the other at its heart.[10] I turned first to William Carey, and his mission in India. First I examined the key text that Carey wrote in which he outlined his initial impulse for mission and saw that in it he was keenly aware of the needs and—to use somewhat anachronistic language[11]—the rights of the other to hear and accept the gospel. Of course, like anyone else, Carey was a man of his time, and the language he used would not, one hopes, be the language of people today. But in his letters and journals there is a struggle between his learned beliefs that the non-Christian is wrong and in some sense fundamentally turned away from God, and his experience of the people among whom he lived. They did not have to be better in order to make an impact, since the other simply by existing as a human being invites or even commands us to know them. And in knowing them Carey found that they were not so different.[12] The step

---

9. I have not looked here at the further developments of Jesuit missions—in China, Japan, India, or Latin America, to name a few places. But, at their best, they give witness to the implementation of Ignatius's vision. For more on Jesuit and Moravian Brethren missions in the Americas, see Noble, "Jesuit and Moravian Brethren Mission."

10. The choice of representatives of Orthodoxy, Protestantism (or more precisely the Radical Reformation), and Roman Catholicism was not accidental. It emphasizes the fact that the other draws near to members of all Christian denominations and all must respond. And it is not surprising that, at their best, Christians of all denominations show similar responses to the blessing and challenge of the other.

11. There is some evidence that Carey was influenced by the language of rights that came out of the French Revolution, which was going on at precisely the time he was founding the Baptist Missionary Society.

12. For the most part. There are, of course, outbursts of frustration, and some of

that I think Carey could never quite take was to acknowledge that these others who came to him—at the indigo works, in Serampore, or wherever else—could actually teach him anything about what it was to be a Christian.

But if he was unable consciously to take this step, it seems to me that he was changed by the experience of his work in India—translation, scientific, botanic, and zoological observation, language teaching, perhaps even in his missionary work as such. Letters and journals are different genres, and so it may be risky to compare them, but the spiritual language of his journals, written in the first few years of his stay in India, and that of his later letters is not the same. The Puritan introspection never entirely disappears, but there is a sense of someone becoming more settled in his role and in his life, especially after his second marriage. He never lost his desire to communicate the Christian message, but he did come to realize that there is more than one way to do this, and he came to appreciate those around him, both the converts and even those who did not convert, but who selflessly helped him in his translation work.

Saint Innocent was a different kind of man. He rarely gives much indication of being troubled spiritually in the way that Carey was. And the world to which he moved was not so strange. Moreover, because his theological starting point was different, Innocent was able to see much more easily the positives in the people among whom he worked and he was much more ready to acknowledge them. With him, there is quite clear evidence that in some things he was able to go beyond the practices of his time, and be changed by the lives of the people among whom he lived. This was limited, it is true,[13] but it happened, as he came to see that rules for fasting and church attendance developed for a different culture and time were simply not going to work in this new setting.

In his catechism and his work, *The Pathway to the Kingdom of Heaven*, there is a response to the faith of the people around him, in which he finds means to communicate not simply what he believes, but what people need and are capable of hearing in ways that will make sense to them. The point of his work was not to give an insight into his own spiritual state, and we do not have a "before" to compare, but it may not be pushing things too far to say that in writing what he did, he found himself pushed to reflect on what was most important for him in this new world in which he was living in

---

the language borders—at the very least—on the racist. We may need (rightly) to say that this is wrong, but to force a late eighteenth-century English Baptist to be like us is simply another form of totality, and is therefore also wrong.

13. See the work of Eliel, referred to earlier, on the almost literal blind spot when it came to using native art and iconography. I suspect that Innocent may not have been the most visual of people, and perhaps he simply did not think about it.

terms of his own faith. And always, at the heart of it, is the need, outlined by Saint Ignatius,[14] to practice love and to act in love.

So, where does all this leave us? I began this book with a question raised by Michael Barram. He asked:

> How does the encounter with the other challenge the power and privilege so often presupposed in the community's understanding of its "sentness"—and indeed, of its appropriation of the gospel? I wonder if a missional hermeneutic would be even more robust if we could come up with a "stream," or at least a focused question, that actually privileged the perspective of the other confronted by mission.[15]

This search for such a "stream" has underlain my work in this book, and it is now time to essay an answer, albeit, as I made clear in the introduction, a provisional one. Barram's first question is about the effect of the encounter with the other on the church's sense of privilege. I want to respond to this question from the best case scenario, though recognizing that this is neither normative, nor perhaps even actually practiced. But a vision of what is possible can serve as a light to guide us through other kinds of world.

To put it simply, then, the encounter with the other can act as precisely a brake on our temptation to see our version and vision of the gospel as "the gospel" *tout court*. It makes us realize that we have no power or privilege, except that of service and response, to the gospel itself, and to the other. We do not and cannot know the fullness of God's Word, and only through the givenness of the other who does not see everything exactly like us can we ever hope to enter more deeply into the mystery of God "in whom we live and move and have our being" (Acts 17:28).[16]

The one who draws near to us in her or his vulnerability and otherness is the one who can teach us at least as much about what it means to be a follower of Christ as we can teach them. The word "mission" is formed from a passive root,[17] and as such it has an implicit agent and an implicit end. We

---

14. The comparison is not quite so strained as it might seem. Saint Nikodimos of the Holy Mountain, apart from his work on the *Philokalia*, also translated (or at least edited a translation of) a version of the *Spiritual Exercises*. On this topic, see Noble, "Hesychasm and Ignatian Spirituality."

15. Barram, "Response."

16. This very quotation from Epimenides's *Cretica* is an excellent example of how exposure to what the other brings can deepen our understanding of who God is for us. By making Epimenides "canonical," Luke is allowing that not just the Hebrew Scriptures have something to say to us about God, but also "pagan" classics.

17. *Missus* is the perfect passive participle of the verb *mittere*, to send, from which is derived the substantive *missio*. In checking this, I discovered that the Proto-

are sent by God to the other. Until that happens, no mission takes place, and the sending has not really happened. Thus the only (human) one who has real power in the missionary endeavor is the other, the *prosēlutos*, the one who sees us coming and takes a step in our direction.

Perhaps deep down this was something that Carey intuited—the success of his mission was not be measured simply in the number of converts, and he seems to have been remarkably sanguine about the slowness of making any. Instead the mission was simply in the going out and waiting for the other to come, allowing the world around him to work its effect on him. This is one way of understanding arguably the greatest missionary novel of all, Shūsaku Endō's magnificent *Silence*.[18] It is only by finally letting Christ talk through the suffering of the people that the main character in the book, the Jesuit Ferreira, can come to understand that in this case to trample on the crucifix is not blasphemy but the way of love.

So, mission can be understood in this sense as response in love to the other who draws near. Admittedly in itself this does not entirely resolve the question of how that mission will take place, but that is because of the way in which the second half of Barram's question must be answered. Like Barram, I too would want to have a question that "privileged the perspective of the other confronted by mission," and when I started I hoped that I would come up with one. Having travelled this far, though, I am less sure. This is not because I do not think the other should be privileged, but rather for that very reason. However, though we can never ask the other's question, we can still ask a question that seeks to privilege their perspective. To that end, I suggest, therefore, that a missional hermeneutics that wants to privilege the perspective of the other will ask something like this: "How can we leave our vision of mission open to the challenge of the other, so that together we travel towards a deeper understanding of who God is?"

At various points throughout this work I have insisted that none of this attention to the other means that mission is unimportant or unnecessary. I would say, rather, that the giving of attention to the other makes mission more important and more necessary, though not any longer solely for the one to whom we are sent. For many years now missiologists have been arguing that Christianity is about mission, and as church numbers plummet in traditional Christian nations and continents and expand rapidly in other parts of the world, church leaders have started to attend to the centrality of mission too.

Indo-European root from which this word derives (*meyth-* or *mith-*) meant "to exchange," which is not too far from what I have argued to be key feature of mission—the exchange of gifts between the two strangers who draw near.

18. Endō, *Silence*.

The proclamation of good news in deed, in love, in word, is still at the heart of what it is to be a disciple of Christ. But it is not a simple one-way knowledge transfer, in which we pass on knowledge of Christ—a content—to those who do not have it. Missionaries are sent to the other, but also to themselves, so that together with the other they can come to understand their own faith and to know, love, and serve God more deeply, fully, and generously. In this book, I have sought to show that Christian mission, at its best, includes the welcoming of the gift of the other with whom we are called to love, honor, and serve God our Lord. It can enable us to see that it is only together with the other that we can receive and respond, and journey on to fullness of life in God, the Lord and Giver of all.

Bibliography

Abraham, Susan. "What Does Mumbai Have To Do with Rome? Postcolonial Perspectives on Globalization and Theology." *Theological Studies* 69 (2008) 376–93.

Adeney, Francis. "Why Biography? Contributions of Narrative Studies to Mission Theology and Mission Theory." *Mission Studies* 26 (2009) 153–72.

Aghamkar, Atul Y. "Traditional Hindu Views and Attitudes toward Christianity." *Global Missiology* 1.5 (2008) 1–42. http://ojs.globalmissiology.org/index.php/english/article/viewFile/244/682.

Alban, Donald, Jr., et al. "The Writings of William Carey: Journalism as Mission in a Modern Age." *Mission Studies* 22 (2005) 85–113.

Aldama, Antonio de. *The Formula of the Institute: Notes for a Commentary*. St Louis: Institute of Jesuit Sources, 1990.

———. *An Introductory Commentary on the Constitutions*. St Louis: Institute of Jesuit Sources, 1989.

———. *Missioning*. St Louis: Institute of Jesuit Sources, 1996.

Allen, W. C. "On the Meaning of ΠΡΟΣΗΛΥΤΟΣ in the Septuagint." *Expositor* 4 (1894) 264–75.

Alphonso, Herbert. *Placed with Christ the Son*. Anand, India: Gujarat Sahitya Prakash, 1993.

Amaladoss, Michael. "Sent on Mission." In *Constitutions of the Society of Jesus: Incorporation of a Spirit*, edited by Joseph Veale et al., 327–50. Gujarat Prakash, India: Secretariatus Spiritualitatis Ignatianae, 1993.

Anderson, Gerald. "Theology of Religions: The Epitome of Mission Theology." In *Mission in Bold Humility: Mission in Bold Humility*, edited by William Saayman and Klippies Kritzinger, 113–20. Maryknoll, NY: Orbis, 1996.

Anderson, Laura. "Healthy Economics or Cautionary Tales? The Narrative Microeconomics of Four Matthean Healing Stories." *HTS Teologiese/Theological Studies* 65.1 (2009). DOI: https://doi.org/10.4102/hts.v65i1.320.

"The Angels of Akun." *Road to Emmaus* 8.2 (2007) 20–33.

Apostolov, Mario. *The Christian-Muslim Frontier: A Zone of Contact, Conflict or Cooperation*. London: Routledge, 2004.

Araya, Victorio. *God of the Poor: The Mystery of God in Latin American Liberation Theology*. Translated by Robert R. Barr. Maryknoll, NY: Orbis, 1987.

Arzhanukhin, Vladislav. "Greek Patristics in Russia of the 17th–18th centuries." *Greek Orthodox Theological Review* 44 (1999) 565–74.

Bachman, Peter. *Roberto Nobili 1577–1656: Ein missionsgeschichtlicher Beitrag zum christlichen Dialog mit Hinduismus*. Bibliotheca Instituti Historici S.I. 32. Rome: Institutum Historicum S.I., 1972.

Balia, Daryl, and Kirsteen Kim, eds. *Witnessing to Christ Today*. Vol. 2 of *Edinburgh 2010*. Oxford: Regnum, 2010.

Bangert, William. *Jerome Nadal S.J., 1507–1580: Tracking the First Generation of Jesuits*. Edited by Thomas McCoog. Chicago: Loyola University Press, 1992.

Barbour, Claude Marie, et al. "Shalom Ministries: An Urban Base Community Comes of Age." *Chicago Theological Seminary Register* 81 (1991) 41–49.

Barram, Michael. "A Response at AAR to Hunsberger's 'Proposals . . .' Essay." https://gocn.org/library/a-response-at-aar-to-hunsbergers-proposals-essay/.

Barry, William, and William Connolly. *The Practice of Spiritual Direction*. New York: Seabury, 1982.

Baziou, Abbé Jean-Yves. "Mission: From Expansion to Encounter." *USCMA Periodic Paper* 1 (Spring 2005).

Beck, James. *Dorothy Carey: The Tragic and Untold Story of Mrs. William Carey*. Grand Rapids: Baker, 1992.

———. "Dorothy's Devastating Delusions." *Christian History* 11.4 (1992) 30–31.

Beck, John. *Translators as Storytellers. A Study in Septuagint Translation Technique*. Studies in Biblical Literature 25. New York: Lang, 2000.

Becker, Dieter, and Andreas Feldtkeller, eds. *Mit dem Anderen Leben: Perspektiven einer Theologie der Konvivenz*. 2 vols. Neuendettelsau: Erlanger, 2000.

Becker, Judith, and Brian Stanley, eds. *Europe as the Other: External Perspectives on European Christianity*. Veröffentlichungen des Instituts für Europäische Geschichte Mainz Supplement 103. Göttingen: Vandenhoeck & Ruprecht, 2014.

Behera, Marina Ngursangzeli, ed. *Interfaith Relations after One Hundred Years: Christian Mission among Other Faiths*. Regnum Edinburgh 2010 Series. Eugene, OR: Wipf & Stock, 2011.

Bellos, David. *Is That a Fish in Your Ear? The Amazing Adventure of Translation*. London: Penguin, 2012.

Benson, Bruce Ellis. *Graven Ideologies: Nietzsche, Derrida and Marion on Modern Idolatry*. Downers Grove, IL: InterVarsity, 2002.

Berryman, Phillip. *Liberation Theology: Essential Facts about the Revolutionary Movement in Latin America and Beyond*. Oak Park, IL: Meyer-Stone, 1987.

Bevans, Stephen. *Models of Contextual Theology*. Rev. ed. Faith and Cultures Series. Maryknoll, NY: Orbis, 2002.

Bevans, Stephen, and Eleanor Doidge. "Theological Reflection." In *Reflection and Dialogue: What MISSION Confronts Religious Life Today?*, edited by Barbara Kraemer, 37–48. Chicago: Center for the Study of Religious Life, 2000.

Bevans, Stephen, and Roger Schroeder. *Constants in Context: A Theology of Mission for Today*. American Society of Missiology Series 30. Maryknoll, NY: Orbis, 2004.

———. *Prophetic Dialogue: Reflections on Christian Mission Today*. Maryknoll, NY: Orbis, 2011.

Black, Lydia T. "Ivan Pan'kov—an Architect of Aleut Literacy." *Arctic Anthropology* 14 (1977) 94–107.

"Blessed John Smirennikov: A Native American Converser with Angels." *Orthodox Word* 33 (1997) 185–95.

Boff, Clodovis. *Theology and Praxis: Epistemological Foundations*. Translated by Robert R. Barr. Maryknoll, NY: Orbis, 1987.
Bonhoeffer, Dietrich. *The Cost of Discipleship*. Rev. and unabridged ed. Translated by R. H. Fuller and Irmgard Booth. New York: Macmillan, 1959.
Bonk, Jonathan. *Missions and Money: Affluence as a Missionary Problem—Revisited*. Rev. and exp. ed. American Society of Missiology Series 15. Maryknoll, NY: Orbis, 2006.
Bosch, David. *Transforming Mission: Paradigm Shifts in Theology of Mission*. American Society of Missiology Series 16. Maryknoll, NY: Orbis, 1991.
Boyle, Marjorie O'Rourke. *Loyola's Acts: The Rhetoric of the Self*. Berkeley: University of California Press, 1997.
Brackley, Dean. *The Call to Discernment in Troubled Times: New Perspectives on the Transformative Wisdom of Ignatius of Loyola*. New York: Crossroad, 2004.
Briggs, John. *The English Baptists of the 19th Century*. London: Baptist Historical Society, 1994.
Brockington, John. "William Carey's Significance as an Indologist." *Indologica Taurinense* 17-18 (1991–1992) 81–102.
Brown, Jeannine. "Direct Engagement of the Reader in Matthew's Discourses: Rhetorical Techniques and Scholarly Consensus." *New Testament Studies* 51 (2005) 19–35.
Brown, Raymond. *The English Baptists of the 18th Century*. London: Baptist Historical Society, 1986.
Brunstetter, Daniel. "Sepulveda, Las Casas, and the Other: Exploring the Tension between Moral Universalism and Alterity." *Review of Politics* 72 (2010) 409–35.
Buckley, Michael. "The Contemplation to Attain Love." *The Way Supplement* 24 (1975) 92–104.
Bultmann, Christoph. *Der Fremde im antiken Juda: Eine Untersuchung zum sozialen Typenbegriff "gēr" und seinem Bedeutungswandel in der alttestamentlichen Gesetzgebung*. Forschungen zur Religion und Literatur des Alten und Neuen Testaments 153. Göttingen, Germany: Vandenhoeck & Ruprecht, 1992.
Bünker, Arnd. "The Function of the Other in Recent German Mission Calls." *International Review of Mission* 91.362 (2002) 342–53.
Burchard, Christoph. "Zu Matthäus 8,5–13." *Zeitschrift für die neutestamentliche Wissenschaft und die Kunde der älteren Kirche* 84 (1993) 278–88.
Burrow, John. *A History of Histories: Epics, Chronicles, Romances and Inquiries from Herodotus and Thucydides to the Twentieth Century*. London: Penguin, 2008.
Butlin, Robin. *Geographies of Empire: European Empires and Colonies c. 1880–1960*. Cambridge Studies in Historical Geography. Cambridge: Cambridge University Press, 2009.
Cadwallader, Alan. "Out of Wordlock: Autobiography and the Syrophoenician Women." *Pacifica: Journal of the Melbourne College of Divinity* 21 (2008) 257–84.
Cairns, Andrew. "Establishing Base Communities in Uptown Chicago: Preliminary Reflections on a Ministry." *Chicago Theological Seminary Register* 81 (1991) 34–41.
Čapek, Karel. *The Gardener's Year*. London: Continuum, 2003.
Caputo, John. "Apostles of the Impossible: On God and the Gift in Derrida and Marion." In *God, the Gift and Postmodernism*, edited by John Caputo and Michael Scanlon, 185–222. Indiana Series in the Philosophy of Religion. Bloomington: Indiana University Press, 1999.

Carey, S. Pearce. *William Carey D.D., Fellow of Linnaean Society*. London: Hodder & Stoughton, 1923.

Carey, William. *An Enquiry into the Obligations of Christians, to Use Means for the Conversion of the Heathens, in which the Religious State of the Different Nations of the World, the Success of Former Undertakings, and the Practicability of Further Undertakings Are Considered*. Leicester, UK: Ireland, 1792.

Carson, Penelope. *The East India Company and Religion, 1698-1858*. Martlesham, UK: Boyder & Bewell, 2012.

Carter, Terry, ed. *The Journal and Selected Letters of William Carey*. Macon, GA: Smith & Helwys, 2000.

Castillo, José Maria. *Los Pobres y la Teología: Que queda de la teología de la liberación?* 3rd ed. Bilbao: de Brouwer, 1999.

Cathcart, William, ed. *The Baptist Encyclopedia*. 2 vols. Rev. ed. Philadelphia: Everts, 1883.

Chandler, H. Im, and Amos Yong. *Global Diasporas and Mission*. Regnum Edinburgh Centenary Series 23. Eugene, OR: Wipf & Stock, 2014.

Charlesworth, Max. "Translating Religious Texts: 'When We Learn to Speak, We Are Learning to Translate' (Octavio Paz)." *SOPHIA* 51 (2012) 423-48.

Chia, Edmund Fee-Kook. "Mission as Dialogue: An Asian Roman Catholic Perspective." In *Mission after Christendom: Emergent Themes in Contemporary Mission*, edited by Ogbu Kalu et al., 144-54. Louisville: Westminster John Knox, 2010.

Chute, Arthur. *John Thomas: First Baptist Missionary to Bengal, 1757-1801*. Halifax: Baptist Book and Tract Society, 1893.

Clements, Keith. *Faith on the Frontier: A Life of J. H. Oldham*. Edinburgh: T. & T. Clark, 1999.

Clooney, Francis. *Comparative Theology: Deep Learning across Religious Borders*. Malden, MA: Wiley-Blackwell, 2010.

———. "Roberto de Nobili, Adaptation and the Reasonable Interpretation of Religion." *Missiology* 18 (1990) 25-36.

Collet, Giancarlo. "German Catholic Mission Science: Comments on the Time of its Commencement." In *Mission and Science: Missiology Revised, 1850-1940*, edited by Carine Dujardin and Claude Proudhomme, 99-110. Kadoc Studies on Religion, Culture and Society 16. Leuven: Leuven University Press, 2015.

Connolly, William. "Story of the Pilgrim King and the Dynamics of Prayer." *Review for Religious* 32 (1973) 268-72.

Constantinescu, Adrian. "Nida's Theory of Dynamic Equivalence." *Linguistic and Philosophical Investigations* 9 (2010) 284-89.

Conwell, Joseph. *Walking in the Spirit: A Reflection on Jeronimo Nadal's Phrase "Contemplative Likewise in Action."* St. Louis: The Institute of Jesuit Sources, 2004.

Coupeau, J. Carlos. "Five *personae* of Ignatius of Loyola." In *The Cambridge Companion to the Jesuits*, edited by Thomas Worcester, 32-51. Cambridge: Cambridge University Press, 2008.

Cousins, Basil. "The Russian Orthodox Church, Tatar Christians and Islam." In *Eastern Christianity: Studies in Modern History, Religion and Politics*, edited by Anthony O'Mahony, 338-71. London: Melisende, 2004.

Cracknell, Kenneth. *Justice, Courtesy and Love: Theologians and Missionaries Encountering World Religions, 1846-1914*. London: Epworth, 1995.

Cracraft, James. *The Church Reform of Peter the Great*. Stanford: Stanford University Press, 1971.
Cro, Stelio. *The Noble Savage: Allegory of Freedom*. Waterloo: Wilfred Laurier University Press, 1990.
Cummins, James S. *A Question of Rites: Friar Domingo Navarrete and the Jesuits in China*. Aldershot, UK: Scolar, 1993.
Cusson, Gilles. *Biblical Theology and the Spiritual Exercises*. St Louis: Institute of Jesuit Sources, 1988.
Cuvillier, Elian. "La construction narrative de la mission dans le premier évangile: un déplacement théologique et identitaire." In *The Gospel of Matthew at the Crossroads of Early Christianity*, edited by Donald Senior, 159–75. BETL 243. Leuven, Belgium: Peeters, 2011.
Dahling-Sander, Christoph, et al., eds. *Leitfaden ökumenische Missionstheologie*. Gütersloh: Kaiser, 2003.
Dalmases, Cándido de. *Ignatius of Loyola: Founder of the Jesuits*. St. Louis: Institute of Jesuit Sources, 1985.
Dalrymple, William. *White Mughals: Love and Betrayal in Eighteenth Century India*. London: Harper Perennial, 2004.
de Guibert, Joseph. *The Jesuits: Their Spiritual Doctrine and Practice*. St. Louis: Institute of Jesuit Sources, 1964.
De Schrijver, Georges. "The Use of Mediations in Theology." In *Mediations in Theology: Georges De Schrijver's Wager and Liberation Theologies*, edited by Jacques Haers et al., 1–64. Annua nuntia Lovaniensia 47. Leuven: Peeters, 2003.
DeBorst, Ruth Padilla. "'At the Table Their Eyes Were Opened': Mission as Renouncing Power and Being Hosted by the Stranger." *International Bulletin of Missionary Research* 39 (2015) 198–202.
DeHass, Medeia Csoba. "Ethnonyms in the Sugpiaq-Alutiiq Region." *Arctic Anthropology* 49 (2012) 3–17.
Deicha, Sophie. "Patristics in Russia, the 19th Century." *Greek Orthodox Theological Review* 44 (1999) 575–83.
Delaney, Joan. "From Cremona to Edinburgh: Bishop Bonomelli and the World Missionary Conference of 1910." *Ecumenical Review* 52 (2000) 418–31.
Derrida, Jacques. *Given Time: I. Counterfeit Money*. Chicago: University of Chicago Press, 1992.
Dolejšová, Ivana. *See* Noble, Ivana.
Donovan, Vincent. *Christianity Rediscovered*. Maryknoll, NY: Orbis, 1982.
Dorr, Donal. *Mission in Today's World*. Maryknoll, NY: Orbis, 2000.
Dowsett, Rose. "Cooperation and the Promotion of Unity: An Evangelical Perspective." In *Edinburgh 2010: Mission Then and Now*, edited by David Kerr and Kenneth Ross, 250–62. Oxford: Regnum, 2009.
Dreyfus, Hubert, and Mark Wrathall, eds. *A Companion to Phenomenology and Existentialism*. Blackwell Companions to Philosophy 35. Oxford: Blackwell, 2006.
Duffy, Stephen. "Experience of Grace." In *The Cambridge Companion to Karl Rahner*, edited by Declan Marmion and Mary Hines, 43–62. Cambridge Companions to Religion. Cambridge: Cambridge University Press, 2005.
Dutta, Mohua. "Bhakti Movement: A Socio-Religious Struggle of the Marginalised Society." *Indian Journal of Applied Research* 4 (2014) 685–87.

Edgar, David Hutchinson. *Has God not Chosen The Poor? The Social Setting of the Epistle of James.* JSNT Supplement Series 206. Sheffield: Sheffield Academic, 2001.

Egan, Harvey. *The Spiritual Exercises and the Ignatian Mystical Horizon.* St. Louis: Institute of Jesuit Sources, 1976.

Eitel, Keith, ed. *Mission in Contexts of Violence.* Pasadena, CA: William Carey Library, 2008.

Eliel, Archimandrite Gerasim. "Russian Icons in a Native Church: Conflict in Culture in Western Alaska." MDiv thesis, St. Vladimir's Orthodox Theological Seminary, Yonkers, NY, 2012.

Ellingson, Ter. *The Myth of the Noble Savage.* Berkeley: University of California Press, 2001.

Elliott, John. *A Home for the Homeless: A Social-Scientific Criticism of I Peter, Its Situation and Strategy.* 1990. Reprint, Eugene, OR: Wipf & Stock, 2005.

Ellis, Ian. *A Century of Mission and Unity: A Centenary Perspective on the 1910 Edinburgh World Missionary Conference.* Dublin: Columba, 2010.

Elolia, Samuel. "Let Us Break Bread Together: The Church and Multiculturalism in America." *Encounter* 66 (2005) 145–63.

Endean, Philip. "Ignatius in Lutheran Light." *The Month* 24 (July 1991) 271–78.

———. *Karl Rahner and Ignatian Spirituality.* Oxford: Oxford University Press, 2001.

———. "The Spiritual Exercises." In *The Cambridge Companion to the Jesuits*, edited by Thomas Worcester, 52–68. Cambridge Companions to Religion. Cambridge Univeristy Press, 2008.

Endō, Shūsaku. *Silence.* London: Owen, 2003.

Engen, Charles E. van. *Mission on the Way: Issues in Mission Theology.* Grand Rapids: Baker, 1996.

Engen, Charles E. van, et al., eds. *Footprints of God: A Narrative Theology of Mission.* Monrovia, CA: MARC, 1999.

Escobar, Samuel. *The New Global Mission: The Gospel from Everywhere to Everyone.* Downers Grove, IL: InterVarsity, 2003.

Evans, A. Steven. "Matters of the Heart: Orality, Story and Cultural Transformation— The Critical Role of Storytelling in Affecting Worldview." *Missiology: An International Review* 38 (2010) 185–99.

Farias, Victor. *Heidegger and Nazism.* Philadelphia: Temple University Press, 1989.

Fiddes, Paul. *Participating in God: A Pastoral Doctrine of the Trinity.* London: Darton, Longman & Todd, 2000.

The First Hindoo Convert: A Memoir of Krishna Pal, a Preacher of the Gospel to His Countrymen More Than Twenty Years. Philadelphia: American Baptist Publication Society, 1852.

Flannery, Kevin. "'Circa missiones': on the Jesuit Fourth Vow." *New Jesuit Review* 1:1 (2009). www.newjesuitreview.org/newjesuitreview/Vol._1_No_1_A._2_files/NJR 0101Flannery.pdf.

———. "'Circa Missiones': On the Founding of the Society of Jesus." http://www.academia.edu/844747/CIRCA_MISSIONES_ON_THE_FOUNDING_OF_THE_SOCIETY_OF_JESUS.

Fleming, David. "Here I Am: Ignatian Ways of Serving." *Review of Ignatian Spirituality* 38.3 (2007) 98–107.

———. *Like the Lightning: The Dynamics of the Ignatian Exercises.* St. Louis: Institute of Jesuit Sources, 2004.

Fletcher, Jeannine Hill. "Rahner and Religious Diversity." In *The Cambridge Companion to Karl Rahner*, edited by Declan Marmion and Mary Hines, 235–48. Cambridge Companions to Religion. Cambridge: Cambridge University Press, 2005.

Flett, John. *The Witness of God: The Trinity, Missio Dei, Karl Barth and the Nature of the Christian Community*. Grand Rapids: Eerdmans, 2010.

Føllesdal, Dagfinn. "Husserl's Reductions and the Role They Play in His Phenomenology." In *Companion to Phenomenology and Existentialism*, edited by Hubert Dreyfus and Mark Wrathall, 105–14. Oxford: Wiley-Blackwell, 2009.

Franks, C. E. S. "In Search of the Savage Sauvage: An Exploration into North America's Political Cultures." *American Review of Canadian Studies* 32.4 (2002) 547–80.

Frazier, Jessica. "Bhakti in Hindu Cultures." *Journal of Hindu Studies* 6 (2013) 101–13.

Freire, Paulo. *Pedagogy of the Oppressed*. Translated by Myra Bergman Ramos. London: Sheed & Ward, 1972.

Gadamer, Hans-Georg. *Wahrheit und Methode: Grundzüge einer philosophischen Hermeneutik*. Tübingen: Mohr/Siebeck, 1960.

Gairdner, William H. T. *"Edinburgh 1910": An Account and Interpretation of the World Missionary Conference*. Edinburgh, UK: Oliphant, Anderson & Ferrier, 1910.

———. "The Vital Forces of Christianity and Islam." *International Review of Missions* 1 (1912) 44–61.

Ganaba, Olga. "Response from Russia." *International Review of Mission* 86.342 (1997) 325–28.

Garcia, Andrew. "Ignatian Obedience in the Light of the Spiritual Exercises." *New Jesuit Review* 1.3 (2010). http://endrtimes.blogspot.cz/2010/06/ignatian-obedience-in-light-of.html.

Garrett, Paul. *St Innocent, Apostle to America*. Crestwood, NY: St. Vladimir's Seminary Press, 1979.

Garvey, John. *Seed of the Word: Orthodox Thinking on Other Religions*. Crestwood, NY: St. Vladimir's Seminary Press, 2005.

George, Timothy. *Faithful Witness: The Life and Mission of William Carey*. Birmingham, AL: New Hope, 1991.

Gerhartz, Johannes. "The Fourth Vow in Respect of Missions and its Influence on the Constitutions: An Historico-Canonical Enquiry." In *Constitutions of the Society of Jesus: Incorporation of a Spirit*, edited by Joseph Veale et al., 75–103. Anand, India: Gujarat Sahitya Prakash, 1993.

Gilliland, Dean. "My Pilgrimage in Mission." *International Bulletin of Missionary Research* 24 (2000) 119–22.

———. "Phenomenology as Mission Method." *Missiology: An International Review* 7 (1979) 451–59.

Gittins, Anthony J. *Ministry at the Margins: Strategy and Spirituality for Mission*. Maryknoll, NY: Orbis, 2002.

Glaser, Arthur, et al. *Announcing the Kingdom: The Story of God's Mission in the Bible*. Grand Rapids: Baker Academic, 2003.

Gnanakan, Ken. "To Proclaim the Good News of the Kingdom." In *Mission in the 21st Century: Exploring the Five Marks of Global Mission*, edited by Andrew Walls and Cathy Ross, 3–10. Maryknoll, NY: Orbis, 2008.

Golder, Frank Alfred. *Father Herman: Alaska's Saint*. Platina, CA: St. Herman of Alaska Brotherhood, 2004.

Goodman, Martin. *Mission and Conversion: Proselytising in the Religious History of the Roman Empire*. Oxford: Oxford University Press, 1994.

Gottwald, Norman. *The Tribes of Israel: A Sociology of the Religion of Liberated Israel, 1250–1050 B.C.E.* Maryknoll, NY: Orbis, 1979.

Grinëv, Andrei. "The First Russian Settlers in Alaska." *The Historian* 75 (2013) 443–74.

Gschwandtner, Christine. *Reading Jean-Luc Marion: Exceeding Metaphysics*. Indiana Series in the Philosophy of Religion. Bloomington: Indiana University Press, 2007.

———. Review of Puntel, *Being and God. Comparative and Continental Philosophy* 4 (2012) 164–65.

Guardiola-Saenz, Leticia A. "Borderless Women and Borderless Texts: A Cultural Reading of Matthew 15:21–28." *Semeia* 78 (1997) 69–81.

Guder, Darrell, ed. *Missional Church: A Vision for the Sending of the Church in North America*. Grand Rapids: Eerdmans, 1998.

Gundry-Volf, Judith. "Spirit, Mercy, and the Other." *Theology Today* 51 (1995) 508–23.

Gutiérrez, Gustavo. *Las Casas: In Search of the Poor of Jesus Christ*. Translated by Robert R. Barr. Maryknoll, NY: Orbis, 1993.

———. *A Theology of Liberation: History, Politics, and Salvation*. Translated by Sister Caridad Inda and John Eagleson. Rev. ed. Maryknoll, NY: Orbis, 1988.

———. *The Truth Shall Make You Free: Confrontations*. Translated by Matthew J. O'Connell. Maryknoll, NY: Orbis, 1991.

Habermas, Jürgen. *Theorie des komunikativen Handelns*. 2 vols. Frankfurt: Suhrkamp, 1981.

Hacham, Noah. "The *Letter of Aristeas*: A New Exodus Story?" *Journal for the Study of Judaism* 35 (2005) 1–20.

Hadas, Moses. *Aristeas to Philocrates (Letter of Aristeas)*. New York: Harper, 1951.

Hall, Gerard. "Conversing with Others: Interreligious Dialogue in Catholic Health and Aged Care." *Compass* 43 (2009) 3–8.

Hardage, Jeanette. *Mary Slessor—Everybody's Mother: The Era and Impact of a Victorian Missionary*. Eugene, OR: Wipf & Stock, 2008.

Hardwick, Susan Wiley. *Russian Refuge: Religion, Migration, and Settlement on the North American Pacific Rim*. Chicago: University of Chicago Press, 1993.

Hartropp, Andrew, and Oddvar Sten Ronsen. "Evangelism Lost? A Need to Redefine Christian Integral Mission." *Mission Studies* 33 (2016) 66–84.

Hastings, Thomas John. *Practical Theology and the One Body of Christ: Toward a Missional-Ecumenical Model*. Grand Rapids: Eerdmans, 2007.

Hauerwas, Stanley, and William Willimon. *Where Resident Aliens Live: Exercises for Christian Practice*. Nashville: Abingdon, 1996.

Hawley, John, ed. *Historicizing Christian Encounters with the Other*. Basingstoke, UK: MacMillan, 1998.

Hayden, Roger. *English Baptist Heritage and History: A Christian Training Programme Course*. Didcot, UK: Baptist Union of Great Britain, 1990.

Heidegger, Martin. *Grundprobleme der Phänomenologie*. GA 58. Edited by Hans Helmuth Gander. Rev. ed. Frankfurt: Klostermann, 2010.

———. *Sein und Zeit*. (GA 2). Frankfurt: Klostermann, 1977. (ET: *Being and Time*. Oxford: Blackwell, 1967.)

Hempton, David. *The Church in the Long Eighteenth Century*. London: Tauris, 2011.

Hesselgrave, David. *Paradigms in Conflict: 10 Key Questions in Christian Missions Today*. Grand Rapids: Kregel, 2005.

———. "Will We Correct the Edinburgh Error? Future Mission in Historical Perspective." *Southwestern Journal of Theology* 49 (2007) 121–49.

Holmes, Stephen. "Three Versus One? Some Problems of Social Trinitarianism." *Journal of Reformed Theology* 3 (2009) 77–89.

Homza, Lu Ann. "The Religious Milieu of the Young Ignatius." In *The Cambridge Companion to the Jesuits*, edited by Thomas Worcester, 13–31. Cambridge Companions to Religion. Cambridge: Cambridge University Press, 2008.

Höpfl, Harro. *Jesuit Political Thought: The Society of Jesus and the State, c. 1540–1630*. Ideas in Context 70. Cambridge: Cambridge University Press, 2004.

Hopkins, C. Howard. *John R. Mott, 1865–1955: A Biography*. Grand Rapids: Eerdmans, 1979.

Horner, Robyn. "The Gifted Self: The Challenges of French Thought." In *Questioning the Human: Toward a Theological Anthropology for the Twenty-First Century*, edited by Lieven Boeve et al., 115–27. New York: Fordham University Press, 2014.

———. *Jean-Luc Marion: A Theo-logical Introduction*. Aldershot, UK: Ashgate, 2005.

Horrell, David. "'Race,' 'Nation,' 'People': Ethnic Identity-Construction in 1 Peter 2:9." *New Testament Studies* 58 (2011) 123–43.

Hsia, R. Po-Chia. *A Jesuit in the Forbidden City: Matteo Ricci, 1552–1610*. Oxford: Oxford University Press, 2010.

Hunsberger, George. *Bearing the Witness of the Spirit: Lesslie Newbigin's Theology of Cultural Plurality*. Grand Rapids: Eerdmans, 1998.

———. "Proposals for a Missional Hermeneutic: Mapping the Conversation." https://gocn.org/library/proposals-for-a-missional-hermeneutic-mapping-the-conversation/.

Hunt, Anne. *Trinity: Nexus of the Mysteries of Christian Faith*. Theology in Global Perspective Series. Maryknoll, NY: Orbis, 2005.

Ignatius. *The Constitutions of the Society of Jesus and their Complementary Norms*. St. Louis: Institute of Jesuit Sources, 1996.

———. *Los Ejercicios Espirituales de San Ignacio de Loyola: Introducción, Texto, Notas y Vocabulario por Cándido de Dalmases*. Santander, Spain: SalTerrae, 1985.

Ingleby, Jonathan. *Beyond Empire: Postcolonialism and Mission in a Global Context*. Milton Keynes, UK: Author, 2010.

Ivens, Michael. *Keeping in Touch: Posthumous Papers on Ignatian Topics*. Edited by Joseph Munitiz. Leominster, UK: Gracewing, 2007.

———. *Understanding the Spiritual Exercises*. Leominster, UK: Gracewing, 1998.

Jackson, Darrell. "'Mission-Shaped Presence' in Europe." *International Review of Mission* 95.378/379 (2006) 341–51.

Jackson, Eleanor. "From Krishna Pal to Lal Behari Dey: Indian Builders of the Church in India or Native Agency in Bengal 1800–1880." In *Converting Colonialism: Visions and Reality in Mission History, 1706–1914*, edited by Dana Robert, 166–205. Grand Rapids: Eerdmans, 2008.

Janciles, Jehu H. "Migration and Mission: The Religious Significance of the North-South Divide." In *Mission in the 21st Century: Exploring the Five Marks of Global Mission*, edited by Andrew Walls and Cathy Ross, 118–29. Maryknoll, NY: Orbis, 2008.

Janicaud, Dominique. *Le tournant théologique de la philosophie française*. Combles: Éditions de l'Éclat, 1991.

Janicaud, Dominique, et al. *Phenomenology and the "Theological Turn": The French Debate*. Perspectives in Continental Philosophy 15. New York: Fordham University Press, 2000.

Jenkins, Philip. *The New Faces of Christianity: Believing the Bible in the Global South*. Oxford: Oxford University Press, 2006.

———. *The Next Christendom: The Coming of Global Christianity*. Revised and expanded edition. Oxford: Oxford University Press, 2007.

Jeong, Paul Yonggap. *Mission from a Position of Weakness*. American University Studies. VII, Theology and Religion 369. New York: Lang, 2007.

Jeschke, Martin. *Rethinking Holy Land: A Study in Salvation Geography*. Scottdale, PA: Herald, 2005.

Jobes, Karen, and Moisés Silva. *Invitation to the Septuagint*. Grand Rapids: Baker Academic, 2000.

Johnson, Galen K. "William Carey's Muslim Encounters in India." *Baptist History and Heritage* 39 (2004) 100–108.

Johnson, Luke Timothy. "Proselytism and Witness in Earliest Christianity: An Essay on Origins." In *Sharing the Book: Religious Perspectives on the Rights and Wrongs of Proselytism*, edited by John Witte Jr. and Richard Martin, 143–57. Maryknoll, NY: Orbis, 1999.

Johnson, Michael W. "Imperial Commission or Orthodox Mission: Nikolai Il'minskii's Work Among the Tatars of Kazan, 1862–1891." PhD diss., University of Illinois at Chicago, 2005.

Johnston, Anna. *Missionary Writing and Empire, 1800–1860*. Cambridge studies in Nineteenth-Century Literature and Culture 38. Cambridge: Cambridge University Press, 2003.

Johnstone, David. "Czarist Missionary Contact with Central Asia: Models of Contextualization?" *International Bulletin of Missionary Research* 31 (2007) 66–72.

Jonkers, Peter and Ruud Welten. *God in France: Eight Contemporary French Thinkers on God*. Leuven: Peeters, 2005.

Jossua, Jean-Pierre. *The Condition of the Witness*. London: SCM, 1985.

Judt, Tony, and Timothy Schneider. *Thinking the Twentieth Century*. London: Vintage, 2013.

Júnior, Nilo Ribeiro. *Sabedoria da Paz: Ética e teo-lógica em Emmanuel Lévinas*. São Paulo: Loyola, 2008.

Justin Martyr. *The Writings of Justin Martyr and Athenagoras*. Ante-Nicene Christian Fathers II. Edinburgh: T. & T. Clark, 1909.

Kaminsky, Joel. "Did Election Imply the Mistreatment of Non-Israelites?" *Harvard Theological Review* 96 (2003) 397–425.

———. "Loving One's (Israelite) Neighbor: Election and Commandment in Leviticus 19." *Interpretation* 62 (2008) 123–32.

Kan, Sergei. "Russian Orthodox Brotherhoods among the Tlingit: Missionary Goals and Native Response." *Ethnohistory* 32 (1985) 196–223.

———. "Russian Orthodox Missionaries at Home and Abroad: The Case of Siberian and Alaskan Indigenous Peoples." In *Of Religion and Empire: Missions, Conversion, and Tolerance in Tsarist Russia*, edited by Robert Geraci and Michael Khodarovsky, 173–200. Ithaca, NY: Cornell University Press, 2001.

———. "Shamanism and Christianity: Modern-Day Tlingit Elders Look at the Past." *Ethnohistory* 38 (1991) 363–87.

Kaplan, Steven, ed. *Indigenous Responses to Western Christianity*. New York: New York University Press, 1995.

Kearney, Richard. *Anatheism: Returning to God after God*. New York: Columbia University Press, 2010.

———. "A Dialogue with Jean-Luc Marion." *Philosophy Today* 48 (2004) 12–26.

Keltie, J. Scott. *The Partition of Africa*. London: Stanford, 1893.

Kemm, William. *John Thomas: Missionary to South India*. Delhi: ISPCK, 2010.

Kharlampovich, Konstantin Vasil'evich. *Archimandrite Makarii Glukharev—Founder of the Altai Mission*. Translated by James Lawton Haney. Studies in Russian History 6. Lewiston, NY: Mellen, 2001.

Kiely, Ray. "The Last Refuge of the Noble Savage? A Critical Assessment of Post-Development Theory." *European Journal of Development Research* 11 (1999) 30–55.

Kilroy, Gerard. *Edmund Campion: Memory and Transcription*. Aldershot, UK: Ashgate, 2005.

Kim, Kirsteen. "Edinburgh 1910 and Edinburgh 2010: Different Theological World-views?" https://www.cccw.cam.ac.uk/wp-content/uploads/2017/08/Kim-Dr-Kirsteen-27-Jan-2010.doc.

Kisskalt, Michael. "Mission as *Convivence*: Life Sharing and Mutual Learning in Mission. Lessons from German Missiology." *Journal of European Baptist Studies* 11.2 (2011) 5–14.

Kobia, Samuel. "Cooperation and the Promotion of Unity: A World Council of Churches Perspective." In *Edinburgh 2010: Mission Then and Now*, edited by David Kerr and Kenneth Ross, 237–49. Oxford: Regnum, 2009.

Kolář, Ondřej. "Hermeneutická misiologie Theo Sundermeiera." *Misiologické forum* 4 (2015) 16–23.

Kollman, Paul. "At the Origins of Mission and Missiology: A Study in the Dynamics of Religious Language." *Journal of the American Academy of Religion* 79 (2011) 425–58.

Kolvenbach, Peter-Hans. *The Road from La Storta: Peter-Hans Kolvenbach on Ignatian Spirituality*. St. Louis: Institute of Jesuit Sources, 2000.

Korsun, Sergei, and Lydia Black. *Herman: A Wilderness Saint: From Sarov, Russia to Kodiak, Alaska*. Jordanville, NY: Holy Trinity, 2012.

Kreider, Alan. "Testimony as Sharing Hope: A Sermon on Matthew 8:5–13; 1 Peter 2:11–12; 3:13–17a." *Vision* 10 (2009) 80–88.

Kruger, René. *Pobres y Ricos en la Epístola de Santiago: El Desafío de un Cristianismo Profético*. Buenos Aires: Lumen, 2005.

Kumar, Prakash. *Indigo Plantations and Science in Colonial India*. Cambridge: Cambridge University Press, 2012.

Küng, Hans. *On Being a Christian*. Translated by Edward Quinn. Garden City, NY: Doubleday, 1976.

Langer, Ruth. "Jewish Understandings of the Religious Other." *Theological Studies* 64 (2003) 255–77.

Lattke, Michael. "The Call to Discipleship and Prosleytising." *Harvard Theological Review* 92 (1999) 359–62.

Ledochowski, Wlodomir. *The Choice and Formation of a Native Clergy in the Foreign Missions*. New York: Kenedy, n.d.

Lévinas, Emmanuel. *Autrement que Savoir: Emmanuel Lévinas*. Paris: Osiris, 1988.

———. *De Dieu qui vient à l'idée*. Paris: Vrin, 1982.

———. *Ethics and Infinity*. Translated by Richard A. Cohen. Pittsburgh: Duquesne University Press, 1985.

———. *Otherwise than Being, or Beyond Essence*. Translated by Alphonso Lingis. Pittsburgh: Duquesne University Press, 1998.

———. *Totality and Infinity*. Translated by Alphonso Lingis. Pittsburgh: Duquesne University Press, 1969.

Livingston, Kevin. *A Missiology of the Road: Early Perspectives in David Bosch's Theology of Mission and Evangelism*. Cambridge: James Clark, 2014.

Logan, Robert. *McCluhan Misunderstood: Setting the Record Straight*. Toronto: Key, 2013.

Lorance, Cody. "Cultural Relevance and Doctrinal Soundness: The Mission of Roberto de Nobili." *Missiology* 33 (2005) 415–24.

Louth, Andrew. "The Influence of the *Philokalia* in the Orthodox World." In *The Philokalia: A Classic Text of Orthodox Spirituality*, edited by Brock Bingaman and Bradley Nassif, 50–60. Oxford: Oxford University Press, 2012.

———. "The Patristic Revival and its Protagonists." In *The Cambridge Companion to Orthodox Christian Theology*, edited by Mary Cunningham and Elizabeth Theokritoff, 188–202. Cambridge Companions to Religion. Cambridge: Cambridge University Press, 2008.

Luzbetak, Louis. *The Church and Cultures: New Perspectives in Missiological Anthropology*. American Society of Missiology Series 12. Maryknoll, NY: Orbis, 1989.

Mackinlay, Shane. "Eyes Wide Shut: A Response to Jean-Luc Marion's Account of the Journey to Emmaus." *Modern Theology* 20 (2004) 447–56.

Malka, Salomon. *Emmanuel Lévinas: His Life and Legacy*. Translated by Michael Kigel and Sonja M. Embree. Pittsburgh: Duquesne University Press, 2006.

Maluleke, Tinyiko Sam. "Christian Mission and Political Power: Commission Seven Revisited." In *Edinburgh 2010: Mission Then and Now*, edited by David Kerr and Kenneth Ross, 204–16. Oxford: Regnum, 2009.

Marambio, José Tomás Alavarado. "Teorías recientes de la Trinidad." *VERITAS* 29 (2013) 189–217.

Marion, Jean-Luc. *Being Given: Toward a Phenomenology of Givenness*. Translated by Jeffrey L. Kosky. Stanford: Stanford University Press, 2002.

———. *The Erotic Phenomenon*. Translated by Stephen E. Lewis. Chicago: University of Chicago Press, 2006.

———. *God without Being: Hors-Texte*. Translated by Thomas A. Carlson. Religion and Postmodernism. Chicago: University of Chicago Press, 1991.

———. *The Idol and Distance: Five Studies*. Translated and with an introduction by Thomas A. Carlson. Perspectives in Continental Philosophy 17. New York: Fordham University Press, 2000.

———. *In Excess: Studies in Saturated Phenomena*. Translated by Robyn Horner and Vincent Berraud. Perspectives in Continental Philosophy 27. New York: Fordham University Press, 2002.

———. "In the Name: How to Avoid Speaking of 'Negative Theology.'" In *God, the Gift and Postmodernism*, edited by John Caputo and Michael Scanlon, 20–42. Bloomington: Indiana University Press, 1999.

———. *Prolegomena to Charity*. Translated by Stephen E. Lewis. New York: Fordham University Press, 2002.

———. "They Recognized Him: And He Became Invisible To Them." *Modern Theology* 18 (2002) 145–52.
———. *Le Visible et Le Révélé*. Philosophie & Théologie. Paris: Cerf, 2005.
———. *The Visible and the Revealed*. Translated by Christina M. Gschwandtner et al. Perspectives in Continental Philosophy. New York: Fordham University Press, 2008.
Marmion, Declan, and Mary Hines, eds. *The Cambridge Companion to Karl Rahner*. Cambridge Companions to Religion. Cambridge: Cambridge University Press, 2005.
Marshman, John Clark. *The Story of Carey, Marshman, and Ward, the Serampore Missionaries*. London: Heaton, 1864.
Martin, Wayne. "The Semantics of 'Dasein' and the Modality of *Being and Time*." In *The Cambridge Companion to Heidegger's* Being and Time, edited by Mark Wrathall, 100–128. Cambridge Companions to Philosophy. Cambridge: Cambridge University Press, 2013.
Marty, Martin. "Introduction: Proselytizers and Proselytizees on the Sharp Arête of Modernity." In *Sharing the Book: Religious Perspectives on the Rights and Wrongs of Proselytism*, edited by John Witte Jr. and Marty Martin, 1–14. Religion & Human Rights Series. Maryknoll, NY: Orbis, 1999.
Matthews, Shelly. *First Converts: Rich Pagan Women and The Rhetoric of Mission in Early Judaism and Christianity*. Stanford: Stanford University Press, 2001.
Matthey, Jacques. "Pilgrims, Seekers and Disciples: Mission and Dialogue in Matthew." *International Review of Mission* 91.360 (2002) 120–34.
Mauz, Andreas. "Theology and Narration: Reflections on the 'Narrative Theology' Debate and Beyond." In *Narratology in the Age of Cross-Disciplinary Narrative Research*, edited by Sandra Heinen and Roy Sommer, 261–85. Berlin: de Gruyter, 2009.
McClendon, James, and James Smith. *Convictions: Defusing Religious Relativism*. Rev. ed. 1994. Reprint, Eugene, OR: Wipf & Stock, 2002.
McCluhan, Marshal. *Counterblast*. London: Rapp & Whiting, 1970.
———. *Understanding Media*. London: Routledge Classics, 2001.
McGavran, Donald, ed. *The Conciliar-Evangelical Debate: The Crucial Documents, 1964–1976*. South Pasadena, CA: William Carey Library, 1977.
McGuckin, John. "The Life and Mission of St Paisius Velichkovsky. 1722–1794. An Early Modern Master of the Orthodox Spiritual Life." *Spiritus* 9 (2009) 157–73.
McNally, Michael D. "The Practice of Native American Christianity." *Church History* 69 (2000) 834–59.
Meyendorff, John. *St Gregory Palamas and Orthodox Spirituality*. Crestwood, NY: St Vladimir's Seminary Press, 1974.
Middlebrook, John B. *William Carey*. London: Carey Kingsgate, 1961.
Mikaelsson, Lisbeth. "'Self' and 'Other' in Biblical Representations in Mission Literature." In *Protestant Missions and Local Encounters in the Nineteenth and Twentieth Centuries*, edited by Hilde Nielssen et al., 87–99. Leiden, Netherlands: Brill, 2011.
Mikula, Maja. "The Island Monastery of Valaam in Finnish Homeland Tourism: Constructing a 'Thirdspace' in the Russian Borderlands." *Fennia* 191 (2013) 14–24.
Milbank, John. *Theology and Social Theory: Beyond Secular Reason*. 2nd ed. Oxford: Blackwell, 2006.

Minns, Denis, and Paul Parvis, eds. *Justin, Philosopher and Martyr: Apologies*. Oxford Early Christian Texts. Oxford: Oxford University Press, 2009.

Moffitt, David, and Jacob Butera. "P.Duk. inv. 727r: New Evidence for the Meaning and Provenance of the Word Προσήλυτος." *Journal of Biblical Literature* 132 (2013) 159–78.

Mooney, Catherine. "Ignatian Spirituality: A Spirituality for Mission." *Mission Studies* 26 (2009) 192–213.

Moran, Dermot. *Introduction to Phenomenology*. London: Routledge, 2000.

Morden, Peter J. *Offering Christ to the World: Andrew Fuller (1754–1815) and the Revival of Eighteenth-Century Particular Baptist Life*. Studies in Baptist History and Thought 8. Carlisle, UK: Paternoster, 2003.

Moreau, Scott, et al. *Introducing World Missions: A Biblical, Historical, and Practical Survey*. Grand Rapids: Baker Academic, 2004.

Mousalimas, Soterios, ed. *Journals of the Priest Ioann Veniaminov in Alaska, 1823–1826*. Fairbanks: University of Alaska Press, 1993.

———. "Patristics in Missionary Work: An Example from the Russian Orthodox Mission in Alaska." *Greek Orthodox Theological Review* 33 (1988) 327–34.

Muck, Terry. "History of Religion and Missiology: Complementary Methodologies." In *Encountering New Religious Movements: A Holistic Evangelical Approach*, edited by Irving Hexham et al., 63–89. Grand Rapids: Kregel, 2004.

Müller, Mogens. *The First Bible of the Christians: A Plea for the Septuagint*. JSOT Supplement Series 206. Sheffield: Sheffield Academic, 1996.

Munitiz, Joseph, and Philip Endean, eds. *Saint Ignatius of Loyola: Personal Writings*. London: Penguin, 1996.

Murshid, Ghulam. "Ramram Basu." *National Encyclopaedia of Bangladesh*. http://en.banglapedia.org/index.php?title=Ramram_Basu.

Myers, Travis. "Tracing a Theology of the Kingdom of God in William Carey's *Enquiry*: A Case Study in Complex Mission Motivation as Component of 'Missionary Spirituality.'" *Missiology* 40 (2012) 37–47.

Nazarius. "St. Herman's Elder, Abbot Nazarius of Valaam." *Orthodox America* 2.1 (1981).

Neely, Alan. *Christian Mission: A Case Study Approach*. Maryknoll, NY: Orbis, 1995.

Neill, Stephen. *Creative Tension*. London: Edinburgh, 1959.

———. *A History of Christian Mission*. Revised by Owen Chadwick. 2nd ed. London: Penguin, 1990.

Nichols, Robert. "Metropolitan Filaret and the Slavophiles." *St. Vladimir's Theological Quarterly* 37 (1993) 315–30.

Nida, Eugene, and Charles Taber. *The Theory and Practice of Translation*. Helps for Translators 8. Leiden: Brill, 1969.

Nikitin, Archimandrite Avgustin. "Russian America." In *The Legacy of St Vladimir: Byzantium, Russia, America*, edited by John Breck et al., 229–42. Crestwood, NY: St Vladimir's Seminary Press, 1990.

(Noble) Dolejšová, Ivana. *Accounts of Hope: A Problem of Method in Post-modern Apologia*. Bern: Peter Lang, 2000.

Noble, Ivana. *Theological Interpretation of Culture in Post-Communist Context: Central and East European Search for Roots*. Farnham: Ashgate, 2010.

Noble, Ivana, and Tim Noble. "A Non-Synthetic Dialectics between the Christian East and West: A Starting Point for Renewed Communication." In *Kommunikation ist möglich: Theologische, ökumenische und interreligiöse Lernprozesse: Festschrift für Bernd Jochen Hilberath*. edited by Christine Büchner et al., 273–81. Ostfildern, Germany: Grünewald, 2013.

Noble, Ivana, et al. *The Ways of Orthodoxy in the West*. Yonkers, NY: St Vladimir's Seminary Press, 2015. Revised translation of *Cesty pravoslavné teologie ve 20: Století na Západ*. Brno, Czech Republic: CDK, 2012.

———. *Wrestling with the Mind of the Fathers*. Yonkers, NY: St Vladimir's Seminary Press, 2015.

Noble, Tim. "Addressing the Other: Mission, Unity and the Question of Place." In *Mission and Unity: Common Witness of Separated Churches?* [Mission und Einheit: Gemeinsames Zeugnis getrennter Kirchen?], edited by Peter De Mey et al., 131–46. Beiheft zur Ökumenischen Rundschau 91. Leipzig: Evangelische, 2012.

———. "Between the Swiss Train and the Eschaton: Mission in a Time of Waiting." *Baptistic Theologies* 5.1 (2013) 147–62.

———. "Budování duchovního místa v hesychasmu a u Ignáce" [The Construction of Sacred Place in Hesychasm and Ignatius]. In *Sensorium Dei: Člověk—prostor—transcendence* [Sensorium Dei: Person—Space—Transcendence], edited by Karel Rechlík et al., 67–80. Brno, Czech Republic: CDK, 2013.

———. "Hesychasm and Ignatian Spirituality: Praying Together." *St Vladimir's Theological Quarterly* 59 (2015) 43–53.

———. "Jean-Luc Marion, Idols, and Liberation Theology." *Communio Viatorum* 48 (2006) 131–54.

———. "Jesuit and Moravian Brethren Mission: Encountering the Native American Other." *Communio Viatorum* 59 (2017) 73–97.

———. *Keeping the Window Open: The Theological Methodology of Clodovis Boff and the Problem of the Alterity of the Poor*. Prague: IBTS, 2009.

———. "Mission as the Place of Encounter between East and West." *Logos* 56 (2015) 289–99.

———. "'The Pathway into the Kingdom of Heaven': The Indigenization of Russian Orthodox Tradition in Alaska." *Mission Studies* 32 (2015) 32–46.

———. *The Poor in Liberation Theology: Pathway to God or Ideological Construct?* Abingdon: Routledge, 2014.

———. "Rights of Indigenous Peoples and the Russian Orthodox Mission to Alaska." *Communio Viatorum* 54 (2012) 164–83.

———. "A Writ Good Guide: The Bible in *The Way of the Pilgrim* and *The Pilgrim's Progress*." *Journal of European Baptist Studies* 12.1 (2011) 20–35.

Nordlander, David. "Innokentii Veniaminov and the Expansion of Orthodoxy in Russian America." *Pacific Historical Review* 64 (1995) 19–36.

Nygren, Anders. *Agape and Eros*. Translated by Philip S. Watson. 1953. Reprint, London: SPCK, 1982.

O'Brien, Peter. "The Great Commission of Matthew 20:18-20: A Missionary Mandate or Not?" *Reformed Theological Journal* 35.3 (1976) 66–78.

Ocaríz, Fernando. "Evangelización, Proselitismo y Ecumenismo." *Scripta Theologica* 38 (2006) 617–36.

Oddie, Geoffrey. *Imagined Hinduism: British Protestant Constructions of Hinduism, 1793–1900*. New Delhi: Sage, 2006.

O'Gara, Margaret. *The Ecumenical Gift Exchange*. Collegeville, MN: Liturgical, 1998.

Okure, Teresa. "The Church in the Mission Field: A Nigerian/African Response." In *Edinburgh 2010: Mission Then and Now*, edited by David Kerr and Kenneth Ross, 59–73. Regnum Studies in Religion. 2009. Reprint, Eugene, OR: Wipf & Stock, 2010.

Oleksa, Michael, ed. *Alaskan Missionary Spirituality*. Crestwood, NY: St Vladimir's Seminary Press, 2010.

———. *Orthodox Alaska: A Theology of Mission*. Crestwood, NY: St Vladimir's Seminary Press, 1992.

———. "The Orthodox Church and Orthodox Christian Mission from an Alaskan Perspective." *International Review of Mission* 90.358 (2001) 280–88.

———. "Orthodoxy and the Evolution of Aleut Culture." In *The Legacy of St Vladimir: Byzantium, Russia, America*, edited by John Breck et al., 243–58. Crestwood, NY: St Vladimir's Seminary Press, 1990.

O'Malley, John. *The First Jesuits*. Cambridge: Harvard University Press, 1995.

———. "The Fourth Vow in its Ignatian Context: A Historical Study." *Studies in the Spirituality of Jesuits* 25.1 (1983).

Omanson, Roger. "Bible Translation: Baptist Contributions to Understanding God's Word." *Baptist History and Heritage* 31 (1996) 12–22.

Orozco, Monica I. "'Not to Be Called Christian': Protestant Perceptions of Catholicism in Nineteenth-Century Latin America." In *Religion and Society in Latin America: Interpretative Essays from Conquest to Present*, edited by Lee Penyak and Walter Petry, 175–89. Maryknoll, NY: Orbis, 2009.

Paas, Stefan. "The Making of a Mission Field: Paradigms of Evangelistic Mission in Europe." *Exchange* 41 (2012) 44–67.

———. "Mission from Anywhere to Europe: Americans, Africans, and Australians Coming to Amsterdam." *Mission Studies* 32 (2015) 4–31.

Pachuau, Lalsangkima. *Ecumenical Missiology: Contemporary Trends, Issues, and Themes*. Bangalore, India: United Theological College, 2002.

Padberg, John. "The Forgotten Founders of the Society of Jesus: Paschase Broët, Jean Codure, Claude Jay." *Studies in the Spirituality of Jesuits* 29.2 (1997) 1–51.

Painter, John. *1, 2, and 3 John*. Sacra Pagina 18. Collegeville, MN: Liturgical, 2002.

Parppei, Kati. "Pagans of Darkness, Cruel Lutherans: Images of Religious 'Others' in the Historical Accounts concerning the Russian Orthodox Valaam Monastery." *Scandinavian Journal of History* 35 (2010) 135–55.

Pears, Angie. *Doing Contextual Theology*. Abingdon, VA: Routledge, 2010.

Pennington, Brian. *Was Hinduism Invented? Britons, Indians, and the Colonial Construction of Religion*. New York: Oxford University Press, 2005.

Pieta, Joseph. *The Land of the Midnight Sun: The Missions of Alaska*. Spokane, WA: Oregon Province of the Society of Jesus, 1925.

Pontifical Council for Inter-Religious Dialogue. "Dialogue and Proclamation: Reflection and Orientations on Interreligious Dialogue and the Proclamation of the Gospel of Jesus Christ." http://www.vatican.va/roman_curia/pontifical_councils/interelg/documents/rc_pc_interelg_doc_19051991_dialogue-and-proclamatio_en.html.

Pospielovsky, Dimitry. *The Orthodox Church in the History of Russia*. Crestwood, NY: St Vladimir's Seminary Press, 1998.

Pozdnyaev, Dionisii. "The Pearl of Great Price: Resurrecting Orthodoxy in China." *Road to Emmaus* 6.4 (2005) 29–54.

Pratt, Douglas. "Christian Discipleship and Interfaith Engagement." *Pacifica: Journal of Melbourne College of Divinity* 22.3 (2009) 317–33.
Presler, Titus. "Mission is Ministry in the Dimension of Difference: A Definition for the Twenty-First Century." *International Bulletin of Missionary Research* 34.4 (2010) 195–204.
Pressler, Carolyn. Review of *The Alien in Israelite Law*, by Christiana van Houten. *Journal of Biblical Literature* 112 (1993) 321–22.
Puntel, Lorenz. *Being and God: A Systematic Approach in Confrontation with Martin Heidegger, Emmanuel Lévinas and Jean-Luc Marion*. Evanston, IL: Northwestern University Press, 2011.
Rahner, Hugo. *The Vision of St. Ignatius in the Chapel of La Storta*. 2nd ed. Rome: Centrum Ignatianum Spiritualitatis, 1979.
Rahner, Karl. "Observations on the Problem of 'The Anonymous Christian.'" In *Theological Investigations* 14, 280–94. London: Darton, Longman & Todd, 1976.
———. "The One Christ and the Universality of Salvation." In *Theological Investigations* 16, 199–224. London: Darton, Longman & Todd, 1979.
Robeck, Cecil. *The Azusa Street Mission and Revival: The Birth of the Global Pentecostal Movement*. Nashville: Nelson, 2006.
Robert, Dana. *Christian Mission: How Christianity Became a World Religion*. Chichester, UK: Wiley-Blackwell, 2009.
Rochcau, Vsevolod. "St Herman of Alaska and the Defense of Alaskan Native Peoples." *St Vladimir's Theological Quarterly* 16 (1972) 17–39.
Ruether, Kirsten. "Heated Debates over Crinolines: European Clothing on Nineteenth-century Lutheran Mission Stations in the Transvaal." *Journal of Southern African Studies* 28 (2002) 359–78.
Russell, Caskey. "Cultures in Collision: Cosmology, Jurisprudence, and Religion in Tlingit Territory." *American Indian Quarterly* 33 (2009) 230–52.
Saayman, William, and Klippies Kritzinger, eds. *Mission in Bold Humility: David Bosch's Work Considered*. Maryknoll, NY: Orbis, 1996.
Salvat, Ignasi. *Servir en Misión Universal*. Bilbao: Mensajero, 2001.
Sanneh, Lamin. *Summoned from the Margin: Homecoming of an African*. Grand Rapids: Eerdmans, 2012.
———. *Translating the Message: The Missionary Impact on Culture*. Rev. and exp. ed. American Society of Missiology Series 42. Maryknoll, NY: Orbis, 2015.
———. *Whose Religion Is Christianity? The Gospel beyond the West*. Grand Rapids: Eerdmans, 2003.
Saulière, Augustine. *His Star Is In The East*. Revised and re-edited by S. Rajamanickam. Madras, India: De Nobili Research Institute, 1995.
Savage, Ann. "Jabez Carey." *Carey Family Newsletter* 16 (2010) 9–11.
Scannone, Juan Carlos. "Situación de la Problemática del Método Teológico en América Latina." *Medellín* 78 (1994) 255–85.
Schineller, J. Peter. "The Pilgrim Journey of Ignatius: From Soldier to Laborer in the Lord's Vineyard and Its Implications for Apostolic Lay Spirituality." *Studies in the Spirituality of Jesuits* 31.4 (1999).
Schnabel, Eckard J. "Israel, the People of God, and the Nations." *Journal of the Evangelical Theological Society* 54 (2002) 35–57.
Schomer, Karine, and W. H. McLeod, eds. *The Sants: Studies in a Devotional Tradition of India*. Delhi: Motilal Banarsidass, 1987.

Segovia, Fernando. *Love Relationships in the Johannine Tradition:* agapē/agapan *in 1 John and the Fourth Gospel*. SBL Dissertation Series 58. Chico, CA: Scholars, 1982.

Seland, Torrey. "The Common Priesthood of Philo and Peter: A Philonic Reading of 1 Peter 2.5, 9." *Journal for the Study of the New Testament* 57 (1995) 87–119.

———. "πάροικος καὶ παρεπίδημος: Proselyte Characterizations in 1 Peter?" *Bulletin for Biblical Research* 11 (2001) 239–68.

Senior, Donald. "Between Two Worlds: Gentiles and Jewish Christians in Matthew's Gospel." *Catholic Biblical Quarterly* 61 (1999) 1–23.

Senyk, Sophia. "Search for Holiness and Pastoral Care: Metropolitan Innocent of Moscow (1797–1879)." *St Vladimir's Theological Quarterly* 45 (2001) 265–83.

Shaffer, Jack Russell. "A Harmonization of Matt 8:5–13 and Luke 7:1–10." *Master's Seminary Journal* 17 (2006) 35–50.

Shenk, Wilbert. *Changing Frontiers of Mission*. American Society of Missiology Series 28. Maryknoll, NY: Orbis, 1999.

———. "Mission and Marginality." In *Anabaptism and Mission*, edited by Wilbert Shenk and Peter Penner, 227–46. Missionary Studies 10. Schwarzenfeld: Neufeld, 2007.

Shishigin, Egor Spiridonovich. "Prelate Innokentii (Veniaminov) and Yakutia." *Greek Orthodox Theological Review* 44 (1999) 597–605.

Sivasundaram, Sujit. "'A Christian Benares': Orientalism, Science, and the Serampore Mission of Bengal." *Indian Economic and Social History Review* 44 (2007) 111–45.

Skedros, James. Review of *The Orthodox Church*, by Thomas Fitzgerald. *Greek Orthodox Theological Review* 44 (1999) 726–30.

Skreslet, Stanley. *Comprehending Mission: The Questions, Methods, Themes, Problems, and Prospects of Missiology*. American Society of Missiology Series 49. Maryknoll, NY: Orbis, 2012.

Šlajerová, Monika. *Palestinská církev dnes: Politická a teologická problematika*. [The Palestinian Church Today: Political and Theological Problems]. Červeny Kostelec, Czech Republic: Mervart, 2009.

Smillie, Gene. "'Even the Dogs': Gentiles in the Gospel of Matthew." *Journal of the Evangelical Theological Society* 45 (2002) 73–97.

Smith, A. Christopher. "The Legacy of William Carey." *International Bulletin of Missionary Research* 16 (1992) 2–9.

———. "The Legacy of William Ward and Joshua and Hannah Marshman." *International Bulletin of Missionary Research* 23 (1999) 120–29.

———. "Mythology and Missiology: A Methodological Approach to the Pre-Victorian Mission of the Serampore Trio." *International Review of Mission* 83.330 (1994) 451–75.

———. *The Serampore Mission Enterprise*. Bangalore, India: Centre for Contemporary Christianity, 2006.

———. "The Spirit and Letter of Carey's Catalytic Watchword: A Study in the Transmission of Baptist Tradition." *Baptist Quarterly* 33 (1990) 226–37.

———. "A Tale of Many Models: The Missiological Significance of the Serampore Trio." *Missiology: An International Review* 20 (1992) 479–500.

Smith, George. *The Life of William Carey, D.D.: Shoemaker and Missionary*. London: Murray, 1885.

Spicq, Ceslaus. *Agape in the New Testament*. 3 vols. Translated by Marie Aquinas McNamara and Mary Honoria Richter. 1963. Reprint, Eugene, OR: Wipf & Stock, 2006.

Spindler, Marc. "The Protestant Mission Study. Emergence and Features." In *Mission and Science: Missiology Revised, 1850–1940*, edited by Carine Dujardin and Claude Proudhomme, 39–52. Kadoc Studies on Religion, Culture and Society 16. Leuven: Leuven University Press, 2015.

Stanley, Brian. *The Bible and the Flag: Protestant Missions and British Imperialism in the Nineteenth and Twentieth Centuries*. Leicester, UK: Apollos, 1990.

———. "Defining the Boundaries of Christendom: The Two Worlds of the World Missionary Conference, 1910." *International Bulletin of Missionary Research* 30 (2006) 171–76.

———. *The History of the Baptist Missionary Society, 1792–1992*. Edinburgh: T. & T. Clark, 1992.

———. *The World Missionary Conference, Edinburgh 1910*. Grand Rapids: Eerdmans, 2009.

Studdert-Kennedy, Gerald. *Providence and the Raj: Imperial Mission and Missionary Imperialism*. New Delhi: Sage, 1998.

Sugirtharajah, Sharada. "Virtuous Christians, Vicious Hindus: A Postcolonial Look at William Ward and his Hinduism." *Studies in World Christianity* 5 (1999) 196–212.

Sundermeier, Theo. "Konvivenz: Ein Modell für Europa?" *International Journal of Orthodox Theology* 3.4 (2012) 33–51.

———. *Konvivenz und Differenz: Studien zu einer verstehenden Missionswissenschaft*. Missionswissenschaftliche Forschungen n.F. 3. Erlangen: Ev.-Lutherischen Mission, 1995.

———. "*Missio Dei* Today: On the Identity of Christian Mission." *International Review of Mission* 92.367 (2003) 567–78.

———. "My Pilgrimage in Mission." *International Bulletin of Missionary Research* 31 (2007) 200–203.

Sunquist, Scott. *Understanding Christian Mission: Participation in Suffering and Glory*. Grand Rapids: Baker Academic, 2013.

Sweetman, Will. "'Hinduism' and the History of 'Religion': Protestant Presuppositions in the Critique of the Concept of Hinduism." *Method & Theory in the Study of Religion* 15 (2003) 329–53.

Synan, Vinson. *The Century of the Holy Spirit: 100 years of Pentecostal and Charismatic Renewal, 1901–2001*. Nashville: Nelson, 2001.

Thiessen, Matthew. "Revisiting the προσήλυτος in 'the LXX.'" *Journal of Biblical Literature* 132 (2013) 333–50.

Trakatellis, Demetrios. *The Pre-Existence of Christ in Justin Martyr*. Harvard Dissertations in Religion 6. Missoula, MT: Scholars, 1976.

Treadgold, Donald. *The West in Russia and China: Religious and Secular Thought in Modern Times*. 2 vols. Cambridge: Cambridge University Press, 1973.

Tsurikov, Vladimir, ed. *Philaret, Metropolitan of Moscow, 1782–1867: Perspectives on the Man, His Works, and His Times*. Jordanville, NY: Variable, 2003.

Tucker, Ruth. "William Carey's Less-Than-Perfect Family Life." *Christian History* 36 (1992). https://www.christianhistoryinstitute.org/magazine/article/william-careys-less-than-perfect-family-life/.

United Nations, "The World at Six Billion." http://www.un.org/esa/population/publications/sixbillion/sixbillion.htm.

Ushimaru, Proclus Yasuo. "Japanese Orthodoxy and the Culture of the Meiji Period." *St Vladimir's Theological Quarterly* 24 (1980) 115–27.

Ustorf, Werner. "Global Topographies: The Spiritual, the Social and the Geographical in the Missionary Movement from the West." *Social Policy and Administration* 32 (1998) 591–604.

Valliere, Paul. "The Liberal Tradition in Russian Orthodox Theology." In *The Legacy of St Vladimir: Byzantium, Russia, America*, edited by John Breck et al., 93–106. Crestwood, NY: St Vladimir's Seminary Press, 1990.

van Houten, Christiana. *The Alien in Israelite Law*. JSOT Supplement Series 107. Sheffield: JSOT, 1991.

van Rensburg, Fika Janse. "Constructing the Economic-Historic Context of 1 Peter: Exploring a Methodology." *Hervoormde Teologiese Studies* 67.1 (2011). DOI: 10.4102/hts.v67i1.939.

Veale, Joseph, et al. *Constitutions of the Society of Jesus: Incorporation of a Spirit*. Rome: CIS, 1993.

Verstraelen, Frans, et al., eds. *Missiology: An Ecumenical Introduction*. Grand Rapids: Eerdmans, 1995.

Vigil, José María. "A opção pelos pobres é opção pela justiça, e não é preferencial. Para um reenquadramento teológico-sistemático da opção pelos pobres." *Perspectiva Teológica* 36 (2004) 241–52.

Wallace, Catherine M. "Storytelling, Doctrine, and Spiritual Formation." *Anglican Theological Review* 81 (1999) 39–59.

Walls, Andrew F. "Commission One and the Church's Transforming Century." In *Edinburgh 2010: Mission Then and Now*, edited by David Kerr and Kenneth Ross, 27–40. Oxford: Regnum, 2009.

———. *The Cross-Cultural Process in Christian History*. Maryknoll, NY: Orbis, 2002.

———. *The Missionary Movement in Christian History: Studies in Transmission of Faith*. Maryknoll, NY: Orbis, 1996.

Walls, Andrew, and Cathy Ross, eds. *Mission in the Twenty-First Century: Exploring the Five Marks of Global Mission*. Mission in the 21st Century. Maryknoll, NY: Orbis, 2008.

Ware, Kallistos. "'The Light that Enlightens Everyone': The Knowledge of God among Non-Christians according to the Greek Fathers and St Innocent." *Greek Orthodox Theological Review* 44 (1999) 557–64.

———. *Orthodox Theology in the Twenty-First Century*. Doxa & Praxis Series. Geneva: WCC, 2012.

Warrington, Keith. *Pentecostal Theology: A Theology of Encounter*. London: T. & T. Clark, 2008.

Watts, John. "Baptists and the Transformation of Culture: A Case Study from the Career of William Carey." *Review and Expositor* 89 (1992) 11–21.

Weaver, Dorothy. *Matthew's Missionary Discourse: A Literary Critical Analysis*. JSNT Supplement Series 38. Sheffield: JSOT, 1990.

Wells, Harold "Christian Mission and the 'Religious Other': Evangelization and Dialogue." *Touchstone* 28.3 (2010) 30–38.

Welten, Ruud. "The Paradox of God's Appearance on Jean-Luc Marion." In *God in France: Eight Contemporary French Thinkers on God*, edited by Peter Jonkers and

Ruud Welten, 186–206. Studies in Philosophical Theology 28. Leuven: Peeters, 2005.
Werner, Dietrich. *Wiederentdeckung einer missionarischen Kirche: Breklumer Beiträge zur ökumenischen Erneuerung.* Hamburg: EB-Verlag, 2005.
Werner, Karel, ed. *Love Divine: Studies in Bhakti and Devotional Mysticism.* Durham Indological Series 3. Richmond: Curzon, 1993.
Wevers, John. *Notes on the Greek Text of Leviticus.* Septuagint and Cognate Studies Series 44. Atlanta: Scholars, 1997.
White, Barry. *The English Baptists of the Seventeenth Century.* History of the English Baptists 1. London: Baptist Historical Society, 1983.
Williams, Ann Elizabeth. "Father Herman: Syncretic Symbol of Divine Legitimation." Master's thesis, University of Alaska Fairbanks, 1993.
Williams, Peter. *The Ideal of the Self-Governing Church: A Study in Victorian Missionary Strategy.* Studies in Christian Mission 1. Leiden: Brill, 1990.
Wilson, Henry S. "Mission and Cultures: Some Paradigms of Encounter." *Asia Journal of Theology* 18 (2004) 14–32.
Wrathall, Mark, and Max Murphey. "An Overview of *Being and Time*." In *The Cambridge Companion to Heidegger's* Being and Time, edited by Mark Wrathall, 1–53. Cambridge Companions to Philosophy. Cambridge: Cambridge University Press, 2013.
Wright, Christopher. *The Mission of God: Unlocking the Bible's Grand Narrative.* Nottingham, UK: InterVarsity, 2006.
Wrogeman, Henning. "Mission as Oikumenical Doxology: Secularized Europe and the Quest for a New Paradigm of Mission. Empirical Data and Missiological Reflections." *Missionalia* 42 (2014) 55–71.
Yakimov, Oleg Dmitrievich. "The Unalaska Period of Ioann Veniamonov's [sic] Life and Activity: The Formation of a Church Leader and a State Leader and an Enlightener." *Greek Orthodox Theological Review* 44 (1999) 623–31.
Yaokum, Ioasaph, and Ioannis Chen. "Beyond the Great Wall: Orthodoxy in China." *Road to Emmaus* 4.2 (2003) 3–48.
Yeh, Allan. "Tokyo 2010 and Edinburgh 2010: A Comparison of Two Centenary Conferences." *International Journal of Frontier Missions* 27 (2010) 117–25.
Young, Doyle. "Andrew Fuller and the Modern Mission Movement." *Baptist History and Heritage* 17.4 (1982) 17–27.
Young, Julian. *Heidegger, Philosophy, Nazism.* Cambridge: Cambridge University Press, 1997.
Zajícová, Lenka. "Vlastní životopis." In *Souborné dílo: Duchovní cvičení, Vlastní životopis, Duchovní deník*, by Ignác z Loyoly, 183–317. Olomouc: Refugium—Rome: Velehrad, 2005.
Zastoupil, Lynn. "Defining Christians, Making Britons: Rammohun Roy and the Unitarians." *Victorian Studies* 44 (2002) 215–43.

Index

Acts of the Apostles, 33, 34
agapē. See love.
Alaska, Russian Orthodox mission to, 146, 149–51
  and the religious other, 154–57
Allen, W. C. 32
Anonymous Christians. *See* Rahner, Karl.
anthropological model of contextual theology, 56–58
Aristeas, Letter of, 24–26, 27, 28
Azariah, V. S. 50–51

Baptist Missionary Society, 118
Baranov, Alexander, 150, 171
Barbour, Claude Marie, 72
Barram, Michael, 3–4, 180
Basu, Ram Ram, 129, 130, 132–34, 137
Being Given. See Marion, Jean-Luc.
Bevans, Stephen and Roger Schroeder, 65, 67, 68, 70, 176
bhakti, 134–35, 141
Boff, Clodovis, 16n6
Bonhoeffer, Dietrich, 74
Bosch, David, 46, 54, 70
  mission and dialogue, 63–65
  and paradigm shifts in mission, 53
Bultmann, Christoph, 21

Campion, Edmund, 7n18
Carey, Charlotte, 136
Carey, Dorothy, 118, 127, 136
Carey, Jabez. *See* Carey, William, advice to son.

Carey, William
  advice to son, 136–38
  death of youngest son, 142
  early life, 117–18
  Enquiry, 119–24
  opposition to caste system, 130, 135
  and religious others, 131–32, 139–141
  spiritual experiences, 125–28
  translation and language learning, 128–30, 137–38
confidence, mission as, 69
Constitutions of the Society of Jesus, 110–13

de Guibert, Joseph, 112
de Nobili, Roberto, 130–31
Derrida, Jacques, 83
Deuteronomy, 21, 27
discernment, mission as, 69–70
discipleship, 9, 59, 74, 102, 176

East India Company, 124–25, 140
Edinburgh 1910. *See* World Missionary Conference.
Edinburgh 2010, 46
Endō, Shūsaku, 181
enemy, love of, 84, 115n110, 153
Enquiry into the Obligations of Christians. See Carey, William, *Enquiry*.
Ephesians, 34
ethnos, 36
Exodus, 20, 21

Flett, John, 54, 66n123
Freire, Paulo, 1

Gadamer, Hans-Georg, 62
Gairdner, W. H. T. 51n34
genos, 36
gēr, 6, 15, 18–23, 174–75
gift, 83–84
givenness, 81–82, 180
Goodman, Martin, 33n84, 34

Hacham, Noah, 26, 27, 28
Heidegger, Martin, 62, 80
Herman, Saint, 148, 150
Horrell, David, 36
Husserl, Edmund, 79–80

Ignatius, Saint
  context of mission, 102
  early life, 96–97
  first encounter in mission, 97–98
  as pilgrim, 98
  understanding of mission, 107, 113
Innocent (Veniaminov), Saint
  appointment as Bishop of Kamchatka, 163
  arrival in Alaska, 153
  and conditions for baptism, 168–69
  death of wife, 162
  early life, 151–53
  effect of encounter with the other on, 179
  and inculturation of church practices, 170–172
  and Ivan Smirennikov, 157–160
  and language learning, 153–54
  later life and death, 163
  missionary instructions, 163–72
  mission as enlightenment, 164–67
  and preaching the gospel, 167–68
  and the Tlingit, 160–62
Ivens, Michael, 99, 103, 104

Janse van Rensburg, Fika, 35, 36–37
Jesuits. *See* Society of Jesus.
Jesus
  and encounter with the other, 38–41, 176

as saturated phenomenon, 87–88
John, Gospel of, 37, 41–42, 87
Justin Martyr, 56, 60–61, 72, 144

Kaminsky, Joel, 17, 18
Kearney, Richard, 85n44
Konvivenz, 7n17, 82n30

laos, 36
Langer, Ruth, 23
Lévinas, Emmanuel, 5, 7n17, 21n25, 45–46, 52–53, 62, 86
Leviticus, 22, 31n84, 90
logoi spermatikoi. *See* Justin Martyr.
love, 10, 11, 22, 51, 77, 84, 89–90, 99, 102, 106, 114, 153, 166, 177, 180, 181
Luke, Gospel of, 5, 55, 84

Marion, Jean-Luc, 77–78, 81, 83, 87
  Being Given, 78–79, 83–84
  and the condition of witness, 88–89
  and conceptual idols, 61, 76
  and givenness, 68, 105
  and love, 89–90, 166
  and saturated phenomenon, 85–86
Mark, Gospel of, 88
Matthew, Gospel of, 5, 33, 38–41, 59, 61, 87, 165
missional hermeneutic, 3–4
missio Dei, 54, 66, 82, 101
mission
  addressee of, 1, 2, 10, 43, 44, 52, 82
  changes in, 54–55
  as encounter, 2, 5, 11, 16, 22, 52–53, 58, 59, 61, 74
  as God's gift, 67, 182
  non-definition of, 5
  as prophetic dialogue, 65–66, 176–77
  as response in love to the other, 181
missionary, 2, 10, 43
  as gardener, 71–73
  as storyteller, 71
  as teacher, 70
  as trail guide, 71

Nadal, Jerome, 106

non-possession, 67

other
  as basis for mission, 62, 180–81
  as given, 76, 84
  as presence of God's goodness, 177
  relational nature of, 29, 30, 42, 51, 74, 82

parepidēmoi, 35
paroikos, 6, 30, 31, 35
Pal, Krishna, 134–35
Peter, First Letter of, 34, 35, 36
phenomenology, 7, 79–80, 83–84
praxis, mission as, 68
praxis model of contextual theology, 58–59
prosēlutos, vii, 6, 23, 30, 31, 33, 74, 86, 175, 180–81

Rahner, Karl, 64n111, 105n63
repentance, mission as, 68–69
revelation as phenomenon, 87
Richard, Timothy, 139n114
Russian American Company, 149, 150, 151, 171

Salvat, Ignasi, 101–2
salvation geography, 49
Sanneh, Lanin, 49, 59–61, 130, 144
Schnabel, Eckard, 17
Schroeder, Roger, 65, 71–72
Seland, Torrey, 37
Septuagint, 23, 24, 26–27, 28

Smirennikov, Ivan. *See* Innocent (Veniaminov), Saint and Ivan Smirennikov.
Society of Jesus, 95, 99n22, 106, 107n74
  Fourth Vow in regard to mission, 107–10
  Jesuits at the Council of Trent, 113–15
Spiritual Exercises, 99–100, 101, 112
  The Call of the King, 100–101
  The Contemplation for Attaining the Love of God, 104–6
  The Incarnation, 101–2
  Presupposition, 113n104
  The Two Standards, 103–4
Stanley, Brian, 50
stranger. *See* other.
Sündermeier, Theo, 7n17, 82n30

Thiessen, Matthew, 32
Thomas, John, 125, 127, 134
Tlingit, 161–62
translation, 15, 23, 28, 29, 128–30, 154, 175–76

Valaam monastery, 146–49
van Houten, Christiana, 19–20, 22, 32
Veniaminov, Innocent, Ioann, Ivan. *See* Innocent (Veniaminov), Saint.
Vulgate, 37–38

Warren, M. A. C., 57–58
World Mission Conference, Edinburgh 1910, 47–48, 50, 52

www.ingramcontent.com/pod-product-compliance
Lightning Source LLC
Chambersburg PA
CBHW052340230426
43664CB00041B/2566